# Contents

**Basic Operational Research**

UNOTT

# Basic Operational Research
## Third edition

**Peter G Moore**
Principal and Professor of Statistics and Operational Research
London Business School

PITMAN PUBLISHING
128 Long Acre, London WC2E 9AN

A Division of Longman Group UK Limited

© Peter G Moore 1968, 1976, 1986

First published in Great Britain 1968
Second Edition 1976
Third Edition 1986
Reprinted 1990

**British Library Cataloguing in Publication Data**
Moore, Peter G.
    Basic operational research.—3rd ed.
    1. Operations research
    I. Title
    658.4′034     T57.6

ISBN 0–273–02025–0  CU003653494

Printed and bound in Singapore

# Preface

Some years ago I gave a series of lectures on operational research to a summer school at an American university. The audience was mainly businessmen who wanted to get an understanding of this relatively new speciality that had sprung up in so many organizations. The discussions I had then first put the idea of writing the present book into my mind, but it was experiences at the London Business School that confirmed me of the need for the book. At the School we have regular three-month executive courses for up-and-coming middle managers and one aim is to introduce the participants to specialities such as operational research, thereby improving their analytical skills, as well as their ability to recognize and formulate problems within a quantitative framework and to interpret the results. The need for some reference book to go with this series of classroom sessions was a compelling motive to go ahead with the book sketched out earlier.

The book has been written for two classes of reader. The first is the manager or executive mentioned above. The second is the more serious student who can use the book as an introduction to the subject before, or at the same time as, studying the more sophisticated texts that are available. The aim throughout has been to speak (or rather to write) through problems and to allow these to dictate the pace and the manner of approach. I suggest that this is valuable in providing a reference point for the majority of the readers I have in mind. Too many books seem to put all their primary effort into the middle, that is the black box, part of the subject and then to work backwards to the problem formulation stage and forwards to the solution interpretation stage. I have deliberately set out to start the discussions with recognizable problems, most of them real or adapted real ones, and to skate over much of the black box manipulations so as to come to grips reasonably quickly with the solution and its interpretation. I have naturally found it necessary to keep to a framework that is broadly technique-based to provide an acceptable thread of continuity, and also an ease of consultation with the recognized formal texts on the subject.

Operational research is not a universal panacea. It is a serious attempt to bring scientific methods to the aid of business problems. A concise definition in the first chapter suggests that it is concerned with the allocation of scarce resources in complex and competing situations. Accepting this necessarily over-simplified definition implies that it must have a very definite relationship with many other subject areas, e.g. accountancy, economics and statistics, to name some of the obvious ones. This will become clear in the book, but what will also, I hope, become clear is the extra power, and indeed dimension, of problem analysis and resolution that is made available by precisely this combination of expertise. For those expecting a do-it-yourself kit there will be disappointment, but for those who want to learn something of the flavour and ethos of the subject, I hope there will be satisfaction.

The book, with its heavy emphasis on case histories and problems, has drawn upon a variety of both published and unpublished sources and quoted from many reports and journals. Wherever the data are substantially in the original form, due acknowledgment has been made through the references appended to each chapter. These references will also enable the reader to pursue many of the case histories further, if he so desires. The occasion of a third edition has been used to update the book at various places and, in particular, to extend the discussion on forecasting and financial modelling and to introduce some new examples. For the first time, a set of exercises is included at the end of the book. My wife has, once more, helped greatly with proof-reading. Any short-comings still remaining must rest with the author and comments from readers will be welcomed.

*London, October 1984*                                    P. G. M.

# 1 The operational research approach

## 1.1 Introduction

In W. S. Gilbert's *The Pirates of Penzance* appears the couplet:

'I'm very well acquainted too with matters mathematical,
I understand equations both the simple and quadratical.'

It is a widely held belief that operational research is an abstruse branch of higher mathematics and that only Cambridge wranglers can hope to appreciate it. Nevertheless, although it is perfectly true that mathematics enters into operational research, many scientists brought up through biology, psychology, economics or other subjects have been able to make very worthwhile contributions to both the development and application of operational research. To understand why this is so, it is necessary to trace briefly the development of the subject.

Until the second half of the last century, most industrial and business organizations were small, employing only a handful of people. The enterprises were usually owned and managed by the same individual. When expansion took place, it was no longer possible for one man to perform all the necessary managerial functions. Consequently, new functions grew up, such as production controller, personnel manager, sales manager, and so on. Each of these functions evolved its own particular sphere and mode of operation and competence.

Following the decentralization of the separate functions, it slowly came to be realized that many problems could not be isolated into the individual compartments that were being set up in large organizations. Although scientific developments were coming to the aid of the individual specialities created by this fragmentation, they were not coming to the aid of the overall executive function being created within the organization as a whole. As a result, it ultimately became imperative to have some method within the organization for coping with problems which spanned the various compartments. This led to the development of the ideas, if not the name, of operational research. For quite a long time, however, this kind of thinking was applied only in a limited number of situations where it had become crystal clear both that a problem existed and that it did not naturally fall within the competence of any single department. Work carried out during the Second World War demonstrated that the range and number of problems to which this kind of thinking could be applied was much larger than previously visualized. The lessons learnt during this time were subsequently taken back, mainly through the redeployment of the personnel concerned, to various civilian industries and businesses.

The United Kingdom Operational Research Society defines operational research as 'the attack of modern science on complex problems arising in the direction and management of large systems of men, machines, materials, and money in industry, business, government, and defence'. It goes on to state that 'the distinctive approach is to develop a scientific model of the system, incorporating measurement of factors such as chance and risk, in order to predict and compare the outcomes of alternative decisions, strategies, and controls. The purpose is to help management to determine its policy and actions scientifically.' Summarizing this definition it could be said that operational research is concerned with allocation and planning in complex situations involving scarce or limited resources. To put it in this way immediately highlights the close affinity which must exist between the operational research worker and those in other branches of management specialities, such as the accountant. Their goals are common and, whilst the tools they bring to the job may differ, they often complement one another.

## 1.2  The complexity of problems

To illustrate the notions of conflict and complexity, consider the extremely common inventory (or stock control) problem. In a large organization, the formulation of the optimum policy to follow with regard to inventory will take into account certain elements of conflict. The production department will argue for a large inventory spread over few products. By this means, they can have long runs on their machinery and thus produce efficiently. The marketing department will tend to urge a large inventory spread over a wide range of products. By this means they can meet the demands and requirements of any customer at a moment's notice. The personnel department will want to produce inventory in slack periods, on the grounds that there is a need to keep up morale and retain the skilled workers who, if dismissed, would be difficult to replace when demand rose again. The finance department will want to reduce the capital that is tied up in stocks and hence will tend to press for small inventories. Ironically, the Finance Department commonly seems to press hardest for reductions in stocks when times are bad, but allows the stocks to rise when times are good without undue comment. This tends to aggravate the operations of the firm when it is at a difficult period. Hence, even in this apparently simple problem, opposing views are likely to be put forward by different departments, and some basis for resolution is needed to decide the optimum policy the firm should follow.

Most of the complex problems arising in a business tend to be solved either by using past experience as a guide, or by applying rules of thumb that have grown up over the years. Whilst many of these rules work quite well in simple situations, they tend to break down as an organization gets larger or more complex. For example, consider the following simple transportation problem.

A firm has three factories located at Watford, Maidstone and Manchester respectively. These factories have available 140 units, 120 units, and 50 units respectively of some product. Delivery of these units is required to three depots: 60 units to Birmingham, 100 units to Sheffield, and 150 units to London. The cost of moving one unit from any one factory to any other depot is shown (in £) in Table 1.1.

Table 1.1  **Costs £ per unit moved from factory to depot**

| Depots | Factories | | | Requirements |
| --- | --- | --- | --- | --- |
| | Watford | Maidstone | Manchester | |
| Birmingham | 18 | 24 | 12 | 60 |
| Sheffield | 12 | 27 | 9 | 100 |
| London | 3 | 6 | 18 | 150 |
| Supplies | 140 | 120 | 50 | 310 |

For example, the cost of moving one unit from the factory at

Manchester to the depot at Birmingham is equal to 12. If 5 units are moved the cost will be equal to $5 \times 12$ or 60. If a transport clerk were now faced with the problem of scheduling these deliveries, he might approach it by looking at the table and selecting first the route that had the least cost. In this case it is the Watford–London route. He would then place as many units as possible on that route. In this case, 140 units would be the maximum, as Watford has only 140 units available for supply. Having done that, he would then select the next cheapest route, which is Maidstone–London, and place as many units as he could on that route. Because the London depot requires only a total of 150 units and 140 have already been supplied by Watford, the maximum he could place is 10. Having done that, he would then pick the next cheapest route, which is Manchester–Sheffield, and place as many as possible upon this route. This would be 50 units, as the Manchester factory only has 50 units available. Proceeding in this way, he would eventually arrive at the distribution pattern shown in Table 1.2, giving a total transport cost of £3720.

Table 1.2   **Transport allocations**

| Depots | Factories | | | Requirements |
|---|---|---|---|---|
| | Watford | Maidstone | Manchester | |
| Birmingham | —   (10) | 60 | —   (50) | 60 |
| Sheffield | —   (100) | 50 | 50 | 100 |
| London | 140   (30) | 10   (120) | — | 150 |
| Supplies | 140 | 120 | 50 | 310 |

(The figures in brackets relate to the optimum allocation.)

Now this is a perfectly logical and straightforward way of proceeding to carry out the allocation. A short study of the table, however, will convince the reader that this is not the optimum method of allocation. Indeed the optimum, which is shown in brackets in the table, gives an overall cost of £2790; this is a very considerable reduction of some 25 per cent in cost on the first attempt. Now although the clerk might, after a fair amount of effort, have reached this optimum solution by juggling around with the various quantities, it is unlikely that he would always reach the optimum before abandoning his efforts. Indeed, if the numbers of factories and depots were very much larger, it is virtually certain that he would never reach the optimum by such methods. Hence, the rule-of-thumb approach used earlier is likely to break down when the situation is at all complex.

A second example (based on an illustration due to P. B. Coaker and A. Battersby) highlights the necessity to define precisely the characteristics it is desired to optimize. A wood-working business, owned by Mr Harvey, works an eight-hour day manufacturing and selling armchairs (A) at £30, bookshelves (B) at £20, coatstands (C) at £20 each. The business has three processes (P, Q, R) available of which only one can be used at a time. The appropriate outputs are shown in Table 1.3.

Table 1.3 **Wood-working business**

| Process | Selling price | Process output (per hour) | | | Daily demand |
|---|---|---|---|---|---|
| | | P | Q | R | |
| Armchairs (A) | £30 | 1 | 2 | 1 | 9 |
| Bookshelves (B) | £20 | 2 | — | 1 | 11 |
| Coatstands (C) | £20 | — | 3 | 2 | 9 |
| Process cost per hour | £50 | £60 | £70 | | |

Thus process P costs £50 per hour and manufactures one A and two B units per hour. The local retailers can sell up to a maximum of 9 A units, 11 B units, and 9 C units in one day, if such units can be supplied by the factory. The problem to be answered is how Mr Harvey should best arrange his operations. If he aims to satisfy the market completely, it will be found that he can use process P for 4 hours, process Q for 1 hour, and process R for 3 hours, and thereby manufacture exactly the amounts demanded of each of the three products. His costs will then total £470, and his sales will realize £670, giving a profit of £200. If, however, he approaches the allocation problem by aiming to maximize his profit within the constraints of demand on each product, he will get a different answer. Indeed, using process P and process Q for 3 hours each, his total costs will be £330 and his sales will be £570, giving him the maximum possible profit of £240. It should be noted that he will then make 9 A units, 6 B units, and 9 C units, so that he will not satisfy all the demand for B units. But he will have maximized his profit at the expense of not satisfying all the demand or working the plant fully.

These examples serve to show that simple rules of thumb may not be wholly adequate in the complex situations that arise in practice. It may be necessary to define both the problem and the associated measure of performance rather more carefully than in the past.

## 1.3  Essential characteristics

The first characteristic of operational research is that it attempts to deal with problems that arise in the operating of systems. The activity of any one part of an organization generally has some effect on the activities of other parts. Hence, to evaluate any decision or action within an organization, it is necessary to identify all the significant interactions and to evaluate their combined impact on the performance of the organization as a whole, not merely on the part originally involved. This orientation is contrary to the natural inclination of many workers who try to cut the problem down to size and to isolate it as far as possible from its immediate environment. Many aspects of a problem are commonly eliminated in this way, although it is reduced to one that can then be handled by standard techniques or by judgment based on experience. Operational research, on the other hand, has a systems orientation and moves in the opposite direction by deliberately expanding and complicating the statement of a problem until all the significantly interacting components are contained within it. Put another way, this approach aims to investigate, over the entire area under the manager's control, the implications of the proposed solution to a problem. Such an enquiry should go to the full limits of the manager's responsibility, not neglecting the effects of policies made outside his area on the activity within his area. If this is not done, solutions can sometimes give misleading results.

As an example, an airline was concerned with the low average rate of utilization of its stewardesses on flying duty (expressed as flying hours per month) and wished to design a new method of scheduling their duties so as to raise this rate of utilization. A possible method to achieve this was found, in a manner which would not have a major effect on the morale of the staff concerned. Only at this point in the study did it become apparent that, because of the terms of duty defined for pilots and other aircrew, the proposed schedules would imply a lowering of their average flying hours. Hence the fact that the problems were so interrelated meant that they should not be considered in isolation, since the optimum solution found for one problem might not be the optimum for the organization as a whole.

Secondly, operational research tends to use the team approach, welding together effectively personnel who have been brought up in a variety of different disciplines. Specialization in sciences became inevitable when the rate of increase of knowledge started to explode in the last century. Such subdivisions are, of course, artificial and not a natural phenomenon. Today more and more subdivision has gone on until the point has been reached where many pressing problems can no longer be treated fruitfully by an individual specialist. Hence, investigation by inter-disciplinary teams has become the only feasible alternative in many areas, although not all members of the team will play an equal part in an investigation. Furthermore, in the early years of development of operational research during the Second World War, there was a great shortage of all kinds of scientists. Consequently, when it was seen that operational research could make a significant contribution to military activities, staff had to be acquired quickly without being able to define very precisely the job specifications, and mixed disciplinary teams were formed out of sheer necessity. Out of this experience, however, came a recognition that the mixed team as such was valuable, and necessity had become a virtue.

As an example, an electronics engineer examining the problem of production and inventory control for a particular product may quickly perceive that fluctuations of inventory are a function of the length of time that elapses between changes in the market demand for the product and adjustments of the production level. His problem is then to design a servo-control system in which the relevant information concerning changes in the market demand is fed back quickly and accurately to the production control centre. At this centre, adjustments in production can be made so as to minimize the appropriate cost function. He has, in fact, translated the problem into one of servo-theory which he knows how to solve. On the other hand, a chemical engineer may look at the same problem and formulate it in terms of flow theory and, having done this, he then has his own methods available for solving it. Which of the alternative methods of approach is the most fruitful depends on the circumstances. The project team must examine the alternatives and select an appropriate approach, possibly borrowing ideas from several different background disciplines.

The third essential characteristic is that of the adaptation of scientific method and the use of models. In research and development, experimental methods are used which are primarily based on the laboratory and pilot-plant scales of operation. With operational research this is not appropriate, in that the experimentation would have to be carried out by making trial changes within an organization which might, in turn, be unwilling to allow such experimentation. There is, however, an alternative approach which is akin to the manner in which the astronomer works. He builds representations of the universe, or part of the universe, and checks whether the model that he builds fits the facts as he knows and can observe them. If it does, he then uses the model to predict future characteristics such as the eclipses of the sun or the states of the tide. When these models were first formulated by early astronomers they were not always very exact, but they were quite good for practical purposes. As time has gone on, the models have been refined and improved so that, whilst even today it is impossible to say that the models themselves are exact, they are nevertheless good enough for virtually all practical purposes. The operational research man can do likewise. He tries to build a suitable model to describe the operations of the system he is considering. This model will be formulated in terms of a number of variables, of which some are under the manager's control and can be altered precisely as required, whilst others are not completely under his control. Provided such a model can be found and formulated, then methods can usually be devised to use them in a predictive manner.

## 1.4  Types of model

There are two basic types of model that the operational research worker commonly concerns himself with (although some other less common types exist which are not discussed here). The first is the *symbolic* type of model where mathematical representations are made to describe the system concerned. As an illustration, many equipment-replacement problems fall into this category, a model being set up in terms of the cost of purchase of a piece of equipment, the costs of maintenance over time, and the resale value. Thus, if $C$ represents the cost of purchase of a new item, $m_i$ the cost of maintenance in the $i$th year, and $S_n$ the resale value at the end of $n$ years, then the cost of purchasing the equipment, using it for $n$ years and selling it again is

$$\left[ C + \sum_{i=1}^{n} m_i \right] - S_n$$

where $\sum_{i=1}^{n} m_i$ is a symbolic representation to denote the sum of the values of $m_i$ from $i = 1$ up to $i = n$, i.e. $m_1 + m_2 + m_3 + \ldots m_n$, i.e. $n$ values in all. If, now, an infinitely long period is considered, the average cost per year, assuming replacement every $n$ years over the time concerned, will be

$$\frac{1}{n} \left[ C + \sum_{i=1}^{n} m_i - S_n \right]$$

The interval between replacements, $n$, would then be chosen such that this average cost is a minimum.

Such a model is extremely simple as it stands, and therefore not entirely realistic. More complex variations can be introduced to remedy this defect. For example, it could be adjusted to include an allowance for any efficiency drop in the equipment which may occur over time. It could again be adjusted to take into account the taxation allowances obtainable on new plant; and the various cash receipts and expenditures can be discounted so as to allow for the precise points of time at which they occur and the rate of interest that has to be paid on capital outstanding. Perhaps, when these extra complexities have been introduced into the model, it may not then be capable of neat and explicit solution by standard mathematical techniques. Mathematical models of this type could then be explored numerically or graphically by substituting various values for the variables concerned, and getting a global view as to the way the effectiveness of the system changes with variations in the variables. Indeed, the ability to display many symbolic representations in either numerical or graphical forms provides a powerful approach to problem-solving in its own right, a point that is stressed on many occasions later in this book.

Modern electronic computers have considerably helped the development of symbolic models. However, the virtue of computers rests basically on their speed of operation and they can only carry out calculations for which the sequence of steps to be followed is well defined. Calculations that would previously have been possible, but impracticable by manual means thus become feasible.

The size and complexity of mathematical models may be extremely great. For example, a model used in the petroleum industry to describe the operations of an inventory system, including its buying and selling procedures, required several hundred equations in order to make it realistic enough to be capable of describing the operations concerned. A computer was then essential in the ensuing analysis. Broadly speaking, it is always possible in principle to formulate a model, provided that it is feasible to get the executives involved in the organization to state the principles on which they currently operate the system under study. The subsequent use of the model may be rather more difficult.

A second type of model is the so-called *analogue* model. Probably the most familiar form of analogue model is that of the slide rule, in which quantities are represented by distances which are proportional to their logarithms. This enables multiplications to be performed by additions and divisions by subtractions. The analogue principle can, however, be taken considerably further with, for example, electronic circuits being used to solve various equations. Thus, many simple forecasting equations used for stock control schemes can be solved by having an electronic circuit with the appropriate responses and delays built into it. By feeding in the basic data concerning, first, the estimate of the current demand, second, the demand which has actually occurred, and, third, the constants of the forecasting equation being used, a new estimate of the forthcoming demand is obtained.

An ingenious analogue model of a mechanical nature can be developed for deciding upon the optimum location of a factory to minimize transport costs. Figure 1.1 (of a simplified situation) shows five towns at which varying levels of demand for a product have to be met from a single factory. The factory is to be located at the point which makes the total transport cost of deliveries to the five locations a minimum. A vertically positioned map is drawn up, with the five locations placed on it, and friction-free pulley wheels put on the map at the five locations, with threads put over the wheels attached to weights which are proportional to the demand at the five points. These five threads are now joined to a single ring. The point at which the ring now settles, i.e. the point of balance of the various forces concerned, will be the point at which the total transport costs are a minimum. The truth of this assertion can be demonstrated mathematically.

One delightful feature of the model is that it is capable of very

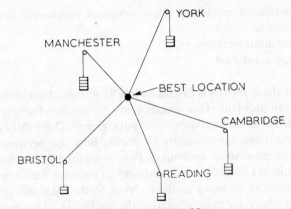

**Figure 1.1   Location of factory**

quick adjustments, without any need to solve complicated equations. For example, if a sixth location is to be introduced, this can be done immediately by putting in a further pulley wheel at the appropriate point and attaching a further thread with the new demand as the weight at the end of the thread. Alternatively, if the cost of moving a unit is twice as high on one route as it is on the others, this can be allowed for by making the weight at the end of that particular thread double what it would otherwise have been.

One important factor in the design of any model is that the number of variables incorporated considerably affects the amount of work involved. The labour of solving problems increases as the square, or even the cube, of the number of variables involved and, whilst it is important to include enough variables for adequate realism, it is desirable to begin with as few variables as seem likely to yield a useful representation. To this end, variables are often combined but it is essential to be able to estimate the errors this form of condensation will incur.

## 1.5   The phases of the study

Any operational research project can be split into <u>six broad phases</u>. These are

 (*a*)  Definition of problem and objective
 (*b*)  Representation (or model) of situation
 (*c*)  Test of model against actual conditions

(*d*) Analysis of model to select optimum conditions to meet objective

(*e*) Pilot implementation test

(*f*) Implementation

Each of these phases is discussed briefly in turn. First, the definition of the problem. This sounds easy, but is often fraught with more difficulty than is apparent at a quick glance. Difficulties commonly stem from the necessity to decide how the performance of some system is to be measured. For example, a post office has frequent queues at its counters and aims to improve the situation. How is the cost of extra counter clerks to be balanced against the improved service to be offered to the public? In addition, some of the variables concerned are controllable, whilst others are apparently uncontrollable. The service times found at the post office counters are, to some extent, controllable, whilst the arrival intervals between customers are virtually uncontrollable. Hence, in setting down the problem, the yardstick by which alternative solutions are to be compared must be defined and, if necessary, a method devised for combining the elements within the system to achieve an overall measure of the effectiveness of each proposed solution.

In the second phase, some model or representation of the system has to be built along the lines already discussed. The complexity of this representation will vary enormously from problem to problem and, whilst complexity is not in itself of any merit, it is essential to have sufficient complexity for realistic results to be achieved. Once the model has been formulated, the third phase, namely its manipulation, is reached. Basically, the model can be manipulated in one of three ways. First of all, it can be examined mathematically by solving the equations concerned in a precise and exact way. Secondly, if the equations defy any unique form of solution, it can be examined arithmetically by a directed system of trial and error. Thirdly, even when it is not possible to put the mathematics in a formal manner, the model can be tackled by simulation techniques, an example of which is described below.

Whichever of these basic procedures is used to examine the model, it is equivalent to applying a form of search procedure which will provide a lead to the fourth phase of the study, namely the selection of the optimum set of conditions. In carrying out this phase, it is important not only to estimate the set of optimum conditions under the various constraints built into the model, but also to examine how sensitive this solution is to changes in these constraints. Such manipulation makes it possible to see how critically the unique solution that was originally obtained depends upon the basic assumptions built into the problem. This, in turn, can be of extreme importance in helping the manager to select precisely the set of conditions under which he is going to operate. If the solution is insensitive to changes in the constraints, he has considerably more flexibility than in a situation where the optimum conditions are poised, so to speak, on a knife-edge.

The two final phases of the study are connected with implementation; first a pilot implementation test, and then the full-scale implementation. Any proposed solution should be tested as stringently as possible before it is completely accepted and put into use. Neglect to do this can lead to vital factors being overlooked whose inclusion would markedly alter the solution. Experience suggests that the best form of pilot implementation is one where the solution is completely implemented for a portion only of the total system. Giving the proposed solution responsibility for running a complete, although small, section of the operations seems to provide a better form of discipline than trying to run the complete solution in parallel with the previous method of operation. Parallel running in practice seems generally to drag on interminably whilst a vast number of doubts are ironed out, with the result that there is no real clear-cut moment when it becomes advisable to cut off the old method and move over to the new. It is also important that, when the final implementation stage is reached, those responsible for the project should still be available. Only by being present then can they see that the solution is being correctly implemented and also arrange, if there are any snags, for these to be ironed out and the experience gained noted for tackling any future problems of the same kind.

## 1.6  Shipping channel illustration

The phases of an operational research study can be illustrated through a problem which arose with a steel works that was accepting ore from ships arriving from a variety of sources. The basic problem is illustrated by Figure 1.2. Ships arrive in the bay outside the port which serves the steel works. They then have to pass through an entrance channel some thousand yards long, which they can do for only an hour or two around high tide. Furthermore, if the

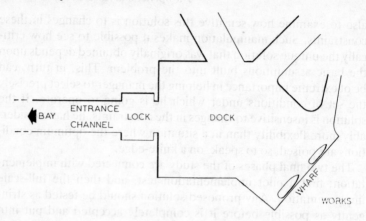

**Figure 1.2    Layout of harbour and docks**

ship is large, it may only be able to go through on certain high tides. Having gone through the entrance channel and lock, it is then moored in the dock area until one of the two berths at the wharf is free, when the ship can go forward for unloading. When the ship has been unloaded it waits in the dock until the next high tide and then passes through the entrance channel back into the bay. Any ship can normally pass through the entrance channel on the way out at the first high tide, irrespective of its size.

Clearly, the actual depth of the entrance channel affects the delays to the ships and their turn-round, in that a deep channel is open to use more frequently than a shallow one. The steel company has some interest in this delay, since they are paid a dispatch bonus which is linked to the turn-round time of ships, measured from their arrival outside the port to their departure from the entrance channel. Furthermore, although the steel company does not own the entrance channel they could pay to have it dredged to a greater depth than it is at present. The problem was to decide whether it would be worthwhile paying to have the entrance channel dredged and, if so, the amount of dredging which should be done. This forms the first phase.

The next phase was to set up a suitable model to describe the situation. It could not be a simple mathematical type of model, because the pattern of intervals between the arrivals of ships, both in terms of time and of the size of ship and type of ore it is carrying, could not be described in simple mathematical terms. What was possible, however, was to set up a flow diagram, such as Figure 1.3, which describes the sequence of decisions that have to be made after each ship arrives. Thus, a ship arrives in the bay; it waits there until the next high tide; if that high tide is suitable it goes through the entrance channel into the dock; if it is unsuitable it waits until the next high tide when it tries to enter the dock again.

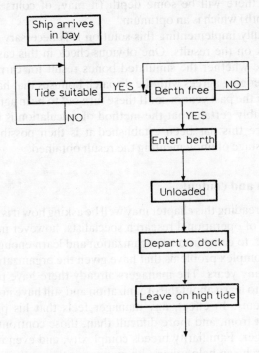

**Figure 1.3 Flow diagram for unloading ships**

This procedure is repeated until the ship arrives in the dock. It will then, subject to any special rules laid down for the presence or absence of queue jumping, go into one of the two berths as soon as one or other is free. The unloading time is defined according to the nature and size of the ship and the type of ore that it is carrying. When that time has elapsed, the ship returns to the dock and then moves out into the bay on the next high tide.

With a table giving the pattern of arrivals of the ships, a corresponding table of the tides and their height and a table of unloading rates, it is possible to simulate what will happen to the whole unloading system for different depths of entrance channel. From these results the corresponding level of dispatch bonus can be estimated. This forms the third phase of the study, namely the simulation analysis of the model. The fourth phase would put together the dispatch bonuses arising from having different depths of channel, against the cost of converting the channel to these different depths. When these two elements of cost and benefit have been combined, there will be some depth (it may, of course, be the present depth) which is an optimum.

Before fully implementing this solution it is necessary to make some check on the results. One obvious check in this case would be to notice whether the simulated bonus result for carrying out no extra dredging agrees with the dispatch bonuses that have been earned over the past year or so. If these turn out to be in agreement, it is reasonably certain that the method of calculation is basically sound. Once this has been established it is then possible to go to the final stage of implementing the result obtained.

## 1.7   Form and content

A manager reading this chapter may well be asking how it is possible for a group of operational research specialists, however ingenious they may be, to come into an organization and learn enough about it to solve complex problems that have given the organization difficulty for many years. The managers already there have probably taken years to learn about the organization and still have not solved these problems. In effect, any manager feels that his problems are different from, and more difficult than, those confronting any other manager. Familiarity breeds complexity, and even if operational research can help others, he may argue 'how can it possibly help me?'

The manager is correct in thinking that his problems are different from anybody else's, but he is wrong in thinking that they are different in every respect. There is a distinction to be drawn between the so-called form and content of problems. In algebra the equation

$$y = a + bx$$

is the standard notation for a straight-line relationship between two variables $y$ and $x$, the letters $a$ and $b$ representing constants. This is an algebraic formula which can be used for a wide range of problems but has no real meaning until it is applied to a particular problem, when specific numbers are put in for the constants $a$ and $b$. For example, if $x$ represents the temperature on the Centigrade scale and $y$ represents the corresponding temperature on the Fahrenheit scale, the equation

$$y = 32 + \frac{9}{5}x$$

which is a particular case of the previous equation, provides a means of converting temperature on one scale to the corresponding temperature on the other. The original form has now been given content and is applicable to the specific problem of temperature conversion.

Any attempt at classification of problem areas is fraught with difficulty. One approach is through a subdivision arranged according to whether or not any of the elements in the problem have a chance factor. If all the relevant facts are known, any decisions needed can be made with complete certainty as to their outcome. Choice of a wrong course of action can then only be because of a flaw in the logical processes of selection. Non-certainty is caused when the decision-maker does not have knowledge or control of all the relevant facts. Such problems are more difficult to handle.

The classical form of linear programming problem (which will be described in Chapter 3), namely the allocation of effort between a number of competing sources, is deterministic (and hence certain) in that the data relating to sources and inputs are completely defined and the outcome of any given allocation can be precisely calculated. Any departure from such definiteness brings the problem into the area of non-certainty. This latter area can be further subdivided into two categories. The category labelled 'risk' is concerned with events having some repetitive nature and whose probabilistic mechanisms are well-known and understood and can generally be computed. The distribution of the intervals between telephone calls, or of the times between successive breakdowns of production machinery are cases in point. The other category, labelled 'uncertainty', is the fuzzier area of non-certainty that arises when, for example, a new product is to be introduced and market forecasts made. This is not a repetitive but a once-and-for-all situation and requires rather different handling.

Table 1.4 shows these three subdivisions and some typical types of problem that fall into each subdivision. Many of these problems will be discussed in the chapters that follow. The book is planned so that three chapters now follow on the first subdivision. Chapters

Table 1.4    **Classification of problems**

| Certainty | Non-certainty | |
| | Risk | Uncertainty |
| (1) | (2) | (3) |
| --- | --- | --- |
| Resource allocation | Simulation | Capital investment |
| Blending (of oils) | Queueing | Bidding problems |
| Transportation | Inventory | Market launching |
| Sequencing | Forecasting | Search problems |
| Critical path | | |

2 and 3 are for all readers, but Chapter 4 may possibly be withheld until a second reading of the book, particularly for those with more limited mathematical equipment. Chapters 5 to 9 deal with problems falling in the second category of risk, whilst Chapters 10 and 11 deal with some concepts and problems in the field of decision analysis under uncertainty. A final chapter discusses applications of operational research in various fields of business operations and the problems associated with both organizing operational research within a firm and implementing the results. The appendices provide additional material, the first for those who wish to further their knowledge of the mathematical approach to programming (particularly allied to Chapter 4), whilst the second appendix provides a useful basic background for the better understanding of Chapters 5 to 11 inclusive. Appropriate references will be found at the end of each chapter.

# References

(1) *A Manager's Guide to Operational Research* by P. Rivett and R. L. Ackoff (Wiley, 1963).
(2) *Management Science: The Business Use of Operations Research* by Stafford Beer (Aldus, 1967).
(3) *Mathematics in Management* by A. Battersby (Penguin, 1966).
(4) *Operational Research for Managers*, edited by S. C. Littlechild (Philip Allan, 1977).

# 2 The programming of resources—Networks

## 2.1 Background

Network analysis (or critical path analysis as it is sometimes called) provides a comprehensive, practical system for planning and controlling many large projects in construction, manufacturing, research and development, and many other fields. Its primary aim is to programme and monitor the progress of a project so that the project is completed in the minimum time. In doing this it pinpoints the parts of the project which are 'critical', i.e. those parts which, if delayed beyond the allotted time, would delay the completion of the project as a whole. It can also be used to assist in allocating resources such as labour and equipment and thus helps to make the total cost of the project a minimum by finding the optimum balance between the various costs and times involved. Basically the method is concerned with the deployment of available resources for the completion of a complex task.

The main financial incentives for using network analysis are to obtain reductions in

(a) lost production time, where productive capacity has to be closed while the work is undertaken;
(b) interest on capital involved, where delay means idle capital;
(c) expenditure on resources, where better planning can increase the utilization of resources that are primarily overheads.

The experience of a number of firms which have used network analysis has shown that on suitable jobs this method can reduce the completion time for a project by 10 per cent or more, and can increase the utilization of resources by at least 5 per cent. The time reduction generally provides the most worthwhile achievement from this technique, and can often be obtained by a relatively low expenditure of effort on the network analysis itself. The following examples illustrate the kind of financial prizes at stake:

(*a*) Alterations made to a paper machine normally operated on a 24-hour continuous basis cause loss of useful production time. If the recovery rate of overheads from operating the machine is £100 per hour, then every day saved on a major machine maintenance yields an increased contribution to profits of £2400.

(*b*) A new factory is being constructed which is expected to achieve an annual profit rate of £1 million once it is operational. For every month by which the construction period of the factory can be reduced, there is a potential gain of about £85 000; for every week a gain of £20 000.

(*c*) The effect of a saving in interest on capital can be illustrated through a major project involving the raising of £10 million capital. Annual interest charges at a rate of 10 per cent would amount to £1 million per annum, so that if better planning could lead to the delay of the expenditure of £1 million of capital for just one month, this alone would result in a saving of £8300.

(*d*) The resources of a department, e.g. the production department or development department, are often under-utilized owing to the fluctuating work load, and at other times may have to be employed at overtime rates to meet peak demands. If the cost of such a department is £300 000 per annum and the utilization can be increased by 5 per cent, this is equivalent to a saving of £15 000 per annum, or may alternatively lead to an increase in output of 5 per cent.

The following are some published examples of actual benefits that have been achieved from the use of networks:

(*a*) The use of PERT version of network analysis is credited with reducing the time taken to implement the Polaris weapon system in the United States by over two years. (PERT stands for Project Evaluation and Review Technique and is broadly equivalent to network analysis.) The use of network analysis is a 'must' for suppliers working on large contracts for the US Government Armed Forces.

(b) Du Pont, the US chemical firm, have used a modified version of network analysis to plan a $10 million project, and credit it with saving $1 million.

(c) Shell's Petite-Couronne refinery is saving 16 per cent in time and 27 per cent in men and money on their maintenance programme.

(d) Mauchley Associates quote the case of a construction project where a 9-month job was reduced to $7\frac{1}{2}$ months, a reduction of nearly 17 per cent.

(e) Du Pont cite a further example in which the use of network analysis reduced the time for a routine maintenance job from 125 to 78 hours, a reduction of over 37 per cent.

Apart from the directly measurable benefits, network analysis can yield other important but less easily measured benefits, e.g. the introduction of a new product to the market earlier than a competitor, or an enhanced ability to deal with last-minute alterations to a programme of work.

The sceptic can argue that there is nothing new in network analysis and that Mrs Beeton's verbal (and indeed verbose) description of how to cook the Christmas dinner is nothing more nor less than a network approach to the need to have everything ready at 1 p.m. on the great feast day. This is perfectly true, but it is also true that once the number of individual activities within a project reaches double figures, most people find it difficult to visualize the project as a whole by conventional means. Network analysis uses a pictorial flow diagram form of approach and aims to squeeze the utmost out of situations where a small saving in time or resources may mean very big money indeed.

## 2.2 The method

The network process consists of two stages as follows:

(a) *Preparing the network,* which entails

(i) Defining the scope and purpose of the whole project.

(ii) Identifying the individual tasks, or 'activities' as they are usually called, which go to make up the project.

(iii) Determining the logical relationships between 'activities' and 'events'—the latter represent the start or end of the individual activities—and constructing the appropriate network diagram.

(iv) Determining, for each activity, the estimated duration, the number of men or other resources to be employed from each trade or skill, and any possible restrictions (such as a specially scheduled starting date for a particular activity).

(b) *Analysing the network and reporting results*, which entails

(i) Analysing the network to find those jobs which are critical in determining the completion time of the project and those which are not so important.

(ii) Determining whether or not it is economically feasible and desirable to shorten the completion time further.

The first stage requires the knowledge and experience of the men responsible for planning the project. Even these preliminaries leading up to the construction of the network can reap considerable benefits: the manager is forced to think in detail about the project well in advance; he will observe the precise way in which the various activities interact or compete for scarce resources; and it is likely that he will be able to improve upon his original plans even before the network has been formally drawn and analysed.

## 2.3　Drawing the network

Each task within the total project is called an ACTIVITY and is represented in the network diagram by an arrow with a circle at either end, as shown in Figure 2.1, the letter A denoting the particular activity concerned.

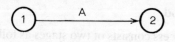

**Figure 2.1**

A circle represents the start or end of the activity and is termed an EVENT, the number in the circle denoting the particular event. An activity can be identified by the pair of numbers belonging to the two events it links. In a typical project, some jobs must be completed before others can begin, whilst others can be carried out concurrently. Consider, for example Figure 2.2 ignoring activity S for the moment. Activity P can be carried out at the same time

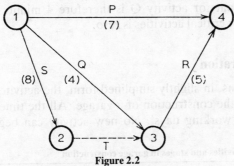

**Figure 2.2**
(Times in brackets are in minutes)

as activities Q and R, but activity Q must be completed before activity R can commence. Suppose now that the further activity S is added. This activity can be performed at the same time as Q but must be completed before R begins. If this is shown as a single loop from event 1 to event 3 this would be ambiguous as both Q and S would be identified by the same pair of events. Hence it is shown by the use of the DUMMY event T, as shown in Figure 2.2. Dummy activities have no duration and, apart from their value in resolving this type of logical difficulty, they have no other meaning. Note that in this particular example, activities Q and S could have been interchanged in position on the network without affecting the logic of the network as a whole.

It should also be noted that, in a network diagram, arrows are used simply to show the relationship between activities; their lengths have no particular significance.

The minimum duration for the sequence of all four activities in Figure 2.2 is 13 minutes. This is because S must be completed before R is started, Q can be done while S is being completed, and P can be done while Q, R and S are being completed. Thus the path from 1 to 4 via 2 and 3 is that of minimum duration and is termed the CRITICAL PATH. Activities which appear on this path are referred to as CRITICAL, others as NONCRITICAL. Thus R and S are critical; P and Q are not. If either R or S is delayed, even by a second, then the whole project is delayed. On the other hand, activity Q could be delayed by as much as 4 minutes before becoming critical, i.e. before it would cause any delay to the completion of the project. The margin available for any activity before it becomes critical is referred to as its TOTAL FLOAT.

The total float for activity Q is therefore 4 minutes, whilst the total float for critical activities is zero.

## 2.4   Illustration

Table 2.1 lists, in slightly simplified form, the activites and stages involved in the construction of a garage. All the times shown are in units of 'working days'. No new activity can begin until the

Table 2.1   **Activities and stages in garage construction**

| Activity reference | Activity nature | Linking events | Estimated days for completion |
|---|---|---|---|
| A | Obtain bricks | 1 and 3 | 5 |
| B | Obtain roof-tiles | 1 and 5 | 12 |
| C | Prepare foundations | 1 and 2 | 7 |
| D | Erect shell | 3 and 4 | 10 |
| E | Construct roof | 5 and 7 | 4 |
| F | Lay drains | 2 and 6 | 7 |
| G | Wiring | 4 and 7 | 10 |
| H | Plastering | 7 and 8 | 6 |
| I | Plumbing | 6 and 7 | 12 |
| J | Flooring | 7 and 10 | 5 |
| K | Landscaping | 9 and 11 | 2 |
| L | Painting and clearing | 10 and 11 | 6 |
| M | Doors and fitting | 8 and 10 | 2 |
| N | Lay pathways | 6 and 9 | 2 |

event logically preceding it (i.e. all the activities leading to that event's completion) has 'occurred'. The corresponding network is shown in Figure 2.3. Notice that a number of dummies have had to be included. Thus activity D cannot be started before both A and C are completed; activity E cannot be started before all the activities A to D inclusive are completed. The events are now numbered in such a manner that any event logically preceding another event has a lower number.

The longest time available for an activity is determined not merely by the time needed for its own completion, but also by the latest time by which it must be completed. Hence, although activity A (obtaining bricks) requires five days, to reach event number 3 needs seven days, because it depends upon the completion of activity C (preparing foundations). The spare time or float available for activity A is therefore at least two days.

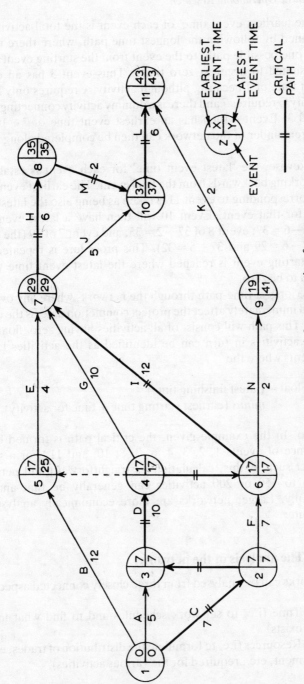

Figure 2.3    Network analysis for construction of garage

The 'earliest event time' of each event is the total activity time obtained by following the longest time path, where there is more than one possible path, to the event from the starting event (which is assumed to occur at zero time). Thus event 3 has an earliest event time of 7 because, although activity A requires only 5 days, activity C requires 7 and there is a dummy activity connecting events 2 and 3. Event 4 then has an earliest event time of $7 + 10 = 17$. The remainder of the network can then be completed along similar lines.

Likewise, the 'latest event time' for each event is established by working backwards from the final event. The earliest event time, 43, corresponding to event 11 is taken as being also the latest event time for that event. Event 10 will then have a latest event time of $43 - 6 = 37$; event 8 of $37 - 2 = 35$; and event 7 of 29 (the earlier of $35 - 6 = 29$ and $37 - 5 = 32$). This procedure is repeated until the starting event is reached where the latest event time will be found to be zero.

The longest time-path through the network, where any over-run would immediately affect the project completion date, is the critical path. This path will consist of all activities having zero 'float', and these activities in turn can be identified as the activities leading to events where the

> Float = (latest finishing time)
>     *minus* (earliest starting time + time for activity)

is zero. In the example given, the critical path is formed by the sequence of events 1, 2, 3, 4, 6, 7, 8, 10, and 11. For a simple project such as this, calculation is straightforward and networks of up to 150 or 200 activities can generally be time-analysed manually. Larger networks are more economically analysed by computer.

## 2.5   The analysis of the network

Networks can be analysed from three closely connected aspects:

(a) Time (i.e. to set work schedules and to find what leeway exists).

(b) Resources (i.e. to formulate the distribution of trades, equipment, etc., required for the various activities).

(c) Cost (i.e. to minimize the total cost of the project).

The result of such analyses can be used as a basis for a plan of action, for example, to attempt to minimize cost for a given total time. These three aspects will now be considered in turn.

## Time

The aim of analysing a network from the point of view of time is to provide

(a) The minimum time in which the project can be completed (based on the estimated times for the various activities); comparison of this with the target completion dates will indicate whether or not the latter can be met.

(b) A list of those activities which are critical, i.e. which must be completed on time if the target completion date is to be met. This focuses attention on those activities which need the closest control, since any reduction in the time taken will reduce the overall time for the project, while any overrun will delay the project. The critical activities are usually emphasized on the network by being shown in red or by a broad strip.

(c) A list of all other activities showing the amount of leeway (float) available, i.e. the amount by which their start or finish can be delayed without affecting the overall completion time.

This form of analysis provides a systematic procedure which identifies those jobs, often relatively few in number, whose improvement in terms of time will shorten the overall duration of the project. In many circumstances there will be possibilities of speeding up selected activities, usually by incurring extra costs. For example, the plumbing could normally be installed in the building in 12 days at a cost of £120 or in 10 days at £150 by working more overtime. Whether this is worthwhile or not will depend upon the value placed upon any time saved in the overall project. If plumbing is on the critical path and each day's saving in completion time for the whole project is worth more than £12, then such a change is worthwhile. If the saving is worth only £10 a day, then it is not worthwhile.

## Resources

The resources available, which are usually limited, may be required for a single project or for several projects running in parallel. The problem is to balance the requests for these resources so that the load on them is as even as possible and yet the projects are each completed in the shortest possible time. The advantage of using networks as the basis for balancing the allocation of resources is that they show clearly which activities can be delayed, and by how much, without causing delays to the whole project. These considerations apply to labour (tradesmen, semi-skilled and unskilled) as well as to various types of capital equipment (bulldozers, cranes, arc-welding equipment, etc.) which may be employed.

The procedure is to

(a) Analyse the requirements for each type of resource according to the various activities, project by project, period by period.

(b) Analyse the total requirements for each particular resource, period by period, assuming that each activity is started at the earliest possible time.

(c) Balance the resource requirements, where it is necessary, by delaying the least critical activities or by proposing a change in the resources available.

The balancing of resources in simple cases can be done by inspection of the tables resulting from these analyses and a re-arrangement of the schedules within the available leeway. For complex situations specialist help may be required in order to reach as satisfactory a solution as possible, without incurring excessive cost. Both the time and resource analyses may have to be re-worked after the total cost analysis has been made (as described in the next section). This specialized procedure is sometimes referred to as RAMPS (resource allocation and multi-project scheduling). Computer programs are available to help, and one such program in general use handles up to six projects utilizing up to 60 resources and containing up to 700 activities. Broadly, by decreasing the input of resources, men, or machinery, there is an increase in their utilization but the project as a whole is delayed. Hence once again the problem of reconciling two conflicting objectives arises. The types of utilization costs that must be borne in mind are threefold. First, there are the premium costs that will be necessary to carry out the scheduled plan during periods when the normally available facilities are overloaded. Second, there are the costs of idle time when no work is available for men or machinery. Third, there are the costs incurred on other projects when they have to wait for individuals or machines that are required on the priority project.

Whenever the availability of a resource is less than its maximum requirement in a network, some choice will have to be exercised in its allocation. Unless a random choice is made, some criterion is needed by which the most efficient allocation may be determined. The criterion used is the utilization, as reflected in the float. By delaying a job with a large float, some of that float tends to be absorbed and the utilization of the resources consumed by that job is thereby enhanced.

## Cost

The object of analysing a network from a cost point of view is to minimize the total cost of the project, i.e. the sum of the direct and indirect costs. By 'direct cost' is meant the cost of labour, material, equipment, etc. required to carry out the project. By 'indirect cost' is meant the penalty for delaying the completion of the project, e.g. loss of profits.

The procedure is to

(a) Estimate the time taken by, and the cost of, the most critical activities if they were carried out normally, and the costs associated with any possible time reductions (e.g. by doing overtime) until the minimum possible time is reached.

(b) Tabulate the direct costs for progressively shorter completion times for the whole project. These costs are calculated by reducing the time taken for those critical activities which cost least to reduce. Note that the critical path may change one or more times during this procedure.

(c) Tabulate the indirect cost for each completion time, since it is likely to be affected by the time taken to complete the project.

(d) Add the direct and indirect costs and hence locate the best time and cost combination.

Figure 2.4 shows graphically the result of carrying out such a procedure, the mimimum cost being shown at point A.

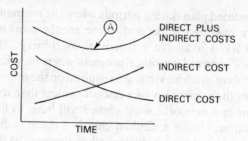

Figure 2.4    Cost versus time

## 2.6    Publishing a book

A further illustration of the use that can be made of a network approach is contained in the various operations necessary for the publication of a book. Table 2.2 shows the thirty-three different activities involved; together with the previous activities that must have been completed in each instance, the normal time involved for each activity, and the associated direct costs. In addition to the direct costs there are fixed overhead costs of £120 per week for the entire duration of the project.

The first step is to construct the network for the publication of the book following the procedures described earlier. The completed network is shown in Figure 2.5, together with the critical path (marked by the double bars) and the earliest and latest event times. As will be seen, the duration is 38 weeks and the total cost is 38 × 120 + 4520 or £9080.

This duration and cost may be acceptable to the publisher in the particular circumstances concerned, but there is the possibility that fourteen of the activities could be completed more rapidly, as indicated in the final columns of Table 2.2, but at a greater cost. A next step in seeing how worthwhile it is to speed up the process is accordingly to re-analyse the network with the rapid as opposed to the normal times. This is done in Figure 2.6 which produces a new critical path, indicated by the revised double bar route through the network. Note that, for a period, the network has parallel critical paths. The new duration is 26 weeks, i.e. a reduction of 12 weeks, and the total cost now involved is 26 × 120 + 6900 = £10020, an increase of £940.

Whilst the shorter duration may well be welcome to the publishers, albeit at increased cost, it is not necessarily the case that

Table 2.2  **Activities in publishing a book**

| Activity | Previous required activities | Description | Normal Duration (weeks) | Cost (£) | Rapid Duration (weeks) | Cost (£) |
|---|---|---|---|---|---|---|
| A | — | Negotiate contract | 4 | 0 | 2 | 800 |
| B | A | Forecast sales | 1 | 40 | 0·5 | 80 |
| C | A | Design book | 2 | 80 | 2 | 80 |
| D | B,C | Estimate cost | 1 | 40 | 1 | 40 |
| E | C | Design jacket | 1 | 40 | 1 | 40 |
| F | B,C | Plan publicity | 8 | 160 | 6 | 180 |
| G | D | Make drawings | 4 | 160 | 2 | 240 |
| H | D | Prepare MS. | 1 | 20 | 1 | 20 |
| J | D | Obtain paper | 8 | 600 | 2 | 1200 |
| K | D | Making binding cases | 4 | 160 | 3 | 200 |
| L | G | Check drawings | 2 | 0 | 1 | 20 |
| M | L | Make bromides | 8 | 80 | 4 | 160 |
| N | M | Check bromides | 2 | 0 | 2 | 0 |
| P | H | Key text | 4 | 800 | 3 | 1000 |
| Q | P | Read galley proofs | 1 | 20 | 1 | 20 |
| R | Q | Correct galley proofs | 2 | 80 | 2 | 80 |
| S | N,R | Paginate | 0·5 | 0 | 0·5 | 0 |
| T | S | Check page proofs | 1 | 0 | 1 | 0 |
| U | S | Index | 2 | 20 | 2 | 20 |
| V | T,U | Impose | 1 | 120 | 0·5 | 160 |
| W | V | Check imposition | 1 | 0 | 1 | 0 |
| X | J,W | Machine (press work) | 4 | 400 | 3·5 | 480 |
| Y | K | Make dummies | 6 | 60 | 4 | 80 |
| Z | Y | Cut binding brass | 2 | 20 | 2 | 20 |
| AA | Z | Block binding cases | 1 | 100 | 1 | 100 |
| BB | X,AA | Bind | 3 | 960 | 1·5 | 1200 |
| CC | E | Make jacket plate | 6 | 80 | 6 | 80 |
| DD | CC | Print jacket | 3 | 160 | 3 | 160 |
| EE | Y,DD | Wrap dummies | 1 | 20 | 1 | 20 |
| FF | F,EE | Sales campaign | 8 | 200 | 8 | 200 |
| GG | FF | Receive orders | 2 | 0 | 2 | 0 |
| HH | DD,BB | Add jacket | 0·5 | 20 | 0·5 | 20 |
| JJ | GG,HH | Distribute | 3 | 80 | 1 | 200 |
| | | Total direct costs | | 4520 | | 6900 |

they need to put all the activities on to the rapid method (and at increased cost) to achieve the lowered duration. Hence some further analysis is desirable and it is assumed for this purpose that an individual activity can be speeded up *pro rata* within the bounds set by the normal and rapid columns of the table; e.g. distribution (activity JJ) could be planned to take 2 weeks at a cost of £140.

Table 2.3 lists the fourteen activities that could be speeded up and, in the final column, the cost per week of speeding up the activity concerned. The derived Table 2.4 provides a sequential

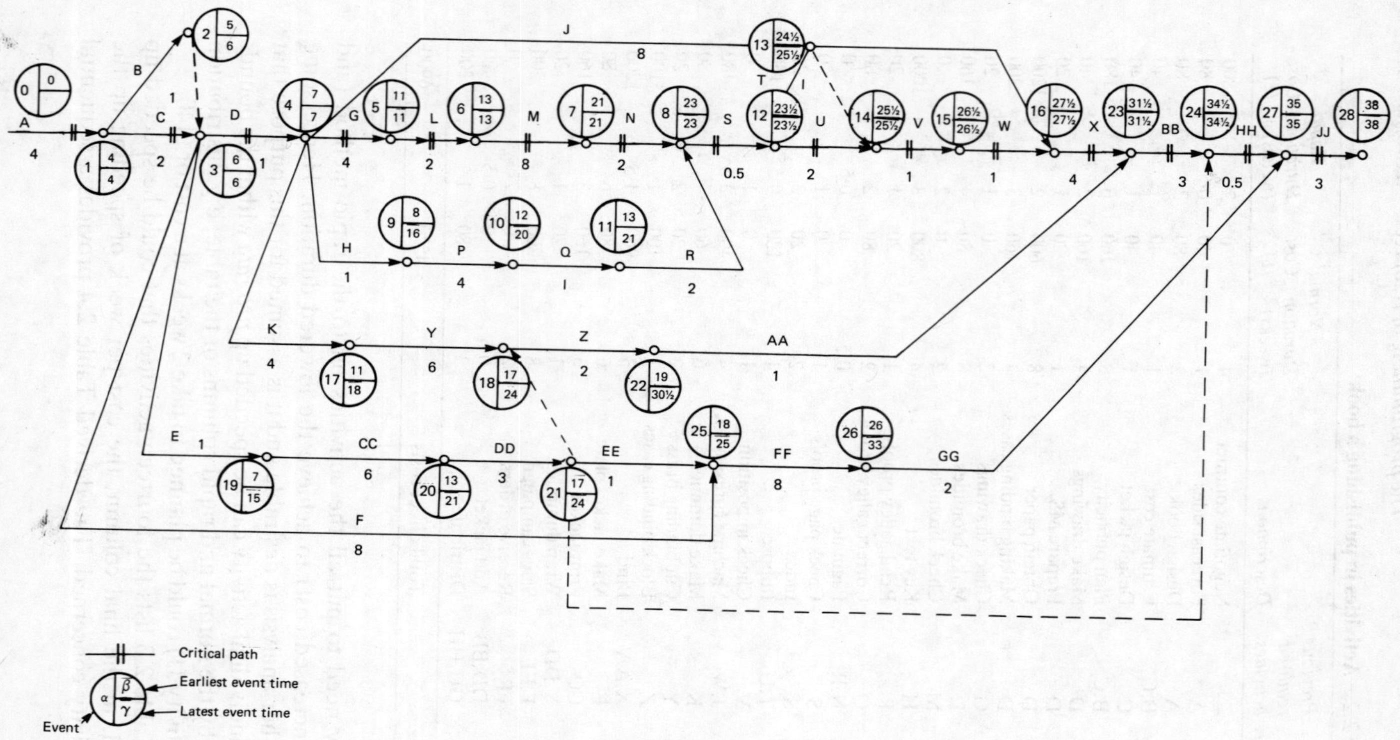

**Figure 2.5  Normal durations**

Critical path

Earliest event time

α / β | γ

Event

**Figure 2.6 Rapid durations**

Table 2.3  **Rapid activities in publishing**

| Activity | Description | Maximum reduction of duration (weeks) | Cost (£/week) |
|---|---|---|---|
| A | Negotiate contract | 2 | 400 |
| B | Forecast sales | 0·5 | 80 |
| F | Plan publicity | 2 | 10 |
| ✓G | Make drawings | 2 | 40 |
| J | Obtain paper | 6 | 100 |
| K | Making binding cases | 1 | 40 |
| ✓L | Check drawings | 1 | 20 |
| ✓M | Make bromides | 4 | 20 |
| P | Key text | 1 | 200 |
| V | Impose | 0·5 | 80 |
| X | Machine (press work) | 0·5 | 160 |
| Y | Make dummies | 2 | 10 |
| BB | Bind | 1·5 | 160 |
| ✓JJ | Distribute | 2 | 60 |

analysis starting with all items at normal duration. It then selects the lowest cost reduction item in the critical path, one at a time, making the maximum reduction until such time as the critical path changes. This occurs after steps 2 to 5 (i.e. reductions for estimates L, M, G and JJ) have been taken, when the duration has been reduced by 9 weeks. Parallel paths have now to be examined and step 6 reduces V and J simultaneously for half a week at a combined cost of £45. Step 7 requires the simultaneous reduction of each of activities BB and Y for half a week at a cost of £85. Finally, with step 8 the contract negotiation, activity A, is reduced by two weeks at a cost of £800. The final duration is now the minimum of 26 weeks at a total cost of $5750 + 120 \times 26 = £8870$, a saving of £1150 on the total cost when all the activities were at rapid.

It will be noted that the mixed strategy, with some activities at normal and some at rapid, has led to a total cost that is *lower* than the situation when all the activities were at normal rates. This raises an interesting question: suppose the publisher has no deadline for the book and can take as long or short a time on it as he likes. What is then the minimum cost duration for publishing the book? Every week that the publisher gains is worth £120 to him and hence, for as long as the cost reduction is below £120, it is worthwhile to make this reduction. From Table 2.4 this is true up to and including step 6, so that the lowest overall cost

Table 2.4  **Steps in network contraction**

| Step | Activity | Rate (£/week) | Cost of reduction (£) | New total cost (£) | Reduced by | New total duration |
|------|----------|---------------|----------------------|--------------------|-------------|-------------------|
| 1 | All at normal | — | — | 4520 | — | 38 |
| 2 | Check drawings (L) | 20 | 20 | 4540 | 1 | 37 |
| 3 | Make bromides (M) | 20 | 80 | 4620 | 4 | 33 |
| 4 | Make drawings (G) | 40 | 80 | 4700 | 2 | 31 |
| 5 | Distribution (JJ) | 60 | 120 | 4820 | 2 | 29 |
| 6 | { Impose (V) / Make dummies (Y) } | 90 | 45 | 4865 | 0·5 | 28·5 |
| 7 | { Bind (BB) / Make dummies (Y) } | 170 | 85 | 4950 | 0·5 | 28 |
| 8 | Negotiate contract (A) | 400 | 800 | 5750 | 2 | 26 |

The column headed *Duration (weeks)* spans the *Reduced by* and *New total duration* columns.

option is a duration of 28·5 weeks with a total cost of
$120 \times 28.5 + 4865$ or £8285.

## 2.7  The cost of using network analysis

The cost of using network analysis is made up of the costs of the
time taken by

(a) the specialist constructing and analysing the network,
(b) those providing the estimates of times, costs, resources, etc.,
(c) clerical assistance or computer time if a computer is used.

These costs are clearly dependent on the project under consideration, but most of them are generally incurred once any planning
at all is done; the use of network analysis, however, considerably
reduces the time taken to revise any project plans compared with,
for instance, revisions of bar or Gantt charts that are commonly
used in project planning.

Since network analysis can commonly be expected to reduce
the time taken for a project by at least 10 per cent, and to improve
the utilization of resources by at least 5 per cent, it is possible
to estimate the amount that can economically be spent on using
it. For example, in a project estimated to take approximately ten
months, for which the penalty for each month's delay in completion
is £1000, it would be economical to spend up to £1000 on network
analysis. Alternatively, if a saving on resources could be made
through network analysis of £15 000 per annum, it would be worth

spending up to some multiple of that amount, say about £60 000. However, it is unlikely that the use of network analysis would ever cost such a high proportion of the savings. If a large project with 1000 activities were considered, the network might require

| 4 weeks' work by a specialist | say £1200 |
| 2 weeks' assistance from those concerned with the project | say £ 400 |
| Computer time or clerical cost | say £ 200 |
| | £1800 |

This could then be justified for a job expected to take roughly ten months at a cost penalty of £1800 or more per month, and few projects of 1000 activities would be found in practice to have such a low penalty.

## 2.8 An algorithm

Networks are concerned with the carrying out of some task in the most effective manner. The decisions made relate to the sequencing of the various components leading to the total task being completed. A related kind of decision process is that commonly referred to as an *algorithm* whose basic definition is 'an exact prescription defining a computational process that leads from various initial data to a desired result'. This definition is something of a mouthful and the following example describes the process in more digestible form.

A car-hire firm at an airport has three tariffs: A, B or C. Each is based on different combinations of the duration for which the car is hired and the mileage covered during the hire period. For example, one tariff has a low duration rate and a high mileage charge; another tariff has the converse. The firm undertakes to charge a client, at the end of his hire period, on the tariff that produces the lowest bill for his particular hiring position. This problem can be straightforwardly solved, in a logical manner, since all the conditions for charging are precisely specified. As inputs there are three sets of rules applicable to tariffs A, B and C; together with the information concerning the duration of hire and the mileage concerned for a particular customer.

The process by which the required change could be arrived at is shown in skeleton form in Figure 2.7. By following the diagram

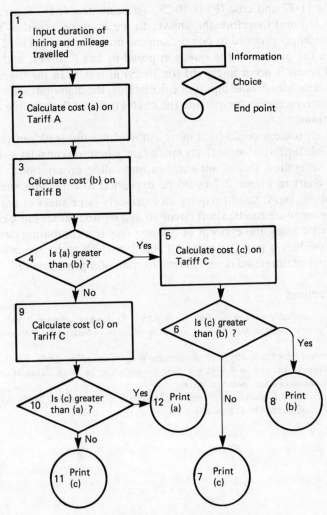

**Figure 2.7 Car-hire tariffs**

through from the start point, marked 1, each step in the calculation is laid out so as to require no conscious analysis as such, only the following of precisely laid-down instructions. Provided the instructions are followed, the correct answer must be obtained, there being no point where judgment as such is necessary.

There are four possible end points, at boxes 7, 8, 11 and 12, and one of these must be reached. For example, suppose that cost

(a) is 11·47 and cost (b) is 10·28. Thus, at step 4, (a) is greater than (b) and therefore the answer to the question posed is Yes. Accordingly proceed to box 5. Suppose now that cost (c) is 12·14. Then the answer to the question posed in box 6 is Yes, and the final result is accordingly (b) (or 10·28) in box 8. In the diagram the rectangles denote inputs or calculations, the diamonds are comparison, or choice, points and the circles indicate the possible end positions.

The problem could be a more complicated one with not three possible tariffs but some thirty tariffs (and when you consider airline fare schedules, this is not such an impossible proposition). The flow-chart in Figure 2.7 could be expanded to cope with such a situation, but it would require an extremely large sheet of paper. The procedure can be short circuited and written rather more concisely by using the concept of a *loop*. This is a computing device that enables a part, or parts, of the flow-chart to be repeated a number of times and is well known to computer programmers.

# References

(1) *An Introduction to Critical Path Analysis* by K. G. Lockyer (Pitman, 1966).
(2) *Network Analysis for Planning and Scheduling* by A. Battersby (Macmillan, 1967).
(3) *Critical Path Method* by A. T. Armstrong-Wright (Longman, 1969).
(4) *Network Analysis in Forming a New Organization* by W. S. Ryan (C.A.S. Occasional Papers, No. 3, HMSO).
(5) *Operational Research for Managers* edited by S. C. Littlechild (Phillip Allan, 1977) (Chapter 4 by J. B. Kidd).

# 3 The programming of resources—the graphical approach to allocation

## 3.1 The wood-working business

In Section 1.2 (page 2) the problem of Mr Harvey's wood-working business was described. Basically his situation was that he had certain productive resources available and could make any or all of three products. The basic data are reproduced in Table 3.1.

Table 3.1 **Wood-working business**

| Product | Selling price | Process output (per hour) | | | Daily demand |
|---|---|---|---|---|---|
| | | P | Q | R | |
| Armchairs (A) | £30 | 1 | 2 | 1 | 9 |
| Bookshelves (B) | £20 | 2 | — | 1 | 11 |
| Coatstands (C) | £20 | — | 3 | 2 | 9 |
| Process cost per hour | | £50 | £60 | £70 | |

As he only works an 8-hour day, there are limitations on the utilization of the productive resources which, together with marketing restrictions, form constraints to prevent Mr Harvey from making as many as he might desire of each product. Assuming that his objective is to obtain maximum profit, one possible line of argument Mr Harvey might pursue runs as follows:

'Suppose that I use process R entirely by itself, as this is the one process that makes all three products. Then, using average outputs and costs, I can operate for only $4\frac{1}{2}$ hours per day and my output per day will be $4\frac{1}{2}$ units of A, $4\frac{1}{2}$ of B, and 9 of C. The total cost will be £315 and the total sales revenue will be £405, giving a profit of £90. I notice that this is well below the potential market for A and B and hence decide to 'fill up' as far as possible with process P which makes both A and B.

'Since process P produces 2 B type units per hour and the untapped market for type B is $(11 - 4\frac{1}{2})$, or $6\frac{1}{2}$ units per day, the maximum time I can take up on process P will be $3\frac{1}{4}$ hours per day. For simplicity, I decide to make my schedule 3 hours on process P, with $4\frac{1}{2}$ hours on process R. This will give total costs of £465 per day and total sales revenue of £615, leaving a profit of £150 per day.

'But this may not be the maximum, particularly as the market is not being completely utilized. I now notice that an hour on process Q produces £60 of profit, whilst on process R an hour produces only £20 of profit. Hence as much substitution from R to Q as is possible would seem desirable. In fact, only 3 hours of process Q are possible, as 9 C type units are the maximum that can be sold per day. The position now would be:

| Production | P: 3 hours at £50 | Q: 3 hours at £60 | Total cost £330 |
|---|---|---|---|
| Yield A | 3 | 6 | 9 sales at £30 = £270 |
| Yield B | 6 | — | 6 sales at £20 = £120 |
| Yield C | — | 9 | 9 sales at £20 = £180 |

With a total cost of £330 and a total selling value of £570, a profit of £240 is left. Can I improve upon this result?'

Trial and error shows that this solution cannot be improved upon, but a trial and error procedure to ensure that this is so is tedious. Cannot, therefore, this type of problem be tackled in some more general way which guarantees obtaining an optimum production schedule?

## 3.2   The general allocation problem

Mr Harvey's wood-working business provides one illustration of an allocation problem. There are three main types of allocation problems.

### (a)  Assignment problems

In this group of problems, each of $n$ units of one type has to be linked with one of $n$ units of a second type in such a way that every unit has just one link. For example, origins of one type are to be associated with a unique destination of the second type, and a table of effectiveness is available showing the cost, or profit, of making each possible link. It is wished to make the associations in such a way as to minimize (or maximize) the summed effectiveness. For illustration, consider the following example, in which the tractors form the origins (!) and the various consumers' premises form the destinations.

A petrol company distributes petrol from its bulk storage depot to industrial consumers. For this purpose, it maintains a fleet of tractors and tank trailers. Since emptying a trailer at a consumer's premises usually takes about two hours, the tractor driver leaves the loaded trailer at the consumer's premises, picks up an empty trailer from either the same or another consumer, and returns it to the bulk storage depot for re-filling.

Assume that on a certain morning ten similar tractors have been sent out to deliver ten loaded trailers to consumers located in different parts of the city. After unhooking the trailers on consumers' unloading premises, the tractors are required to haul back ten empty trailers from the premises of ten other consumers. The problem is to assign these ten tractors to empty trailers in such a way that the cost of hauling back empty trailers is minimized.

The cost of taking back an empty trailer is known to depend on

(i) the total distance travelled by the tractor from the place where it was unloaded back to the bulk storage depot, and

(ii) the speed of travel.

Knowing these factors, one naive method of approaching this problem would be to determine the cost associated with every feasible assignment and then to pick the minimum cost assignment. Note, however, that the total number of feasible assignments is 3 628 800. Hence some quicker and more systematic method of approach seems necessary and efficient algebraic procedures and computer codes have been developed to achieve this result.

## (b) Transportation problems

This class of problem is a generalization of the type described under (a) above. The table of effectiveness of the various possible linkages is no longer necessarily square: it defines the precise effectiveness when each of a number of origins is associated with each of a possibly different number of destinations. The total movement from each origin is known, together with the total movement to each destination. It is required to determine how the associations should be made subject to the limitation on totals. An illustration of such a problem, involving the transportation of goods from factories to warehouses, was described in Section 1.2, and again efficient algebraic procedures and computer codes have been developed to solve general problems of this type.

## (c)  Programming problems

In describing this group, the earlier groups of problems (a) and (b) are included as special cases. Since rather easier computational procedures are available for (a) and (b) these are used whenever possible. The general group involves a broad class of optimization problems dealing with the interaction of many variables subject to certain constraints.

For example, certain steel products may be obtained in a steel mill by using various combinations of raw material and hot-rolling, cold-rolling, annealing, normalizing and slitting operations. To be able to reach an optimal programming decision, all possible combinations of these operations and materials must be considered simultaneously. Here profit might be the objective to be optimized. Note, incidentally, that there is usually a big difference between programmes which maximize profits and those which minimize costs. Only if the product quantities are fixed or if the sales prices are directly proportional to the costs will the two programmes give the same allocation.

The constraints imposed on the process could include, for example:

   (i)   capacity limitations of each operational facility,
  (ii)   minimum amounts required for each product,
 (iii)   production requirements, quantity and/or quality,
  (iv)   delivery requirements,
   (v)   limitations on availability of operating fuels,
  (vi)   limitations on availability of raw materials.

To illustrate this general type of problem and the method by which its solution can be approached, an example is described below in some detail. The technique used for its solution provides a demonstration of the *linear programming* method. Such a method is applicable when the key elements are related directly (e.g. total variable costs are proportional to the volume of production). This property is called linearity and is referred to further in Section 3.8. In this chapter a graphical approach to linear programming is described, whilst in the following chapter, and in Appendix A a more mathematical approach is discussed.

## 3.3 The Transrad Company

A small company, the Transrad Company, assembles and markets two types of portable black and white TV sets, A and B. Currently 200 sets of each type are manufactured per week. It is clear to management that not all the facilities are being fully utilized and it is desired to formulate the production schedule that will maximize the profits. Some relevant facts concerning these TV sets are as follows:

| Type | Total component cost per set | Man-hours of assembly time per set | Average man-minutes of inspection and correction time per set | Selling price per set |
|------|------|------|------|------|
| A | £50 | 12 | 10 | £100 |
| B | £40 | 6 | 35 | £70 |

The disparity in inspection and correction time is due to the fact that some of the components in the B sets are of cheaper and lower quality than those in A sets. The company employs 100 assemblers, who are paid £2·50 *per hour actually worked* and who will work up to a maximum of 48 hours per week. The amount of inspection and correction time used per week cannot be exactly forecast for any particular week, as long runs of successes or failures may occur. The inspectors, of whom there are currently four, have agreed to a plan whereby they average 40 hours of work per week each. However, the four inspectors have certain other administrative duties which have been found to take up an average of $8\frac{1}{3}$ hours per week between them. The inspectors are each paid a fixed wage of £200 per week.

Each TV set, of either type, requires one speaker, the type being the same for each set. Speakers are scarce, and the company can obtain a maximum supply of 600 in any one week. Their cost has been included in the components cost given for each set in the table above. Only speakers actually used need be paid for. The only other costs incurred by the company are fixed overheads of £5000 per week.

Under the present production schedule the company has a sales income of

$$200 \times 100 + 200 \times 70 = 34\,000$$

(All monetary values from now on are expressed in £ unless otherwise stated and the £ sign will be omitted when there is no risk of ambiguity.)

The company's costs consist of

| | | |
|---|---|---|
| Components | $50 \times 200 + 40 \times 200$ | $= 18\,000$ |
| Assemblers | $2.5\,(12 \times 200 + 6 \times 200) =$ | $9\,000$ |
| Inspection | | $800$ |
| Overheads | | $5\,000$ |

giving a total cost of 32 800 and a profit of 1200. The company now has to ask itself whether this is the maximum profit it can make. Clearly, any decision to change from the present manufacturing schedule must partially depend upon the marketing opportunities available. On being pressed, the sales manager believes he could sell up to 600 of either type, and 600 is clearly the maximum that could ever be sold because of the limitation on the availability of speakers.

To study the problem formally, let $a$ represent the number of TV sets made of type A, and $b$ represent the number made of type B. Then the cost statement given earlier can be re-stated formally as follows:

| | | |
|---|---|---|
| Sales income | $100a + 70b$ | |
| Costs: | | |
| Components | | $50a + 40b$ |
| Assemblers | $2.50(12a + 6b) =$ | $30a + 15b$ |
| Inspection | | $800$ |
| Overheads | | $5000$ |

Hence the profit is

$$(100a + 70b) - (50a + 40b) - (30a + 15b) - 800 - 5000$$

or

$$20a + 15b - 5800 \qquad (3.1)$$

It is important, however, to realize that $a$ and $b$ cannot be chosen at will. There are three constraints involved which affect the permissible range of $a$ and $b$ values. These constraints are derived from the availability of the speakers, the availability of labour for the assembly of the TV sets, and the limitation on inspection time.

| Constraint | Resources | Amount needed | Maximum amount available | Form of constraint† |
|---|---|---|---|---|
| | | (1) | (2) | (3) |
| I | Speakers | $a + b$ | 600 | Col. (1) ≤ Col. (2) |
| II | Assembly | $12a + 6b$ (hours) | 4800 (hours) | Col. (1) ≤ Col. (2) |
| III | Inspection | $10a + 35b$ (minutes) | 9100* (minutes) | Col. (1) ≤ Col. (2) |

* This figure represents the total available minutes less the time required for other duties (in minutes) or $4 \times 60 \times 40 - 500$.

† The symbol ≤ is shorthand for the phrase 'is less than or equal to'.

The values of $a$ and $b$ should now be chosen to maximize the profit function, at equation (3.1) above, subject to the three constraints given in the table. To illustrate this, Figure 3.1 shows the complete range of values of $a$ and $b$ that are permissible. The figure is in the form of a simple graph with $a$ and $b$ forming the two axes. Since $a$ and $b$ must both take positive (or zero) values, only the top right-hand part of the straightforward four-quadrant graph is permissible. But even within this quadrant not all values of $a$ and $b$ are allowable. Constraint I states that the sum of the values of $a$ and $b$, or $a + b$, must be less than or equal to 600. What combinations of values of $a$ and $b$ meet this restriction? Suppose that $a + b$ exactly equals 600. Then it will be found that this condition will be satisfied for all the values of $a$ and $b$ falling along the line marked I in Figure 3.1. Thus the points (400, 200) or (300, 300) or (0, 600) all satisfy the constraint exactly. Remember that in the shorthand notation (400, 200), the first figure 400 refers to the $a$ or horizontal axis, whilst the second figure 200 refers to the $b$ or vertical axis. For any point (i.e. combination of $a$ and $b$) which falls to the south-west of line I the combined value of $a$ and $b$ will be less than 600, since the value of either $a$ or of $b$, or of both, must be less than those for some point falling on the line I. Hence all points that fall in the area KPQ satisfy

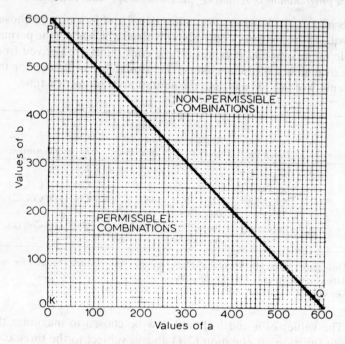

**Figure 3.1    The constraint due to loudspeakers**

constraint (I). This already limits the possibilities, but further limitations must also be put down.

## 3.4   Additional constraints

Not only are there constraints due to the availability of speakers, but also constraints due to the time required for assembly and inspection. These two forms of constraint can be dealt with in precisely the same way. For example, the constraint due to assemblers (II) can be expressed as

$$12a + 6b \leqslant 4800$$

The line RS in Figure 3.2 shows the boundary between what is and is not permissible. Any combination of values of $a$ and $b$ to the north-east side of this line is inadmissible; any combination to the south-west is admissible. But the values of $a$ and $b$ must satisfy both the restrictions due to speakers and those due to assemblers. Taking restrictions I and II together, the area for

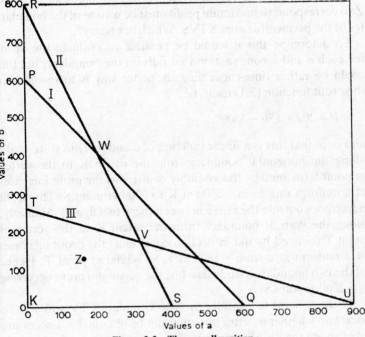

**Figure 3.2 The overall position**

permissible combinations of *a* and *b* values is now KPWS, a four-sided area.

The final constraint, that of inspection time, leads to the boundary line TU and the overall permissible area of combinations of *a* and *b*, taking into account all three constraints, becomes KTVS.

It is now necessary to find the particular combination of *a* and *b* values within the area KTVS which leads to the greatest profit. The profit function which is to be maximized is

$$20a + 15b - 5800 \qquad \text{(from (3.1) above)}$$

Consider the pair of values of *a* and *b* corresponding to an arbitrarily chosen point Z inside the allowable area KTVS. The profit corresponding to these values for *a* and *b* could be calculated from equation (3.1). Call this profit $P_1$. But as the point Z is *inside* the allowable area, it would be possible to increase $P_1$ by increasing the value of either *a* or *b* or both. Note that this is because the coefficients (multipliers) of both *a* and *b* in (3.1) are positive. The value of *a* or *b* or both can go on increasing until a boundary of the area KTVS is reached. Hence the optimum location for Z to correspond to maximum profit must be on one of the boundaries of the permissible area KTVS. Which boundary?

To determine this it would be possible to evaluate the profit for each $a$ and $b$ combination that falls on the boundary, but this could be rather time-consuming. A better way is to re-consider the profit function (3.1) itself, i.e.

$$P = 20a + 15b - 5800$$

and note that this is a linear function of $a$ and $b$. Thus if we move along the horizontal boundary from the origin K to the vertex at point S (defined by the assembly constraint) the profit increases at a uniform rate from $-5800$ at K to 2200 at point S. The profit never goes outside the range between these two figures. Similarly, along the vertical boundary from the origin K to the vertex at point T (defined by the inspection constraint) the profit increases at a uniform rate from $-5800$ at K to $-1900$ at point T. Hence of the two boundaries studied so far, the maximum profit occurring is $+2200$ at point S.

There remains to consider the two boundaries TV and VS. To ascertain whether a better optimum can be obtained it is necessary to evaluate the profit at point V. The coordinates of point V represent the junction of the pair of lines.

$$12a + 6b = 4800 \text{ (assembly constraint)}$$
$$\text{and } 10a + 35b = 9100 \text{ (inspection constraint)}$$

If these are solved as a pair of simultaneous equations they give

$$a = 315 \text{ and } b = 170$$

and hence the corresponding profit at point V from equation (i) is equal to 3050. The same principle applies as before, namely that all points on the boundary TV must have profits between $-1900$ and 3050, whilst on VS the profits fall between 3050 and 2200. Thus the optimum solution occurs at point V, when the production schedule would be 315 sets of Type A and 170 sets of Type B, to give a resultant weekly profit of 3050. This profit can be compared with the current weekly profit of 1200. In general terms, the optimum can be found by evaluating the profit at the production combinations corresponding to each of the vertices of the permissible area and picking out the best.

## 3.5   Relaxation of constraints

At the optimum point V, two constraints are being called into play, namely those of assembly and inspection time. The number of speakers is not a constraint in this situation, only 485 out of the available 600 being used up for the optimum schedule. This raises the question as to what would happen were it possible to relax those constraints which are critical to the solution, say by working overtime or by taking on extra staff. To answer this, a form of marginal analysis is carried out. Suppose that constraint II, relating the availability of assemblers, were made to read

$$12a + 6b \leq 4801$$

in place of

$$12a + 6b \leq 4800$$

This is recording formally that one extra hour of assembler's time can be permitted. The whole analysis outlined above could now be repeated and a new and modified solution found along the same lines as before. The revised solution is

$$a = 315\frac{7}{32} \qquad b = 169\frac{35}{36}$$

and the new profit $P' = 3051\frac{19}{36}$.

Ignore, for a moment, the fractional nature of the values of $a$ and $b$ and note that an increase of 1 hour in the amount of assembly time available has led to an increase in the total profit of $1\frac{19}{36}$. The method of calculation used has automatically included the £2·50 cost of an hour of assembler's time. Hence what this result is saying is that, at £2·50 per hour, an extra hour of assembler's time increases profit by £$1\frac{19}{36}$. If it proved necessary to pay a premium rate of £5 per hour for such extra time, the change in profit would be $1\frac{19}{36} - (5 - 2\cdot50)$ or $-\frac{35}{36}$, converting a marginal profit into a marginal loss. Thus overtime at such a rate is not worthwhile. Note also that the revised production schedule, whilst increasing the number of A sets produced, decreases the number of B sets produced.

Alternatively, consider the effect of changes in the amount of inspection time available. If the total number of inspection minutes available are raised by 1 (i.e. from 9100 to 9101), leaving the other constraints unaltered, then the revised solution is

$$a = 314\frac{59}{60} \qquad b = 170\frac{1}{30}$$

and the total profit is

$$P'' = 3050\tfrac{1}{6}$$

Hence 1 extra minute of inspection time is worth 1/6, or 1 extra hour would be worth $60 \times 1/6$ or 10. Note that the profit evaluation used here considers inspection as a fixed cost in the total costs. Hence the cost of inspection time would have to be deducted from this apparent profit of any extra units. If such time could only be obtained at a rate of 10 per hour, then there would be no overall profit in obtaining the extra time. If it were to cost only 7·5 per hour, then there would be a further profit of 2·5 per hour obtained. Note also that, in this case, the revised production schedule calls for more B-type sets, but fewer A-type sets.

The summarized position, if marginally extra amounts of assembly or inspection time were available, is shown in Table 3.2.

Table 3.2   **Marginal profit-changes**

| Extra hour of | Extra profit excluding cost of provision of manpower | Normal cost of 1 hour of manpower |
|---|---|---|
| Assembly time | 4·03 (i.e. $1\tfrac{19}{36} + 2\tfrac{18}{36}$) | 2·50 |
| Inspection time | 10·00 | 5·30* |

\* This includes an allowance for 'non-inspection' time in the inspectors' working week. If this is ignored the normal cost falls to 5·00.

Of course it would not actually be possible to operate extra single hours of either assembly or inspection time, owing to the fractional values for $a$ and $b$ that result. Nevertheless, these figures demonstrate the *rate* of improvement in profits achieved as the level of availability of time improves. Such rates must not, however, be extrapolated indefinitely. It would, for example, be quite wrong to assume from the marginal calculation that 100 extra hours of inspection time would automatically net precisely 1000 extra profit, less the cost of the provision of the time. The amount may be affected by whether or not other constraints come into play. Hence for large changes it would be necessary to re-establish the profit actually achievable in the same way as before and the reader is invited to investigate the revised situation for himself. Like the correct use of marginal costing figures, these marginal profit figures are valuable in showing the trends.

## 3.6   A minimum cost problem

The problem just discussed aimed to maximize profits. Linear programming can equally well be concerned with minimizing some function. For example, the quality of a product is specified by the number of units of a certain attribute Z contained in each tonne. It is desired to make 1 tonne of this product containing at least 50 units of Z at minimum cost. The raw materials shown in Table 3.3 are available—how much of each should be purchased?

Table 3.3   **Ingredients and costs**

| Material | Units of Z per tonne of material | Cost per tonne (£) |
|---|---|---|
| A | 30 | 80 |
| B | 40 | 50 |
| C | 80 | 70 |
| D | 100 | 90 |

Here the total cost is to be minimized and the solution will consist of finding the cheapest mixture of the four materials which contains at least 50 units of Z per tonne.

The problem can be solved graphically, through a slightly different approach to that used earlier. Figure 3.3 shows the cost per tonne of each material and the units of Z per tonne. Now any compound formed from A, B, C and D will have costs and Z-content represented by a point inside the area ABCD on Figure 3.3. For example, if a mixture is made consisting of A and C in a 50:50 ratio, then the characteristics of the mixture as to cost and Z-content will correspond to the point in Figure 3.3 which bisects the line joining A to C. Now MN divides the allowable mixtures, from a Z-content point of view, from the non-allowable mixtures. Only mixtures to the right of MN need be considered. As the cost is to be minimized, a mixture is required which is as far down the graph as is possible. This is achieved at point N where the line MN crosses the line BC. At this point $BN = \frac{1}{4}BC$ (found either by measurement on the graph or by simple algebra) and hence the mixture consists of 3 parts of B to 1 part of C. The cost, read from the graph, is £55 per tonne.

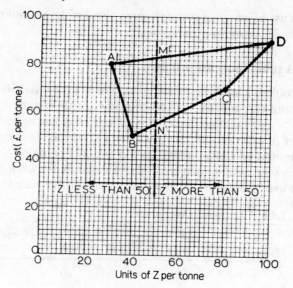

**Figure 3.3   Allowable compounds**

## 3.7   Power and limitations

In general, the use of linear programming obtains a specific solution to a particular problem. For example, if a factory can manufacture ten different products and only one constraint is placed on the manufacturing schedule, say time, then the optimum production schedule will contain just one product. This would be the product whose profit per unit of production time is highest. If two constraints were placed on the system, say time and material availability, the optimum solution need only contain at most two products. As an illustration that this is so, suppose that the solution to a particular programming problem containing three products, A, B and C, appeared to suggest the schedule in Table 3.4.

Then it would be possible to improve the proposed allocation, which gives a profit of £280 by transferring all the time spent on A to B, since that provides an increase in profit per unit time and a reduction in usage of material. The solution would now read:

   B 8 hours     C 2 hours     Profit £320

and not all the material would be used, some 8 units being left over. A further improvement could be made by increasing the

Table 3.4 **Trial allocation**

| Product | Profit per unit (£) | Material used per product unit | Machine time used per product unit | Initial allocation of product units |
|---|---|---|---|---|
| | | Constraints | | |
| A | 20 | 5 | 1 | 4 |
| B | 30 | 3 | 1 | 4 |
| C | 40 | 7 | 1 | 2 |
| Total availability of constraints — | | 46 | 10 | Profit = 280 |

time spent on product C; each extra hour taken from product B would provide $40 - 30 = 10$ extra units of profit but use up a further $7 - 3 = 4$ units of material. Hence only 2 hours can be so transferred, giving a final solution of

   B 6 hours     C 4 hours     Profit £340

Note that two products appear in the solution (in some cases only one product may appear) but no higher profit solution exists involving all three products. In general, if there are $n$ constraints (time, labour, raw materials, marketing, etc.), then only $n$ or fewer products will appear in the final optimum solution.

Linear programming provides a technique which can achieve, in a systematic manner, the optimum choice from amongst a great number of alternative allocations. Thus, suppose a small firm is faced with the problem of selecting its product line from amongst ninety possible goods. Imagine that the firm has ten scarce resources or constraints on its programme of manufacture, so that it may be expected to produce ten items or less for the optimum situation. The number of theoretically feasible solutions to the problem can be shown from standard permutation and combination theory to be in excess of $17 \times 10^{12}$. Therefore, if a conscientious management were to devote even one second to the examination of each of these possible product-line combinations and were to spend 12 hours per day and 365 days per year on the task, the job would require over 1 million years to complete!

What happens, of course, when such a decision has to be taken by traditional methods is that only a very small subset of the possible combinations is actually considered and, as a result, some of the best possibilities will be likely to be overlooked. Linear programming has to its credit a very noteworthy achievement in devising methods of solutions to such large problems so that, with the aid of computers, they can be solved in a matter of minutes or even seconds.

## 3.8  Linearity

Like all techniques, the results achieved depend to some extent upon the validity of the assumptions made, in particular the assumption of linearity, i.e. that the constraints can be expressed as simple linear or straight-line relationships between the variables. Although this may well be true for a certain range of problems, e.g. many transportation problems, this is not likely to be true for a wide range of economic problems. If one or more of the constraints can be represented only by a curved boundary, rather than by a straight line, the principle is still very similar to that shown earlier, although it may now be found that the optimum solution does not lie at a vertex of the allowable region, but on some edge of the curved part of its boundary round the allowable region. (Note that this is theoretically possible with a set of linear boundaries, but if this is so, then any point on the boundary concerned within the allowable region will give rise to the same optimum profit, i.e. there are an infinite number of optimum solutions, each giving rise to the same profit.) If, however, the profit function itself is non-linear, then, whether or not the constraints are linear, the optimum solution need not be at the edge of the allowable region, but could be in the interior.

Provided that the profit function can be formulated explicitly, this condition is easily detected by a sensitivity analysis. The problem is then usually dealt with by a related but more complicated technique known as separable programming or, more simply, by adding additional linear constraints. Recourse should be made to the specialist in such situations.

Sensitivity analyses can be developed and implemented to indicate how far the profit function can deviate from being linear and the linear programming solution still remain optimal. Troubles may be experienced if the extent of these non-linearities are difficult to estimate. In certain circumstances, even if the non-linearity is extremely slight, the error made by using linear programming can be substantial. W. J. Baumol, for instance (in reference 5 at the end of the chapter), has shown that the unmodified linear programming solution to a number of problems of a practical type can give poorer results than a more or less randomly selected initial allocation. This is not to say that linear programming is of no use, but merely to point out that it needs to be applied with care, and specialists should be consulted whenever doubt arises as to its applicability. In the following chapter some more complex problems in linear programming, where there are quite a large number of variables and constraints concerned, are discussed from the point of view of the user of the technique.

# References

(1) *Linear Programming and Extensions* by G. B. Dantzig (Princeton) (particularly chapters 1 to 3).
(2) *Linear Programming, Methods and Applications* by S. I. Gass (McGraw-Hill, 1964).
(3) *Quantitative Approaches to Management* by R. I. Levin and C. A. Kirkpatrick (McGraw-Hill) (Chapter 8).
(4) *Linear Programming and the Theory of the Firm* by K. E. Boulding and W. A. Spivey (Macmillan) (Chapter 3).
(5) Errors produced by linearization in mathematical programming, by W. J. Baumol and R. C. Bushnell, *Econometrica*, vol. 35, 1967, pp. 447–71.
(6) *Applied Linear Programming* by J. R. Frazer (Prentice-Hall, 1968).

# 4 The programming of resources— the mathematical approach to allocation

## 4.1 The approach

In the previous chapter the portable TV set problem was examined graphically to a large extent. This was possible because there were only two types of TV set involved, A and B. If a third type, C, were added, this method would be impossible except by visualizing it in a three-dimensional geometrical form. If a fourth type, D, were added, the problem would become completely impossible in a geometrical idiom. Hence other approaches must be found. The most common approach is a mathematical procedure known as the simplex method. This is described in detail in Appendix A, and appropriate computer programs are widely available. It is not necessary to understand the appendix in order to follow the material in this chapter which discusses in some detail two examples, although for those readers possessing a knowledge of elementary algebra it could be helpful to study the appendix at this stage. The examples will be discussed from three angles: first, the nature of the problem being tackled and its formulation in a linear programming context; secondly, the form in which solutions are obtainable from the simplex procedure; and thirdly, some of the practical implications inherent in the solution.

## 4.2 A handling equipment problem

The first problem is concerned with the feasibility of reconciling marketing policy with production restrictions in a firm which manufactured materials handling equipment. The firm found itself in a position where it seemed to be getting orders for 'specials' without consequent orders for standard equipment. As a result, it was unable to take advantage of a flow-line type of production; it also gained the reputation for the manufacture and supply of specials, thus aggravating its existing problem. The firm decided that they must rationalize their products and product groupings. In doing this the firm was prepared to revise drastically their ideas as to which were the most profitable lines. It realized that it might then prove best to reduce the manufacture of certain products to a much lower level.

Talks with the management revealed that one of their basic concerns was with the amount of capital tied up in stocks. The large sum involved arose to a considerable extent because of the willingness to build specials which, in turn, required components of non-standard dimensions. The special components often had to be bought in from outside and, as a result, there were long lead times attached to these parts, causing the associated components to be held over this same long lead time. Even for certain standard items bought in from outside, the firm did not appear to be given the same attention as larger customers by the manufacturers of these components. It was felt that if the specials could be eliminated or reduced, then the overall stock-holding would be drastically cut. The problem thus resolved itself into determining which product groups were the most profitable to make, and which groups could be dropped from production or run at a nominal level.

## 4.3 The basic data

The basic data are set out in tabular form in Table 4.1. The range of products manufactured was divided into eleven basic product groups. Information on the average number of hours taken for single units in each product group to pass through each of the five production departments was collected and analysed to give the figures in the left-hand portion of Table 4.1. The five production departments are shown as column headings and the eleven product groups are shown down the left-hand side. The total daily capacity of the five departments is given in the bottom row, two of the departments having so much capacity that they do not contribute any constraints in practice. Other data, shown in the right-hand portion of the table, relate to the various costs, giving rise to an estimated profit margin for each product.

In obtaining all this information, so effortlessly summarized and presented in Table 4.1, a great deal of work was necessary, and

Table 4.1  Basic data

| Product group | Hours required per item | | | | | Financial data (£) per unit | | | |
| --- | --- | --- | --- | --- | --- | --- | --- | --- | --- |
| | Fabricating | Machining | Assembling | Spraying | Inspecting and testing | Direct labour cost | Cost of material | Average selling price | Margin |
| Transporting units | 45·00 | 35·00 | 12·00 | 3·50 | 0·50 | 50 | 257 | 650 | 343 |
| Conveying units | 45·00 | 35·00 | 12·00 | 3·50 | 0·50 | 43 | 247 | 600 | 310 |
| Lifting (N) units | 50·00 | 30·00 | 14·00 | 4·50 | 0·50 | 57 | 417 | 1100 | 616 |
| Storing units | 50·00 | 30·00 | 15·00 | 5·00 | 0·50 | 65 | 392 | 1250 | 893 |
| Loading units | 50·00 | 100·00 | 22·00 | 6·00 | 0·75 | 116 | 625 | 1828 | 1087 |
| Lifting (L) units | 55·00 | 100·00 | 26·00 | 10·00 | 0·75 | 106 | 1290 | 2100 | 704 |
| Lifting (M) units | 50·00 | 100·00 | 15·00 | 10·00 | 0·75 | 94 | 858 | 1900 | 948 |
| Carrying units | 175·00 | 100·00 | 75·00 | 15·00 | 3·00 | 211 | 3522 | 5100 | 1367 |
| Handling units | 4·00 | 12·50 | 3·00 | 1·50 | 0·75 | 11 | 32 | 100 | 57 |
| Hoisting (G) units | 0·25 | 5·00 | 0·50 | 0·10 | 0·25 | 3 | 5 | 22 | 14 |
| Hoisting (H) units | 1·50 | 13·00 | 2·00 | 1·00 | 0·50 | 9 | 33 | 105 | 63 |
| Approx. total daily capacity (standard hours) | 438 | 1043 | 633 | — | | | | | |

Note: Fabricating includes cutting, pressing and welding.
      Margin = Selling price − (Direct labour + Materials).

management was forced to focus their attention on a number of matters which had previously been neglected under the pressure of time. This in itself proved to be an extremely valuable part of the exercise.

The data are now in a form to which the linear programming approach may be applied. The problem is to find the mix of products which should be made so that the total margin achieved is a maximum, while at the same time the constraints due to the capacities of the various departments are met. The information can be laid out in the form of a matrix array as described in Appendix A and analysed appropriately. After a number of trial solutions which are successively improved, a final and optimum solution is obtained. The form in which this appears is shown in Tables 4.2 and 4.3 and attention will now be concentrated on the information to be extracted from those tables.

## 4.4 The solution and its interpretation

The optimum combination, indicated in Table 4.2, is to make 6·8 storing units and 64·5 hoisting (H) units per day. This corresponds to 1705 storing units and 16 125 hoisting (H) units per annum, and will give a total margin of £10 152 per day, or £2 538 000 per

Table 4.2  **Optimum solution from linear programme**

| Product | Output per day |
|---|---|
| Storing units | 6·8 |
| Hoisting (H) units | 64·5 |
| All other units | nil |
| Total margin per day | £10 152 |
| *Spare capacity* | *Hours per day* |
| Assembly shop | 401·7 |
| Fabricating | nil |
| Machining | nil |

annum (which compared with an existing margin of approximately £1·3 million (per annum).

If this optimum combination is made, Table 4.2 also indicates that there would be 401·7 hours per day capacity still available in the assembly shop, but that the capacity of the other two departments with capacity constraints would be fully utilized. Note that the original conditions for this problem suggested three constraints, whilst the final solution contains just two products. This arises because the constraint of assembly time is dominated by the other two constraints.

The reason that the other product groups do not appear in the optimum solution is that the margin on them is not high enough to justify using the scarcest resources, namely fabricating and machining, on them. Clearly if the margin on any one of these omitted products was steadily increased, there would come a point when it would be worthwhile to include this product in favour of one or other of the two products in the current solution without diminishing the overall margin achieved. The increase in margin which would be necessary to bring each of the product groups in turn into the optimum solution without diminishing the overall margin achievable can be obtained from the linear programming solution and is indicated in Table 4.3.

Table 4.3  **Minimum increase in margin on each product group to make production worthwhile**

| Product group | Minimum increase in margin necessary (£) | % increase on selling price |
|---|---|---|
| Carrying units | 1744·0 | 34 |
| Conveying units | 517·5 | 86 |
| Transporting units | 484·5 | 75 |
| Lifting (L) units | 478·4 | 24 |
| Lifting (N) units | 277·0 | 25 |
| Lifting (M) units | 154·0 | 8 |
| Handling units | 44·1 | 44 |
| Loading units | 15·0 | 1 |
| Hoisting (G) units | 4·9 | 22 |

For example, if the margin on lifting (M) units were increased by 154 from 948 to 1102, then it would be found that the optimum solution would just include some lifting (M) units and the total margin would still be at least £2 538 000 per annum. Any smaller increase than 154 would make it impossible, whilst including some

(M) units in the optimum solution, to raise the total margin obtainable. An alternative way of looking at the situation is to argue that each lifting (M) unit included in the production schedule at current prices loses a possible margin otherwise obtainable of 154. The list above gives the minimum margin increase per product group to ensure incorporation in the overall optimum solution. The final column of the table shows these increases expressed as a percentage of the existing selling prices. This is a form of sensitivity analysis.

The value of an additional productive hour in the departments fully used is also obtainable from the linear programming solution, as was done for the Transrad Company in Chapter 3. Thus the availability of an extra hour in the fabricating department would produce an extra margin of 16.1 (and of course, the previously found production schedule would have to be revised to achieve this gain). The cost of providing this extra hour of capacity would also have to be borne in mind as, up to now, the costs of provision of the five departments have been treated as overhead (i.e. constant) items. Any additional cost would, therefore, have to be deducted from the profit of 16·1 apparently obtainable. An extra hour of machining time would similarly be worth 3·0.

## 4.5   Further Implications

The 'robustness' of the optimum solution, in terms of the products which appear in it, may be critically dependent upon the accuracy of the margins imputed to each of the product groups. To test whether or not this is so, the margins were altered by 5 per cent, in such a way that the margins on each of the two products currently appearing in the final solution were reduced by 5 per cent, whilst the margins on each of the nine products not appearing in the current solution were increased by 5 per cent. The linear programme was then reworked and the revised solution was found to be as follows, all quantities expressed per day:

|  | *Revised solution* | *Original solution* |
|---|---|---|
|  | 8·2 Loading units | 6·8 Storing units |
|  | 16·7 Hoisting (H) units | 64·5 Hoisting (H) units |
| Profit | £10 350 | £10 152 |

Hence, although the total profit changes by very little, the optimum mix of product changes quite markedly. Such an alteration suggests that the cost data in this instance ought really to be accurate to something better than 5 per cent in order to be entirely confident with the solution obtained in terms of products to be produced.

The solution pursued so far in this analysis has treated as constraints only the capacity restrictions of the various production departments. It has been implicitly assumed that the firm could sell everything that it could produce. This initial linear programme solution gave the manager a clear view of the apparently ideal programme under such circumstances and, once that was known, he could redirect the firm's sales effort so as to sell more of the high profit items and so replan its production facilities to make its sales pattern as profitable as possible.

The next step was to introduce several marketing restrictions according to what it was believed could be sold. This would have the effect of limiting the production of individual products to specified quantities. After a full discussion with the managers concerned, limitations were placed on each product, due either to production considerations or to marketing restrictions, and whichever restriction was the harsher was the one incorporated in the final re-work. When these restrictions were incorporated—details are not given here—the optimum combination gave a margin of £7780 per day and included a varying degree of production from eight of the eleven product groups. Further analysis would give the marketing department a choice of different price–quantity combinations to choose from.

Additional points which emerge from the solution are suggestions as to those areas where method study might ease the bottlenecks, i.e. in fabricating and machining, and where preventative maintenance may yield a high return.

## 4.6   A problem in paper-making

The second problem to be discussed concerns paper-making. Paper mills produce paper in reels of a given width, the width depending upon the particular paper machine concerned. Customers require reels of paper of varying widths (less than the machine width) and these are 'fitted' together to come as near as possible to the width of the manufacturing machine. The machine reels are, therefore, cut to meet the customer's requirements, and there will usually be some waste at the edge of the reel in the form of an offcut which provides too small a width for any customer. The manufacturer aims to put the reel widths ordered from him together in such a way as to make the total edge (or trim) loss as small as possible. This 'putting together' of ordered reels to fit the paper machine is commonly referred to as the deckling problem.

The basic deckling problem starts with a single paper machine of given width making one grade of paper only and a set of orders. These orders will normally be for reels of a standard length, but of varying widths, each width usually only a fraction of the width of the paper machine. It is then required to fit the orders together in such a way that the best possible use is made of the machine. For example, suppose the paper machine width is 270 cm and the only sizes of paper ordered are 63 and 39 cm wide respectively, for each of which a number of orders has been obtained. Then the possibilities as to ways in which orders of these widths can be put together are shown in Table 4.4.

Table 4.4 **Permissible combinations of reels**

| Combination | Number of 63 cm reels | Number of 39 cm reels | Trim (deckle) loss (cm) |
|---|---|---|---|
| 1 | 4 | 0 | 18 |
| 2 | 3 | 2 | 3 |
| 3 | 2 | 3 | 27 |
| 4 | 1 | 5 | 12 |
| 5 | 0 | 6 | 36 |

Combination 3, for example, shows that two 63 cm reels can be combined with three 39 cm reels to be cut out of a complete 270 cm width to leave 27 cm trim loss which will be wasted. In practice the trim loss paper is repulped, so that the material is not completely wasted, but the processing costs are lost. It is assumed that the weight of paper produced is proportional to its area, so that, for example, the production of 1 tonne of 63 cm paper using combination 4 will lead to the simultaneous production of $5 \times \frac{39}{63}$ (= 3·1) tonne of 39 cm paper and $\frac{12}{63}$ (= 0·19) tonne of trim loss.

Now if the overall requirement is to make 40 tonnes of 63 cm paper and 70 tonnes of 39 cm paper, linear programming shows that the best solution is

Combination 2    20·06 tonne of 63 cm plus 8·28 tonne of 39 cm together with

Combination 4    19.94 tonne of 63 cm plus 61·72 tonne of 39 cm

giving a deckle loss of 3·80 tonne or 3·3 per cent. Note that there are two constraints in this problem, namely that the amount of 63 cm paper is at least 40 tonnes and the amount of 39 cm paper is at least 70 tonnes. The solution, therefore, will only involve one or, at most, two of the five possible combinations.

As the number of order sizes increases, the magnitude of the programming problem grows disproportionately large and the difficulties of producing an optimum solution by inspection or by trial and error become very great. Similarly, if more than one paper machine is brought into the problem, possibly of different widths, the complexity is considerably increased. In such circumstances, the resulting linear programming problem can be solved only on an electronic computer using the appropriate program.

Briefly, all feasible combinations are produced on the computer. From these, potentially useful solutions are extracted, bearing in mind the various machine restrictions, and eliminating those combinations which are inferior to simple mixtures of other combinations. An optimum solution, in which total deckle loss is a minimum, is then selected. This procedure tacitly assumes that deckle loss is the required quantity to minimize, which may well be so if there are no further processes through which the paper passes, although frequently delivery and storage problems have to be considered as well. But a new factor of a different kind enters if the paper also has to pass through further processes, such as a more expensive coating process. It may then be more profitable to use the coating capacity as efficiently as possible, even at the expense of increasing the trim loss on the paper machines making the base paper.

Figure 4.1 illustrates a typical situation where 300 cm base reels of paper are slit into two parts for cutting into sheet paper of 63 cm and 54 cm width, the lengths required being in the ratio of 3:2. Two cutters are available, one 270 cm wide and the other 132 cm wide. Trim waste on the reels of base paper is minimized by slitting and cutting as shown in the figure. If, however, the paper has to be coated before it is cut into sheets and the available coaters are also 270 cm and 132 cm wide, then the method of slitting and cutting shown in Figure 4.1 will waste coating capacity (81 cm on the 270 cm coater and 24 cm of the 132 cm coater). If the objective

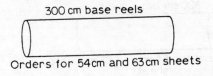

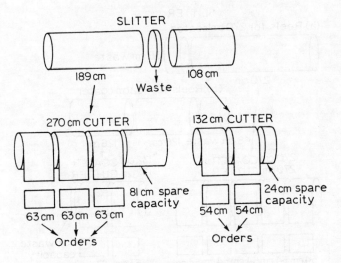

**Figure 4.1 Typical slitting and cutting arrangements**

of the planning were to reduce the coating waste capacity to a minimum, in place of reducing the base paper trim loss to a minimum, the paper should be slit and cut as shown in Figure 4.2. There is now, however, a much larger trim loss. Clearly there will be costs involved, both from wastage of base paper and from leaving coating machine capacity spare. The most profitable overall method of programming the production may lie anywhere between these two extremes.

## 4.7 The optimum solution

To choose the best schedule, the relative profitabilities of all possible schedules have to be assessed. This must be done keeping the machine capacities fixed because, with some methods of scheduling, spare capacity may be available for alternative forms of production. The principle is illustrated in Figure 4.3 which considers only one base machine and one coating machine for the

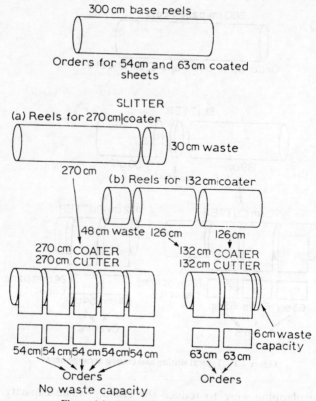

**Figure 4.2   Reduction of coating waste**

two alternative objectives, i.e. minimum paper trim or maximum use of coater capacity. Suppose that the programme is for minimum trim, when for the coater to produce $X$ tonnes per week requires $Y$ tonnes of base paper, made in $Z$ hours on the paper machine. Alternatively, suppose that the programme is designed for maximum use of coater capacity. The coater output will now be increased, say to $X + x$ tonnes per week, requiring $Y + y$ tonnes of base paper. The time taken to make this base paper will be longer than $Z$, for two reasons: (*a*) more base paper is required (an increase of $y$ tonnes), and (*b*) the paper trim loss is larger. If the time required on the paper machine is $Z + z$ hours, alternative allocations of the $z$ hours' production not used by the first allocation must be included in the comparison. Costs can then be properly estimated and the relative profitabilities of the two allocations compared.

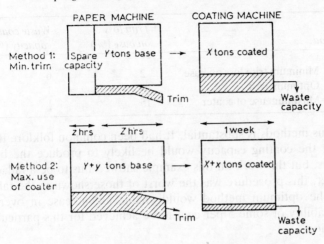

Figure 4.3 **Alternative extremes of machine arrangement**

Paper companies have applied these principles to a complex system involving three or more mills and a number of machines of various widths. Orders for several different types of paper have to be met, some coated on one side and some on both sides. Two distinct coating mixes are applied by dissimilar coating systems on coating machines of six different sizes (widths) and running speeds. Finishing adds a further variety of equipment, and there is a considerable interchange of base paper and partly coated paper from machine to machine and from mill to mill. All this has to be integrated into one coherent and efficient operation of optimum profitability, bearing in mind the various costs involved. The revised optimum method of allocation will not necessarily be one where the base paper trim is minimized, or the coater capacity utilization is maximized: it may fall somewhere between these two extremes.

Some results of specimen calculations made with the aid of an appropriate computer program are shown below for the two extreme methods of planning and for the intermediate method which was found after detailed investigation to be the best amongst a wide range of possibilities examined (see page 68).

Note that the optimum method is a long way, in its waste and utilization figures, from either of the two extremes of production which might have been used if programming techniques had been applied blindly, and the difference in profitability between the

| Method | Trim loss on base (%) | Waste coater capacity (%) |
|---|---|---|
| (a)  Minimum trim loss on base | 2 | 6 |
| (b)  Optimum cost | 8 | 1 |
| (c)  Maximum use of coater | 15 | $\frac{1}{2}$ |

various methods is substantial. It had been common folklore that filling the coating capacity would be likely to produce the best results, but the work on this example showed this to be a fallacy. In fact, this procedure was the worst of those shown in the table and the optimum method would enable an increase in overall profitability of some 5 per cent to be achieved for this particular situation.

## 4.8    Planning over time

In many of the illustrations given above, linear programming was used to deduce the optimum allocation of resources at a given moment of time. Planning, for production or investment in the general sense, involves not only decisions about which products to make and in what quantity, but also decisions about the choice of raw materials and plant to use, the timing of operations, and whether to buy or hire additional resources such as extra processing or storage capacity. Planning may also include decisions about where to manufacture various products, taking account of availabilities of materials, processing methods and efficiencies at various plants, and the costs of transport of raw materials and of products to customers.

Linear programming can assist with all these problems, coupled as well with the allocation over time. Linear programming cannot be used to forecast future events, and so all estimates of future sales, selling prices, raw material prices and availabilities must be made by other methods. Given such data, the linear programming technique will then provide the optimum solution. For example, if sales are seasonal, a linear programming model can be used to decide how stocks should be built up during the slack season. A company whose sales are seasonal may choose to keep stocks low and work maximum overtime during the busy period, or to build up stocks before the heavy selling season and then work less overtime. Decisions of this kind will depend upon the relative costs of storage and of overtime working, as well as on the storage facilities, plant availabilities and forward sales forecasts.

If there is uncertainty about some or all of the estimates, it is usually possible, once the programme is formulated, to feed in a succession of different estimates and obtain a new optimum solution for each. The resulting set of solutions will then provide a good indication as to how changes in circumstances are likely to affect the company's plan. If some not improbable set of circumstances could cause serious difficulties, the company may be able to take appropriate cautionary action in good time.

## References

Those of Chapter 3 and, in addition, the following:

(1) *Quantitative Approaches to Management* by R. I. Levin and C. A. Kirkpatrick. (McGraw-Hill) (Chapter 9).
(2) *Readings in Mathematical Programming* by S. Vajda (Pitman, 1962) (Chapters 2 to 6).
(3) *Linear Programming* by C. Hedley (Addison-Wesley, 1969).
(4) *Mathematical Programming* by K. B. Haley (Macmillan, 1967).
(5) *Linear and Non-linear Programming in Industry* by N. Williams (Pitman, 1967).
(6) *Mathematical Programming in Practice* by E. M. L. Beale (Pitman, 1968).

Some examples of specific applications are:

(7) Machine programming, by W. S. Harvey and E. Jowett, *The Paper Maker* (1965), vol. 150, pp. 59–64.
(8) A case study in mathematical programming of portfolio selections, by N. R. Paine, *Applied Statistics* (1966), vol. 15, pp. 24–36.
(9) Separable programming applied to an ore purchasing problem, by E. M. L. Beale *et al.*, *Applied Statistics* (1965), vol. 14, pp. 89–101.
(10) A warehouse location problem, by W. J. Baumol and P. Wolfe, *Operations Research* (1958), vol. 6, pp. 252–63.
(11) Forest management and operational research—a linear programming study by P. A. Wardle, *Management Science* (1965), vol. 11B, pp. 260–70.

# 5 The planning of operations— queueing

## 5.1 Introduction

After selecting goods in a supermarket, a shopper must take them to a desk for checking and payment. The customer may be served immediately, or may have to wait for previous customers to be served. Most customers would naturally like to be served immediately, which would imply that there should always be empty desks with cashiers awaiting customers. The store manager, on the other hand, would like to have his cashiers busy all the time. These requirements conflict because customers do not arrive at the desks at fixed and regular intervals, and some take longer to be served than others. If a cashier is to be kept fully occupied, a queue will develop at the desks when customers arrive more frequently than usual, or take longer than usual to be served. If the queues get too long, they will begin to block the shop and customers, finding that they often have a long wait, may decide to shop elsewhere. For this reason the manager would then have to consider employing a further cashier. Obviously this should reduce the customers' waiting times and cut down the queue length, but at the same time it will add to his costs. The manager, in deciding whether to pay for one or more extra cashiers, will want to know the consequential effects on both the average waiting time and the queue length.

The basic features of a problem of this sort are that: there is some form of *input* of units requiring some kind of *service*; this service may not always be immediately available, in which case a *waiting-line* will be formed; when a unit has been serviced it leaves, forming the *output* of the queueing system. This is shown diagrammatically in Figure 5.1.

The input in the example above is formed by the customers arriving at the cash desks to pay. If no desk is free they form a queue or waiting line. The queue could be a common one for

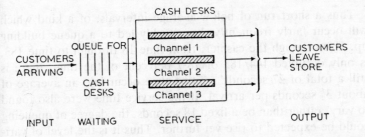

**Figure 5.1 Basic queueing situation**

all the cash desks, or a separate queue for each desk. When a cash desk becomes vacant, the next customer moves forward for payment or service and finally, when each finishes paying for her goods, they leave the store, forming the output.

A queueing problem arises because of the irregularity of the rate of input or of service, or both, so that input and service cannot be matched exactly in an arithmetic or deterministic fashion. If a cashier always took exactly 20 seconds to deal with a customer and a customer arrived every 20 seconds precisely, then there would be no queue and, correspondingly, the cashier would be 100 per cent occupied. The system could then be said to be 100 per cent effective. If the time taken by the cashier to deal with each customer were reduced from exactly 20 seconds to exactly 18 seconds and the customers still arrived at 20-second intervals, then whilst there would still be no queue, the cashier would only be 90 per cent (i.e. $\frac{18}{20} \times 100$) occupied. But suppose that the interval between arrivals varied from 10 seconds to 30 seconds, retaining an average interval of 20 seconds, what effect would this have? A typical short-run situation, still retaining the constant 18 second service time, might then be:

| Arrival number | 1 | 2 | 3 | 4 | 5 | 6 | 7 | 8 |
|---|---|---|---|---|---|---|---|---|
| Inter-arrival times | 18 | 12 | 19 | 14 | 20 | 28 | 25 | 19 |
| Time (cumulative) | 18 | 30 | 49 | 63 | 83 | 111 | 136 | 155 |
| Time into cashier | 18 | 36 | 54 | 72 | 90 | 111 | 136 | 155 |
| Time exit from cashier | 36 | 54 | 72 | 90 | 108 | 129 | 154 | 183 |
| Queueing time | 0 | 6 | 5 | 9 | 7 | 0 | 0 | 0 |

(All times expressed in seconds)

Thus a short run of below-average intervals, of a kind which will occur fairly frequently, has quickly led to a queue building up. Even though the cashier, from time 18 through to time 183, is only occupied 144/183 or 78·7 per cent of the time, there is still a total of 27 seconds' waiting time occurring, an average of about $3\frac{1}{2}$ seconds per arrival. If the service time were also found to vary, rather than be a fixed 18 seconds, the degree of queueing could be expected to rise yet further. Thus it is the level of variability, both in the arrival intervals and in the service times, that induces the queueing (in a system that would otherwise appear to be capable of having neatly balanced activities).

One of the earliest examples of this kind of problem arose in connexion with the design of telephone exchanges where the inputs are the callers and the service channels are the lines at the exchange. Anyone with a working knowledge of a small manually operated internal switchboard in an organization will be familiar with the kinds of difficulties that occur. Work on problems of this type was first published by K. Erlang, a Danish engineer, in 1909. He applied his results to a number of problems and, in particular, to estimating the optimum number of channels that should be available from one telephone exchange to another. The detailed solutions of most queueing problems met with in practice are intricate and require heavy mathematics. The present discussion will be confined to illustrating the principles through a number of examples.

## 5.2   Traffic intensity

Many queueing problems make use of a quantity labelled the *traffic intensity*. This is defined as the demand expressed as a proportion of the service capacity, or more explicitly as the average service time divided by the average interval between successive arrivals at the service point. The calculation of the traffic intensity for a single server system is relatively simple. The intervals between the arrivals of individual items at the point of input are measured, and the average of these intervals determined. Next a similar calculation is made for the average service time. The traffic intensity would then be the quotient of these two averages, that is

$$\frac{\text{average service time}}{\text{average inter-arrival interval}}$$

For example, a post office counter has an average interval between arrival of customers of 4·8 minutes, whilst the average time taken to serve a customer is 3·2 minutes. Then the traffic intensity, denoted here by the symbol $t$, will be $t = 3 \cdot 2 / 4 \cdot 8 = 0 \cdot 67$.

In a simple queueing system with only one service point (and hence only one queue as in the case of a post office with a single clerk serving) a value of $t$ less than one indicates an absence of queues, provided that the service times and arrival intervals do not vary from one occasion to the next. If they do vary, the precise queues generated depend upon the form of the variation, but it has been demonstrated mathematically that, under certain assumptions regarding the variability of service times and arrival intervals, the customer's average total time in the system (including the time being served) will be

$$\frac{1}{1 - t} \text{ multiplied by the average service time.}$$

His average waiting time (excluding from this the time spent in actually being served) will be

$$\frac{t}{1 - t} \text{ multiplied by the average service time}$$

This relationship is only strictly true over a long period of observation, where the arrival intervals and service times both vary with the particular kind of distribution known as the 'negative exponential'. This distribution is, however, quite common in queueing situations, so that the relationship provides a reasonable approximation for a large number of practical problems. Applying this to the post office example, the estimated average total time in the system would be

$$\frac{1}{1 - 0 \cdot 67} \times 3 \cdot 2 = 9 \cdot 6 \text{ minutes}$$

of which 3·2 minutes would be for actual service, while 6·4 minutes would be spent waiting for service. This may or may not be considered tolerable, but the fine balance of the system should be noted, in that a marginal increase in demand, with a new average arrival interval of, say, 4·0 in place of 4·8 minutes, raises the average total time in the system to 16 minutes, of which the queueing element rises from 6·4 to 12·8. Thus a 17 per cent reduction in the mean arrival interval leads to a doubling of the average waiting time.

In fact, with traffic intensities above 0·7 or so, waiting times increase very rapidly indeed, as Figure 5.2 demonstrates. For any particular traffic intensity the vertical axis gives the ratio of average waiting time to average service time. For example, with a traffic intensity of 0·7 and an average service time of 3 minutes, the average waiting time will be $3 \times 2·3$ or 6·9 minutes. This is in accordance with the observable fact that bottlenecks arise when a very marginal increase in traffic intensity occurs in systems where the intensity is already high. It should be noted that when the system starts from rest—say at the opening of the post office in the morning—the congestion may take a long while to build up, but once congestion is built up it may be very slow to disperse unless the traffic intensity level can be considerably reduced, for example, by employing extra servers. It is, therefore, wise not to allow the traffic intensity of any servicing point to approach unity unless considerable flexibility is available for reducing it should occasion arise.

## 5.3   The avoidance of bottlenecks

Queueing and allied bottleneck situations that are unacceptable must be examined to see how they can be improved. In the queueing situation illustrated in Figure 5.1 the two factors that could be susceptible to change are

(a)  the input pattern,
(b)  the service facilities.

Before examining these factors in detail, however, it ought to be pointed out that some method study of the operation itself may be worthwhile, as bottlenecks may be caused purely by poor attention to planning.

Consider the layout of a supermarket and, in particular, the two supermarkets illustrated in Figure 5.3. What is the basic difference between them? The sizes differ, of course, but consider the way in which shoppers will tend to go round the supermarket. In case I there are three aisles only, an odd number. Hence if a customer is to go down *every* aisle, and the layout of goods in a supermarket is usually carefully arranged to try and ensure that this happens, then it follows that he (or more usually she) must

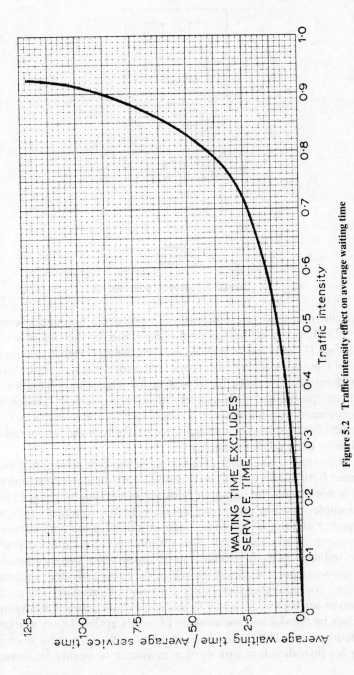

**Figure 5.2  Traffic intensity effect on average waiting time**

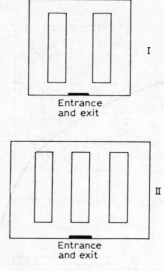

**Figure 5.3   Layout of supermarkets**

go down at least one aisle twice. In practice a bottleneck would probably occur at the top right-hand corner of the supermarket. In case II there are four aisles, an even number. Hence customers could go down every aisle once and arrive back near the exit, without any necessity for repeat visits. The second situation is clearly preferable. This problem of layout design—if it is indeed recognized by supermarket planners as a problem—is of a kind which can be solved by a straightforward study of the system rather than by detailed mathematics.

Reverting to the more common queueing-type situation, sometimes both factors need to be changed, sometimes only one. Indeed it is not always the case that both are susceptible to change. For example, patients arrive at a doctor's surgery in a fairly random manner and there tend to be large variations in the time intervals between successive arrivals. This variation in arrival intervals could be reduced by having some kind of appointment system whereby there was a predetermined interval between the arrivals of patients, with a consequent reduction in the amount of queueing. The variation in service times, which in this context are actual consultation times by the doctor, are unlikely to be susceptible to any marked modification. There may be a case for having an extra doctor, or for providing him with nursing assistance to modify his service time distribution, but the basic distribution is likely to be intractable.

It must be accepted, too, that the ideal situation is not necessarily one where all queues are eliminated. Frequently this would mean enormous idle time amongst the service facilities, and a balance must be struck between costs of queues and costs of extra servicing facilities. Consider, for example, a port with unloading facilities and ships arriving for unloading in a higgledy-piggledy fashion. The amount of unloading facilities available could be varied and the total costs computed for each level of facilities. Clearly, if there were infinite loading facilities the costs would be infinite (and the waiting zero). As the facilities decrease the costs decrease, but there comes a time when queues of ships start to form and extra costs for demurrage are thereby incurred. As loading facilities are further reduced there comes a point when the saving on an extra marginal decrease in unloading facilities is just outweighed by the extra costs of ships queueing incurred as a consequence. This would provide the overall optimum situation, which is shown schematically in Figure 5.4.

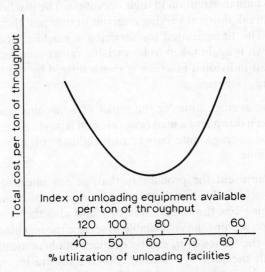

Figure 5.4   Optimum balance of resources

The optimum utilization of the unloading facilities will not always be at the 60 per cent figure shown. It is a function of many factors such as costs of berths, cranes, rate of arrivals of ships, demurrage charges, etc. However, for each set of conditions, there will be some optimum balance which is the point to aim at, and this point of balance will almost certainly envisage some idle time both amongst the ships arriving and amongst the unloading facilities available in the port. In a number of situations the costs of waiting and the costs of the facilities may often be borne—at least initially—by different organizations, so that there may be nobody who is charged with, or indeed interested in, finding the overall optimum.

## 5.4  The servicing of machines

The range of queueing problems which can be handled on a straightforward mathematical basis is not large, for reasons that will be discussed in Section 5.6. Nevertheless a great deal of pioneering work has been done using formal mathematical procedures.

To illustrate a queueing problem which can be handled mathematically, consider the following, based upon a Swedish article by C. Palm (see reference 5 at end of chapter). This article describes the servicing of completely automatic machines that normally require no human attention in their operation. The machines may, however, break down at varying intervals of time and then require servicing. The time needed for servicing a machine once it has broken down is again taken to be variable rather than fixed. Suppose that an individual machine is characterized by the two constants, $r$ and $s$, where

>  $r$ is the average time for the repair of a machine once it has broken down and a man is working on it, and
>  $s$ is the average time between breakdowns of an individual machine.

Let $p_n$ represent the probability that, at any one time, there will be $n$ machines broken down amongst a group of $m$ machines. Each machine has the same value of $r$ and also the same value of $s$. A single repair-man is available to service the machines. Palm shows how the values of $p_n$ can be deduced mathematically, once the value of the ratio $r/s$ is fixed. For the illustrative values in Table 5.1 below, it is assumed that there are six machines ($m = 6$) and that the value of the ratio $r/s$ is taken as $0 \cdot 1$ for each machine. Such a ratio would mean, for example, that when considering one individual machine, the average time between breakdowns was 10 hours, but, once it had broken down and was being serviced,

Table 5.1  **Probabilities for six machines, one repair-man**

| Number of machines broken down (n) | Machines being serviced | Machines awaiting service (excluding machines being serviced) | Probability ($p_n$) |
|---|---|---|---|
| 0 | 0 | 0 | 0·485 |
| 1 | 1 | 0 | 0·291 |
| 2 | 1 | 1 | 0·145 |
| 3 | 1 | 2 | 0·057 |
| 4 | 1 | 3 | 0·018 |
| 5 | 1 | 4 | 0·004 |
| 6 | 1 | 5 | 0·000 |
| | | Total | 1·000 |

the average time for its repair was 1 hour. If both $r$ and $s$ are multiplied by the same factor, then the ratio $r/s$, and hence the probabilities for $p_n$, would remain unaltered.

Table 5.1 shows that there will be at least one machine broken down for approximately 51 per cent of the time, i.e. $(1 - 0·485) \times 100$. Furthermore there will be at least one machine waiting in the queue to get attention for about 22 per cent of the time, i.e.

$$(0·145 + 0·057 + 0·018 + 0·004) \times 100$$

The average number of machines broken down and awaiting service at any one time will be the sum of the products of the individual entries in the third and fourth columns of the table, i.e. 0·329. The argument for this is that there is at any moment of time a probability of 0·145 that one machine is awaiting service, or a probability of 0·057 that two machines are awaiting service, etc., so that the average number of machines awaiting service is

$$1 \times 0·145 + 2 \times 0·057 + 3 \times 0·018 + 4 \times 0·004 = 0·329$$

## 5.5  Generalization of servicing problem

The scope of the problem can be widened by assuming that more than one repair-man is available. It is assumed that only one repair-man is needed on each broken-down machine, and so it is logical that there should be no more repair-men than the total number of machines in the system. The amended mathematical equations that arise from the changed conditions still have explicit solutions. Suppose there are 20 machines and 3 repair-men, then the appropriate values are as tabulated in Table 5.2, the ratio $r/s$ again being taken as $0.1$.

Table 5.2  **Probabilities for 20 machines, three repair-men**

| Number of machines broken down (n) (1) | Machines being serviced (2) | Machines awaiting service (excluding machines being serviced) (3) | Repair-men idle (4) | Probabilities ($P_n$) (5) |
|---|---|---|---|---|
| 0 | 0 | 0 | 3 | 0·136 |
| 1 | 1 | 0 | 2 | 0·273 |
| 2 | 2 | 0 | 1 | 0·259 |
| 3 | 3 | 0 | 0 | 0·154 |
| 4 | 3 | 1 | 0 | 0·088 |
| 5 | 3 | 2 | 0 | 0·047 |
| 6 | 3 | 3 | 0 | 0·024 |
| 7 | 3 | 4 | 0 | 0·011 |
| 8 | 3 | 5 | 0 | 0·005 |
| 9 | 3 | 6 | 0 | 0·002 |
| 10 | 3 | 7 | 0 | 0·001 |
| 11 | 3 | 8 | 0 | 0·000 |

From Table 5.2 various calculations and comparisons can be made. If there were 20 repair-men available, so that any machine breaking down would never under any circumstances have to wait for service, the machine efficiency (i.e. proportion of the time for which a machine was open for work that is useful production time) would be $s/(s + r)$, or $0.91$. If there were only 3 repair-men, then the further fraction of productive time lost could be estimated from the column (5) of Table 5.2 as

$$(1 \times 0.088 + 2 \times 0.047 + 3 \times 0.024 + \ldots)/20 = 0.017$$

since on a fraction $0.088$ of occasions there will be 1 machine awaiting service, on $0.047$ of occasions 2 machines waiting, and so on. The revised machine efficiency is now $0.89$ (or $0.91 - 0.017$), a small drop at the saving of 17 repair-men.

It is instructive to compare Tables 5.1 and 5.2, since the ratio of arrival interval to service time used is the same in both cases. The ratio of machines to repair-men is slightly higher at 20 machines

to 3 repair-men, or 20/3 to 1, in the second table, as opposed
to the equivalent ratio of 6 to 1 in the first table. A comparison
of the final columns of the two tables does reveal, however, some
surprising features which suggest that the repair-men and machines
in the situation underlying the second table are being used very
much more efficiently. To formulate the differences, consider the
following two coefficients:

Machine Loss Coefficient
(MLC)

$$= \frac{\text{Average number of machines awaiting service}}{\text{Number of machines in system}}$$

Repair-men Loss Coefficient
(RLC)

$$= \frac{\text{Average number of repair-men idle}}{\text{Number of repair-men employed}}$$

The numerical values of these coefficients can be calculated from
the two tables. For example, from Table 5.1 the MLC for the
6-machine situation is equal to

$$(1 \times 0.145 + 2 \times 0.057 + 3 \times 0.018 + 4 \times 0.004)/6 = 0.055$$

whilst the RLC for the first situation is equal to

$$(1 \times 0.485)/1 = 0.485$$

as the single repair-man is only idle when no machines are broken
down.

Table 5.3  **Comparison of repair systems**

|  | *Table 5.1 situation* | *Table 5.2 situation* |
| --- | --- | --- |
| Number of machines | 6 | 20 |
| Number of repair-men | 1 | 3 |
| Machines per repair-man | 6 | 20/3 |
| Machine loss coefficient | 0·055 | 0·017 |
| Repair-men loss coefficient | 0·485 | 0·404 |

The coefficients for the two situations are summarized in Table
5.3. Both coefficients are much lower in the second situation, showing that 3 repair-men servicing a total of 20 machines would be
a more economic proposition than having 3 repair-men, each of

whom services a separate group of 6 machines. This difference comes about because of the 'averaging' effect that is allowed to have more rein in the situation described in Table 5.2. Nevertheless, the difference is a startling one in that the machine loss time has simultaneously been drastically cut. It should be noted that if 18 machines were served by 3 repair-men, but divided into three rigid sets of 6 machines to 1 repair-man, with no overlap allowed, then the overall situation would effectively be that shown in Table 5.1. It is only because each of the 3 repair-men is allowed to service *any* machine in the group which breaks down that the large gains shown have been achieved.

## 5.6   Alternative analysis

The systems described in the two foregoing sections were both capable of explicit mathematical analysis. Some systems, however, are so complicated that they defy straightforward mathematical form. For example, the distribution of service times may not follow any well-known statistical distribution that can be written down in straightforward mathematical form. To set about analysing such a situation it is useful to put down once again just what quantities are needed to define a queueing situation in order to build a model to represent the system. For a situation where units arrive (input), are then serviced and finally leave (output), data are needed about:

(a) The distribution of intervals between arrivals
(b) The distribution of service times (e.g. how long the cashier takes to add up and take the money)
(c) The processing or service facilities available (e.g. the number of counters and whether these are all general or have some restriction on the type of service offered)
(d) The priority system, if any, operated in the queue or waiting line, i.e. the queue discipline which determines whether there is a common queue or a separate one for each service facility.

Given these quantities, a schedule could be written up—maybe rather a lengthy one—of the appropriate times for service and exit for a set of arrivals under the various alternatives which it was desired to investigate, say changes in the service facilities available. This might well be a very laborious procedure for which a computer could be of great assistance, but the principle is a simple and straightforward one which goes under the general heading of *simulation*. This technique is of sufficient importance for the next chapter to be devoted to it. Meanwhile, a straightforward illustration of what is implied by simulation is afforded by the following example relating to the Post Office.

## 5.7 Post office counter problem

A working party carried out some investigations a few years ago into the relative efficiencies of working the counters in Crown post offices using different principles. The two principal methods of working considered were

- (a) *Team working*—counters divided into two categories, banking and stamps. Within these two categories postal officers deal with any item categorized as banking or stamps, but the two types of work do not overlap.
- (b) *Composite working*—a customer entering the office for any class of business (except parcels and one or two specialized transactions) can go to any counter for service.

As a first step a pilot investigation was made concerning the time taken under the existing system of team working then operative in the bulk of Crown offices. For example, at Harrogate head post office the following observations were made:

The Banking team concerned served 634 customers in a period of 739 available 'banking minutes', spread over a period of one week. The total waiting (idle) time for the team contained in this study was 185 minutes spread over 202 occasions. Hence the actual average service time per customer was $(739 - 185)/634$, or 0·87 minutes. When a server found himself idle, his idle time lasted on average $185/202 = 0·92$ minutes. Similarly with the Stamp team, 367 customers were studied over a period of 360 minutes. The actual average service time was 0·58 minutes per customer, and there were 187 instances of waiting (idle) time averaging 0·79 minutes per occasion.

Clearly in each team a reserve of service was available equal to some portion of the waiting (idle) time, and this reserve could be utilized provided one team could help the other. Under team working conditions this was virtually impossible, and the enquiry was thus directed into the possibility of using composite working (i.e. breaking up the teams) in offices of this size.

It will be appreciated that the measurement of the results of composite working compared with team working is not a simple arithmetical calculation based on figures such as those quoted above, mainly because of the random pattern of arrival of the customers and the fluctuation in the service times. Short of an actual trial of composite working, it was believed that the construction of a mathematical model to simulate counter operation would be the most beneficial approach and this was done, based on the operations of Colchester post office.

The constituents of the queueing situation were first determined by observation, namely:

(a)  The number of servers.
(b)  The number of possible queues.
(c)  The queue discipline (e.g. whether a customer sticks to the queue he first joins or moves from one queue to another).
(d)  The customer 'input' expressed as a distribution of intervals between arrivals (estimated by sampling methods).
(e)  The service time expressed as a distribution of the length of time taken to serve each customer concerned (estimated by sampling methods).

By means of such information, the actual situation was replaced by a model in the form of a flow diagram. The originally intractable mathematical problem of the effects of alternative methods of operation could now be tackled by simulation techniques. A check can be made against the existing situation by taking observations to determine such quantities as waiting time and queue length and seeing how well these agree with the results from simulations.

Based on a simulation of two hours of counter operations, when 600 customers were served, using identical customer arrival times and service times for both methods of working, Table 5.4 shows the percentage of customers who had to wait for the lengths of time shown in the various bands given in the left-hand column.

The results from Table 5.4 can be alternatively summarized in the comparative form shown in Table 5.5. They show that a considerable reduction in waiting time and queue length would be achieved by a change from team to composite working and, as a consequence, further simulations were carried out and composite

Table 5.4 **Waiting time distributions**

| Waiting time (minutes) | | Percentage of customers | |
|---|---|---|---|
| over | up to | Team working | Composite working |
| | 0 | 47·9 | 72·5 |
| 0 | 1 | 18·5 | 17·0 |
| 1 | 2 | 9·2 | 7·2 |
| 2 | 3 | 7·0 | 1·0 |
| 3 | 4 | 6·5 | 0·9 |
| 4 | 5 | 2·8 | 0·8 |
| 5 | 6 | 2·5 | 0·3 |
| 6 | 7 | 3·5 | 0·3 |
| 7 | 8 | 1·8 | — |
| 8 | 9 | 0·3 | — |
| 9 | — | — | — |
| | | Total   100·0 | Total   100·0 |

Table 5.5 **Comparative performance characteristics**

| | Team working | Composite working |
|---|---|---|
| Average waiting time (minutes) | 1·28 | 0·31 |
| Average queue length | 1·78 | 0·92 |
| Average number of people in office | 10·1 | 5·2 |

working adopted experimentally at a number of post offices. Subsequently special tables were computed to show the staffing requirements for different levels of customer arrival rates and service times under composite working.

This illustration shows how simulation provides a method whereby alternative operating systems can be painlessly 'lived through' on a piece (or pieces) of paper and all the possible outcomes evaluated before the manager becomes committed to putting any particular scheme into physical operation. The principle has wide applications, some of which are considered in more detail in the following chapter.

## References

(1) *Queues, Inventories and Maintenance* by P. M. Morse (Wiley, 1958).
(2) *Queues* by D. R. Cox and W. L. Smith (Methuen, 1961).

(3) *A Guide to Operational Research* by W. E. Duckworth (Methuen, 1962) (Part II).

(4) *Operations Research* by M. Sasieni, A. Yaspan and L. Friedman (Wiley, 1959) (Chapter 6).

(5) The distribution of repair-men in servicing automatic machines, by C. Palm, *Industritidningen*, vol. 75, 1947, p. 75.

# 6 The planning of operations — simulation

## 6.1 Introduction

In many situations direct experimentation is possible. For example, the housewife may rearrange the bedroom furniture by directly experimenting with different layouts. Essentially she (or perhaps her husband under her supervision!) moves the furniture and observes the results. This process may be repeated, and perhaps further moves made, until all logical possibilities have been exhausted. Eventually one such move is judged best, the furniture is returned to this position, and the experiment is completed.

Direct experimentation such as this could in theory be applied to the effects of a rearrangement of machinery in a factory. Such a procedure would, however, be costly, time-consuming, and disruptive. Hence, simulation, or indirect experimentation, is employed, using a model to represent the factory and templates to represent the items of machinery to be moved. Again direct experimentation in aircraft design would involve constructing a full-scale prototype which could be flight-tested under real conditions. Although this is an essential step at a particular phase in the evolution of a new design, it would be very costly as a first step. The usual procedure is to evaluate several proposed configurations by building a model of each and then testing in a wind tunnel. Again this is the process of simulation.

A succinct definition of simulation is that 'Models represent reality; simulation imitates it'. Simulation indeed involves the manipulation of a model so that, in effect, it yields a motion picture of reality. Logical models are used in an attempt to copy the dynamics of a real-life situation. Such logical models do not usually use mathematics directly, they are best represented in the form of a flow-chart which shows how, and in what sequence, the factors relevant to a situation interact. By this means attempts are made to copy the dynamics of the real situation and to predict actual behaviour under changed assumptions. A simulation model will not in itself generate policies or improvements; all it can do is to evaluate possibilities put forward by managers or others concerned with the system.

## 6.2 The Monte Carlo technique

A standard technique for simulation is the system commonly referred to as the Monte Carlo technique, linked to the gambling casinos rather than the car rally. To illustrate the principles, a simple example will be described. Consider a new product which contains two independent and distinct parts, each of which will eventually fail. These parts might be a condenser and a transistor. From past tests and records, the probability of failure of each item in terms of its time in use has been estimated, i.e. the life curve of each item is available. What is wanted is the life curve of the product which contains one of each of these elements—assuming the product fails when the first component fails. Denote the original life distributions of the components by the symbols $f$ and $g$ respectively, whilst the symbol $h$ denotes that of the combined derived distribution. Now in some cases $h$ can be derived by mathematical analysis. This will occur when $f$ and $g$ can be represented by simple mathematical functions. But in other instances it is not possible or practical to evaluate the derived function $h$ in this way. In such instances the Monte Carlo technique may be the best method available.

Assume that the frequency of incidence of time to failure of the two components is as shown in Figure 6.1. In the assembly of the product, one item from each class of component will be selected at random. To simulate this, items must be selected in such a way that each has an equal chance of being selected. Since there are clearly more items of the first component with life spans in some intervals (say the interval from 95 to 105) than in other intervals (say the interval from 75 to 85), the procedure must be such that the chance of selecting an item in any chosen interval on the time scale is equal to the proportion of items falling in that interval. Now a simple random sample drawn from the set of possible time values laid out along the horizontal axis would lead to giving the same chances to the drawing of an item with

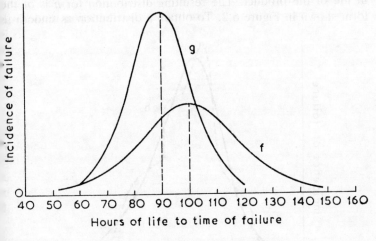

**Figure 6.1** **Distribution of component lives**

a life span between 95 and 105 as to one between 75 and 85. This is clearly an inflexible and incorrect procedure. Hence a technique must be devised for sampling from frequency distributions, taking into account the relative frequencies of the different intervals.

One time-honoured way of doing this is by drawing discs from a drum. The discs would have numbers on them representing the possible values of the variable (e.g. the life of component *f*) concerned. To achieve the necessary weighting of the values of this variable, the number of discs given any particular value would need to be proportional to the frequency with which such a value occurs in the frequency distribution in question. In theory a large number of discs would be needed, to ensure sufficiently good representation of the distribution, and the discs must be well shuffled before each drawing to ensure that each disc stands an equal chance of being selected. To obtain a series of values for the variable concerned, a series of discs would be drawn, each drawn disc being replaced and the drum reshuffled before the next disc is drawn.

A second drum, with a second set of discs, would be required for component *g*. If one disc is now drawn from each drum and the lower length of life noted, this gives one simulation for the length of life of the product. The whole process would now be repeated a large number of times so as to formulate the distribution

of life of the product. The resulting distribution for *h* is of the
form shown in Figure 6.2. To obtain a distribution as smooth as

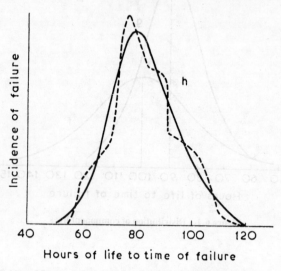

**Figure 6.2　Distribution of combined product lives**

that shown would require a large number of simulations, and the
jagged dotted distribution shows the form that it might have
reached at a somewhat earlier stage. Note that this technique can
be applied whatever the shape of the original distributions of component lives. The distributions do not have to be smooth and bell-
shaped as shown in Figure 6.1, but could equally well be of an
irregular form.

## 6.3　Random numbers

In practice the drum and the shuffling of numbered discs can be
avoided through the use of so-called *random numbers* (or random
digits). Published tables of random numbers consist of pages on
which the decimal digits 0, 1, 2...9 are set down as they might
appear if they had been generated by means of some random-choice
device, giving each digit the same probability of 1/10 of appearing
at any given place in the table. Such a device would be achieved
by having one set of 10 cards in a drum, this time bearing the
numbers 0, 1, 2...9 respectively. One card is drawn out, the
number noted in the table and then replaced. The process is

repeated indefinitely and the series of numbers noted to fill up the page of random numbers. In general any page of random numbers will be different from any other page.

Table 6.1 shows a specimen page taken from a large volume of random numbers (generated in this case not from drawing discs from a drum, but by an electronic procedure which need not detain us here). To illustrate its use a model for a well-known queuing system, the appointments system at a hospital's outpatients department will be studied.

## 6.4 The hospital clinic

In the outpatients clinic there are obvious stochastic elements—consultations take different times, some patients arrive late for appointments and a few do not turn up at all. Initially a simplified system will be studied where the only stochastic element is the variation in consultation time. Suppose the hospital makes appointments for patients to see a particular consultant at 10-minute intervals from 9.00 a.m. to 12.20 p.m. inclusive. The consultations take either 5, 9 or 15 minutes, depending upon the type of examination or treatment the consultant has to give. This pattern of consultation time may not be unreasonable for some types of clinic. Patients at the clinic may need either a brief examination (5 minutes) to decide that no further treatment is needed; others who need new treatment require a long consultation (15 minutes); while those who are found to require continuation of an existing treatment require a 9-minute consultation. From past experience it is known that in the long run one-fifth of all patients require a 5-minute consultation, one-half a 9-minute consultation and the remaining three-tenths require a 15-minute consultation. These proportions represent the probabilities that individual consultations will be of those lengths. The fact that we know these probabilities, but not the categories into which individual patients will fall, introduces the probabilistic or stochastic element and makes it impossible to schedule appointments to fit the precise consultation times required for individual patients.

To obtain the average consultation time, we multiply each possible consultation time by its probability and add to get $\frac{1}{5} \times 5 + \frac{1}{2} \times 9 + \frac{3}{10} \times 15$, or 10 minutes.

Thus the average time of 10 minutes per consultation is the same as the systematic interval built into the appointments system.

Table 6.1  Random number table

| | 1–4 | 5–8 | 9–12 | 13–16 | 17–20 | 21–24 | 25–28 | 29–32 | 33–36 | 37–40 |
|---|---|---|---|---|---|---|---|---|---|---|
| | | | | | First thousand | | | | | |
| 1 | 23 15 | 75 48 | 59 01 | 83 72 | 59 93 | 76 24 | 97 08 | 86 95 | 23 03 | 67 44 |
| 2 | 05 54 | 55 50 | 43 10 | 53 74 | 35 08 | 90 61 | 18 37 | 44 10 | 96 22 | 13 43 |
| 3 | 14 87 | 16 03 | 50 32 | 40 43 | 62 23 | 50 05 | 10 03 | 22 11 | 54 38 | 08 34 |
| 4 | 38 97 | 67 49 | 51 94 | 05 17 | 58 53 | 78 80 | 59 01 | 94 32 | 42 87 | 16 95 |
| 5 | 97 31 | 26 17 | 18 99 | 75 53 | 08 70 | 94 25 | 12 58 | 41 54 | 88 21 | 05 13 |
| 6 | 11 74 | 26 93 | 81 44 | 33 93 | 08 72 | 32 79 | 73 31 | 18 22 | 64 70 | 68 50 |
| 7 | 43 36 | 12 88 | 59 11 | 01 64 | 56 23 | 93 00 | 90 04 | 99 43 | 64 07 | 40 36 |
| 8 | 93 80 | 62 04 | 78 38 | 26 80 | 44 91 | 55 75 | 11 89 | 32 58 | 47 55 | 25 71 |
| 9 | 49 54 | 01 31 | 81 08 | 42 98 | 41 87 | 69 53 | 82 96 | 61 77 | 73 80 | 95 27 |
| 10 | 36 76 | 87 26 | 33 37 | 94 82 | 15 69 | 41 95 | 96 86 | 70 45 | 27 48 | 38 80 |
| 11 | 07 09 | 25 23 | 92 24 | 62 71 | 26 07 | 06 55 | 84 53 | 44 67 | 33 84 | 53 20 |
| 12 | 43 31 | 00 10 | 81 44 | 86 38 | 03 07 | 52 55 | 51 61 | 48 89 | 74 29 | 46 47 |
| 13 | 61 57 | 00 63 | 60 06 | 17 36 | 37 75 | 63 14 | 89 51 | 23 35 | 01 74 | 69 93 |
| 14 | 31 35 | 28 37 | 99 10 | 77 91 | 89 41 | 31 57 | 97 64 | 48 62 | 58 48 | 69 19 |
| 15 | 57 04 | 88 65 | 26 27 | 79 59 | 36 82 | 90 52 | 95 65 | 46 35 | 06 53 | 22 54 |
| 16 | 09 24 | 34 42 | 00 68 | 72 10 | 71 37 | 30 72 | 97 57 | 56 09 | 29 82 | 76 50 |
| 17 | 97 95 | 53 50 | 18 40 | 89 48 | 83 29 | 52 23 | 08 25 | 21 22 | 53 26 | 15 87 |
| 18 | 93 73 | 25 95 | 70 43 | 78 19 | 88 85 | 56 67 | 16 68 | 26 95 | 99 64 | 45 69 |
| 19 | 72 62 | 11 12 | 25 00 | 92 26 | 82 64 | 35 66 | 65 94 | 34 71 | 68 75 | 18 67 |
| 20 | 61 02 | 07 44 | 18 45 | 37 12 | 07 94 | 95 91 | 73 78 | 66 99 | 53 61 | 93 78 |
| 21 | 97 83 | 98 54 | 74 33 | 05 59 | 17 18 | 45 47 | 35 41 | 44 22 | 03 42 | 30 00 |
| 22 | 47 46 | 06 04 | 79 56 | 23 04 | 84 17 | 14 37 | 28 51 | 87 27 | 55 80 | 03 68 |
| 23 | 25 96 | 68 82 | 20 62 | 87 17 | 92 65 | 02 82 | 35 28 | 62 84 | 91 95 | 48 83 |
| 24 | 81 44 | 33 17 | 19 05 | 04 95 | 48 06 | 74 69 | 00 75 | 67 65 | 01 71 | 65 45 |
| 25 | 11 32 | 25 49 | 31 42 | 36 23 | 43 86 | 08 62 | 49 76 | 67 42 | 24 52 | 32 45 |

## Table 6.1 (contd)

| | | | | Second thousand | | | | | |
|---|---|---|---|---|---|---|---|---|---|
| 1–4 | 5–8 | 9–12 | 13–16 | 17–20 | 21–24 | 25–28 | 29–32 | 33–36 | 37–40 |
| 1 64 75 | 58 38 | 85 84 | 12 22 | 59 20 | 17 69 | 61 56 | 55 95 | 04 59 | 59 47 |
| 2 10 30 | 25 22 | 89 77 | 43 63 | 44 30 | 38 11 | 24 90 | 67 07 | 34 82 | 33 28 |
| 3 71 01 | 79 84 | 95 51 | 30 85 | 03 74 | 66 59 | 10 28 | 87 53 | 76 56 | 91 49 |
| 4 60 01 | 25 56 | 05 88 | 41 03 | 48 79 | 79 65 | 59 01 | 69 78 | 80 00 | 36 66 |
| 5 37 33 | 09 46 | 56 49 | 16 14 | 28 02 | 48 27 | 45 47 | 55 44 | 55 36 | 50 90 |
| 6 47 86 | 98 70 | 01 31 | 59 11 | 22 73 | 60 62 | 61 28 | 22 34 | 69 16 | 12 12 |
| 7 38 04 | 04 27 | 37 64 | 16 78 | 95 78 | 39 32 | 34 93 | 24 88 | 43 43 | 87 06 |
| 8 73 50 | 83 09 | 08 83 | 05 48 | 00 78 | 36 66 | 93 02 | 95 56 | 46 04 | 53 36 |
| 9 32 62 | 34 64 | 74 84 | 06 10 | 43 24 | 20 62 | 83 73 | 19 32 | 35 64 | 39 69 |
| 10 97 59 | 19 95 | 49 36 | 63 03 | 51 06 | 62 06 | 99 29 | 75 95 | 32 05 | 77 34 |
| 11 74 01 | 23 19 | 55 59 | 79 09 | 69 82 | 66 22 | 42 40 | 15 96 | 74 90 | 75 89 |
| 12 56 75 | 42 64 | 57 13 | 35 10 | 50 14 | 90 96 | 63 36 | 74 69 | 09 63 | 34 88 |
| 13 49 80 | 04 99 | 08 54 | 83 12 | 19 98 | 08 52 | 82 63 | 72 92 | 92 36 | 50 26 |
| 14 43 58 | 48 96 | 47 24 | 87 85 | 66 70 | 00 22 | 15 01 | 93 99 | 59 16 | 23 77 |
| 15 16 65 | 37 96 | 64 60 | 32 57 | 13 01 | 35 74 | 28 36 | 36 73 | 05 88 | 72 29 |
| 16 48 50 | 26 90 | 55 65 | 32 25 | 87 48 | 31 44 | 68 02 | 37 31 | 25 29 | 63 67 |
| 17 96 76 | 55 46 | 92 36 | 31 68 | 62 30 | 48 29 | 63 83 | 52 23 | 81 66 | 40 94 |
| 18 38 92 | 36 15 | 50 80 | 35 78 | 17 84 | 23 44 | 30 14 | 63 33 | 21 86 | 81 28 |
| 19 77 95 | 88 16 | 94 25 | 22 50 | 55 87 | 51 07 | 30 10 | 70 60 | 79 84 | 19 61 |
| 20 17 92 | 82 80 | 65 25 | 58 60 | 87 71 | 02 64 | 18 50 | 64 65 |  | 81 70 |
| 21 94 03 | 68 59 | 78 02 | 31 80 | 44 99 | 41 05 | 41 05 | 31 87 | 43 12 | 15 96 |
| 22 47 46 | 06 04 | 79 56 | 23 04 | 84 17 | 14 37 | 28 51 | 67 27 | 55 80 | 03 68 |
| 23 47 85 | 65 60 | 88 51 | 99 28 | 24 39 | 40 64 | 41 71 | 70 13 | 46 31 | 82 88 |
| 24 57 61 | 63 46 | 53 92 | 29 86 | 20 18 | 10 37 | 57 65 | 15 62 | 98 69 | 07 56 |
| 25 08 30 | 09 27 | 04 66 | 75 26 | 66 10 | 57 18 | 87 91 | 07 54 | 22 22 | 20 13 |

The further simplifying assumption is made that all patients turn up precisely on time—neither early nor late. If the doctor is free he will see a patient as soon as he arrives. If a previous consultation is still in progress, the patient joins any other waiting patients who are seen in their order of arrival, as soon as the doctor is free, up to 12.30 p.m. The doctor completes any consultation he starts before 12.30 p.m., but patients who are still waiting at that time have to make a fresh appointment for another day.

Interest lies in three measures: the average time a patient has to wait to see the doctor; the total time the doctor is idle between consultations awaiting the next patient; and the number of patients forced to make fresh appointments because they have not been seen by 12.30 p.m. In an effective system all these measures would be small.

The problem has obviously been greatly simplified from reality for illustrative purposes by ignoring the possibility of late arrivals and missed appointments, and by allowing only three discrete consultation times rather than a continuous range of times. The model could be extended to remove these restrictions if the appropriate information were available, e.g. the probability that a patient does not turn up, arrives 5 minutes late, etc. Such features complicate the system, but do not introduce new basic principles, and we discuss variations of this nature later when we have examined our basic or prototype clinic.

Although this particular system could be handled on a mathematical basis, a hand-simulation is used since it is capable of further generalizations that cannot be readily handled mathematically. It is essential to remember that the results from each simulated or 'mock' clinic are only applicable to what happens in a real clinic, provided the assumptions made in setting up the simulation model are correct. This is equally true whether the results have been obtained through mathematics or by the use of random numbers.

To use the table of random numbers to assign consultation times with correct probabilities, the digits 0 or 1 are associated with 5-minute consultation time (thus assigning to it a probability of $\frac{1}{5}$). Digits 2, 3, 4, 5 or 6 are then associated with a consultation time of 9 minutes (thus assigning a probability of $\frac{1}{2}$). Finally, digits 7, 8 or 9 are associated with a consultation time of 15 minutes, thus assigning it the correct probability of $\frac{3}{10}$.

In Table 6.2 this procedure has been followed for a complete

Table 6.2 **Simulation of hospital appointment system (1)**

| Random digit (1) | Arrival time (2) | Consultation time (min) (3) | Start time (4) | End time (5) | Doctor idle (min) (6) | Patient wait (min) (7) |
|---|---|---|---|---|---|---|
| 5 | 9·00 | 9 | 9·00 | 9·09 | 1 | 0 |
| 3 | 9·10 | 9 | 9·10 | 9·19 | 1 | 0 |
| 6 | 9·20 | 9 | 9·20 | 9·29 | 1 | 0 |
| 5 | 9·30 | 9 | 9·30 | 9·39 | 1 | 0 |
| 0 | 9·40 | 5 | 9·40 | 9·45 | 5 | 0 |
| 0 | 9·50 | 5 | 9·50 | 9·55 | 5 | 0 |
| 5 | 10·00 | 9 | 10·00 | 10·09 | 1 | 0 |
| 4 | 10·10 | 9 | 10·10 | 10·19 | 1 | 0 |
| 4 | 10·20 | 9 | 10·20 | 10·29 | 1 | 0 |
| 1 | 10·30 | 5 | 10·30 | 10·35 | 5 | 0 |
| 2 | 10·40 | 9 | 10·40 | 10·49 | 1 | 0 |
| 0 | 10·50 | 5 | 10·50 | 10·55 | 5 | 0 |
| 3 | 11·00 | 9 | 11·00 | 11·09 | 1 | 0 |
| 8 | 11·10 | 15 | 11·10 | 11·25 | 0 | 0 |
| 3 | 11·20 | 9 | 11·25 | 11·34 | 0 | 5 |
| 7 | 11·30 | 15 | 11·34 | 11·49 | 0 | 4 |
| 8 | 11·40 | 15 | 11·49 | 12·04 | 0 | 9 |
| 8 | 11·50 | 15 | 12·04 | 12·19 | 0 | 14 |
| 8 | 12·00 | 15 | 12·19 | 12·34 | 0 | 19 |
| 0 | 12·10 | 5 | not seen | | | not seen |
| 1 | 12·20 | 5 | not seen | | | not seen |
| | | | | Totals | 29 | 51 |

morning, using the column of random numbers headed *17* from Table 6.1 to generate the consultation times. Columns (6) and (7) give the idle time of the doctor and the waiting time for the patients. Note first that two patients are not seen at all and have to be referred back to another day. Of the other 19 patients, the total waiting time is 51 minutes (all incurred in the last hour and a half of the morning) or an average of 2·7 minutes per patient seen. The idle time for the doctor totals 29 minutes in an overall working period of 214 minutes, or 13·6 per cent. Note also that once a doctor has had idle time, he can never make up that time, which makes such a system particularly vulnerable when the total working time is just equal to the number of patients multiplied by the average consultation time. (A similar situation arises in many industrial disputes—a stoppage on a daily newspaper at 9 p.m. for 2 or 3 hours will generally mean the loss of a day's production with no possible restoration of the lost revenue at a later stage.)

## 6.5    Modified consultation system

To try to overcome the objection of having expensive doctor time idle, a common feature of appointment systems is to ask two patients to arrive at the first consultation time, and then for subsequent patients to arrive at 10-minute intervals afterwards. Reworking the same simulation as the one in Table 6.2 with this revised arrival pattern (but the same consultation pattern) gives the results shown in Table 6.3. The first major change to note is that all 21 participants are now seen. However, the total patient waiting time has been increased from 51 minutes to 125 minutes, an average of 5·95 minutes, whilst the idle time of the doctor has been reduced to a total of 19 minutes, or 8·9 per cent of his working session. Thus there is a direct trade-off between the use of the doctor's time and the use of a patient's time. (A similar trade-off occurs in other situations: queues at a supermarket check-out, the use of courts of law where cases have to wait for the court to be free rather than vice versa, etc.)

A further frequently occurring complication is that patients arrive early or late, and this affects the operation of the system. Suppose that observation of past occasions shows that, whilst 60 per cent of patients arrive precisely on time, 20 per cent arrive 5 minutes early, 10 per cent 5 minutes late and 10 per cent 10 minutes late. The pattern shown in Table 6.2 is now re-worked with the late/early/on-time arrival pattern simulated by the column of random numbers next to the one used earlier for the consultation time, the new random numbers being shown in column 1(a) of Table 6.4. (Digits 2 to 7 correspond to on-time, 0 and 1 to 5 minutes early, 8 to 5 minutes late and 9 to 10 minutes late.) Table 6.4 shows that the situation has reverted to one where two patients are not seen, whilst the average waiting time for the 19 patients seen is 6·26 minutes, with the total idle time of the doctor 29 minutes, or 13·6 per cent of his available time.

The results obtained for the three different appointment systems discussed are summarized in Table 6.5. These results must be

Table 6.3  **Revised arrival pattern in hospital appointment system (2)**

| Arrival time (2) | Consultation time (min.) (3) | Start time (4) | End time (5) | Doctor idle (min.) (6) | Patient wait (min.) (7) |
|---|---|---|---|---|---|
| 9·00 | 9 | 9·00 | 9·09 | 0 | 0 |
| 9·00 | 9 | 9·09 | 9·18 | 0 | 9 |
| 9·10 | 9 | 9·18 | 9·27 | 0 | 8 |
| 9·20 | 9 | 9·27 | 9·36 | 0 | 7 |
| 9·30 | 5 | 9·36 | 9·41 | 0 | 6 |
| 9·40 | 5 | 9·41 | 9·46 | 4 | 1 |
| 9·50 | 9 | 9·50 | 9·59 | 1 | 0 |
| 10·00 | 9 | 10·00 | 10·09 | 1 | 0 |
| 10·10 | 9 | 10·10 | 10·19 | 1 | 0 |
| 10·20 | 5 | 10·20 | 10·25 | 5 | 0 |
| 10·30 | 9 | 10·30 | 10·39 | 1 | 0 |
| 10·40 | 5 | 10·40 | 10·45 | 5 | 0 |
| 10·50 | 9 | 10·50 | 10·59 | 1 | 0 |
| 11·00 | 15 | 11·00 | 11·15 | 0 | 0 |
| 11·10 | 9 | 11·15 | 11·24 | 0 | 5 |
| 11·20 | 15 | 11·24 | 11·39 | 0 | 4 |
| 11·30 | 15 | 11·39 | 11·54 | 0 | 9 |
| 11·40 | 15 | 11·54 | 12·09 | 0 | 14 |
| 11·50 | 15 | 12·09 | 12·24 | 0 | 19 |
| 12·00 | 5 | 12·24 | 12·29 | 0 | 24 |
| 12·10 | 5 | 12·29 | 12·34 | 0 | 19 |
| | | | Totals | 19 | 125 |

treated with caution, in that they are based on a simulation for just one morning clinic. At their face value they suggest that the second situation is the best of the three, in that all patients are seen, whilst the doctor's idle time is relatively small and there is only a modest increase in the average patient's waiting time. Patients' arrival indiscipline in the third situation, whilst no doubt realistic, makes it a more expensive system, since to give the same level of patient service as in the second case would require a greater ratio of doctor/patient time.

However, to be sure that these results are reliable further simulation runs, say about 25 half-day clinics, would be desirable and the average results obtained examined. Individual clinics would undoubtedly vary but, in carrying out a large number of such

Table 6.4   **Second revised pattern in hospital appointment system (3)**

| Random digit (1a) | Arrival time (2) | Consulta- tion time (min.) (3) | Start time (4) | End time (5) | Doctor idle (min.) (6) | Patient wait (min.) (7) |
|---|---|---|---|---|---|---|
| 9 | 9·10 | 9 | 9·10 | 9·19 | 0 | 0 |
| 5 | 9·00 | 9 | 9·00 | 9·09 | 1 | 0 |
| 2 | 9·10 | 9 | 9·19 | 9·28 | 0 | 9 |
| 8 | 9·25 | 9 | 9·28 | 9·37 | 0 | 3 |
| 8 | 9·35 | 5 | 9·37 | 9·42 | 3 | 2 |
| 8 | 9·45 | 5 | 9·45 | 9·50 | 0 | 0 |
| 6 | 9·50 | 9 | 9·50 | 9·59 | 1 | 0 |
| 4 | 10·00 | 9 | 10·00 | 10·09 | 0 | 0 |
| 1 | 10·05 | 9 | 10·09 | 10·18 | 2 | 4 |
| 5 | 10·20 | 5 | 10·20 | 10·25 | 5 | 0 |
| 6 | 10·30 | 9 | 10·30 | 10·39 | 1 | 0 |
| 3 | 10·40 | 5 | 10·40 | 10·45 | 5 | 0 |
| 7 | 10·50 | 9 | 10·50 | 10·59 | 11 | 0 |
| 9 | 11·10 | 15 | 11·10 | 11·25 | 0 | 0 |
| 6 | 11·10 | 9 | 11·25 | 11·34 | 0 | 15 |
| 1 | 11·15 | 15 | 11·34 | 11·49 | 0 | 19 |
| 3 | 11·30 | 15 | 11·49 | 12·04 | 0 | 19 |
| 8 | 11·45 | 15 | 12·04 | 12·19 | 0 | 19 |
| 2 | 11·50 | 15 | 12·19 | 12·34 | 0 | 29 |
| 7 | 12·00 | 5 | not seen | | not seen | |
| 7 | 12·10 | 5 | not seen | | not seen | |
| | | | | Totals | 29 | 119 |

Table 6.5   **Summary of simulation results**

| | Regular arrivals | Regular arrivals (two at start) | Variable arrival times |
|---|---|---|---|
| No. of patients sent away | 2·0 | 0·0 | 2·0 |
| Average waiting time (for those seen), minutes | 2·7 | 5·95 | 6·26 |
| Percentage of doctor's time idle | 13·6 | 8·9 | 13·6 |

simulations a pattern of results would emerge that could provide a basis for action—whether it be to have more medical staff, a reduction in consultation times, the use of ancillary staff for some routine tasks, etc. Readers are left to carry out a substantial number of simulations for themselves on one or more of the appointments systems to assess the representativeness of the results given in Table 6.5.

## 6.6 The rolling mill

A further illustration of the simulation process relates to a problem where a rolling mill has material waiting to be rolled, thus forming a queue. It is a particular case of a single server queue with variable service times and arrival intervals, for the time ($t_1$) between arrivals of material and the time ($t_2$) taken to process it once it is in the rolling mill are probabilistic. In a simulation model these times have, therefore, to be generated as samples from their respective probability distributions (which might be obtained by gathering facts from the real-life situation. Figure 6.3 illustrates the situation, and the corresponding distributions of the times $t_1$ and $t_2$.

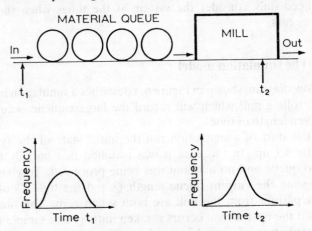

**Figure 6.3   Rolling mill queue**

The distribution of service times in the rolling mill will be independent of the size of the queue of raw material. A known distribution of process times for the furnace allows the times for $t_2$ to be estimated, and hence the output times from the system can be determined. An item of raw material will be taken from the queue into the mill in accordance with some rule. This rule describes the 'queue discipline'. There are basically three possible rules:

FIFO (first in, first out)
LIFO (last in, first out)
Random selection from the waiting queue.

The optimum solution to such a problem could depend upon the viewpoint taken. The works manager's aim would no doubt be to reduce the size of the queue; the queue discipline used would be immaterial. From the point of view of the rolling mill machinery the aim would be to reduce idle time to a minimum; queue discipline again being irrelevant. Finally if the items themselves were cooling steel (and heat is money) they would have as their aim the reduction in the total time taken for service.

Adopting the works manager's criterion as the most desirable, note that the queue size changes only when there is an arrival or a departure. Therefore using this approach the rest of the time (in which all the real work is done) is of no interest to the simulator, who need only consider the system at the times when such an event occurs.

## 6.7 The simulation model

The flow diagram shown in Figure 6.4 describes a simulation model of the rolling mill which will record the largest queue occurring in a given length of time.

At the start of a simulation run the initial state of the system must be set up. In this case it was assumed that initially there was no queue and no material was being processed. To give this initial state the current queue length $Q$ and the time $T_2$ of the next departure from the mill are both set to zero. The time $T_1$ at which the next arrival occurs is taken initially as a sample from the distribution of arrival intervals $t_1$. The initial conditions are completed by setting the largest queue size recorded, $n$, to zero and setting the total time $L$ it is required to simulate.

At each stage of the simulation the nature of the next event to occur is determined by comparing the values of $T_1$ and $T_2$. If it is an arrival then the right-hand fork of the diagram will be taken and the current queue length increased by 1. The largest

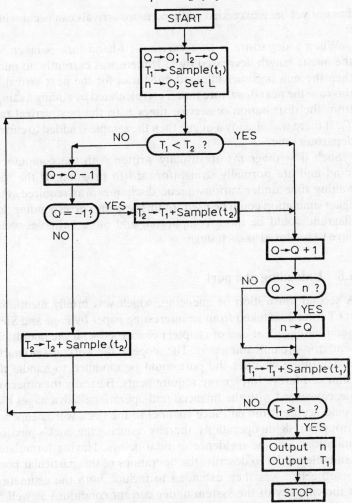

**Figure 6.4    Flow diagram**

$Q$ = current size of queue
$n$ = largest size queue recorded
$L$ = length of time to be simulated
$T_1, T_2$ = times in and out of the system, respectively

queue length $n$ is updated if necessary, and the time of the next arrival is calculated by sampling from $t_1$. The simulation is halted, after the appropriate data has been obtained, as soon as the next arrival time $T_1$ becomes greater than $L$; at this stage the time limit has not yet been exceeded while no more arrivals can occur within it.

When a departure is to occur the left-hand fork is taken and the queue length decreased by 1. If there was currently no queue then the mill becomes idle and must wait for the next arrival. In this case the next departure time $T_2$ is calculated by adding a sample from the distribution of service times $t_2$ to the next arrival time $T_1$. If there was already a queue then the sample is added to current departure time.

Such flow diagrams are usually written with the computer in mind and are normally straightforward to program. If the total waiting time under various queue disciplines was required, then again simulation could be used. In this case the corresponding flow diagram would be more complicated and more variables would have to be stored at each stage.

## 6.8　Unloading at a port

A second illustration of queueing, which was briefly mentioned in Chapter 1, is taken from an interesting paper by Page and Steer (see reference 5 at end of chapter) concerned with the operations of an iron-ore unloading port. The scope of the work was primarily to determine whether the port could be modified to handle the estimated future foreign ore requirements. Basically the objective was concerned with the financial and operational advantages that would accrue if the entrance channel to the dock were deepened through dredging operations, thereby reducing the dock's physical limitations and the incidence of tidal delays. Having formulated a suitable model to describe the operations of this particular port, the objective was then extended to include both the estimation of the capacity of the system under current conditions as well as the increase in capacity that could be expected from relatively inexpensive modifications. These modifications would incorporate a deeper entrance channel together with reduced service times that might be derived from the application of a method study of the unloading operations at the wharf itself.

Various basic pieces of information were obtained, such as the arrival pattern of the ships, by size as well as by time, the delays that occurred outside the lock, the service times once the ships had arrived at the unloading quay, and the pattern and height of the tides.

In the first instance, attempts were made to obtain a formal mathematical solution. Several mathematical models were formulated but failed to reproduce current or future conditions accurately enough when tested against wharf records and the results of hand simulations. The reason for these failures was that mathematical formulations could not adequately incorporate the wide variety of ships visiting the wharf, the sporadic nature of their arrivals, or the operating methods of the lock which connected the dock to the sea. For this reason Monte Carlo simulation techniques turned out to be essential. A flow diagram of the complete programme of operations was drawn up and a basic procedure for generating arrivals was compiled. To effect the random sampling involved in carrying out the simulation, it was found convenient from the programming point of view to follow the concept of generating pseudo-random numbers internally in the manner mentioned above, rather than to store random numbers in the machine.

At the commencement of a run on the computer, the program, together with the data relating to the various relationships and distributions, was fed into the machine and stored. On initiating the program, the data for four tides contained on the arrival tape were read in and processed. This took about 43 seconds and was repeated until the data for some 700 tides had been processed. The computer then printed out the following information for each ship when it had been unloaded: type of ship; arrival tide; hours neaped (i.e. waiting for a tide high enough for the ship to enter the dock); hours queued; berth hours; turn-round time (tides); and cargo weight (tons).

At the end of each simulated week the berth occupancy was calculated as a percentage, whilst at the end of each simulated year a great deal more information was printed out relating to the ship-hours lost through various causes, the turn-round times, service times, etc., and the tonnage of ore actually imported.

It is interesting to note that the ratio of simulated to actual time achieved with this computer program once it was written proved to be approximately 1:4200, which may be compared with approximately 1:35 for earlier simulations that were done by hand. This gain would in itself have been sufficient justification of the decision to use the computer in this context, apart from the fact that the program could, without much difficulty, be made to cater for future changes in the various constants of the model.

The results obtained from the simulation showed that the company would gain significant financial and operational benefits by deepening the entrance channel. Further, the present system of use was shown to be incapable of handling the required future changes in throughput without considerable capital expenditure to change the nature of the dock concerned.

# References

(1) *The Art of Simulation* by K. D. Tocher (English Universities Press, 1963).
(2) *Industrial Dynamics* by J. W Forrester (MIT Press, 1961).
(3) *Cybernetics and Management* by S. Beer (English Universities Press, 1959).
(4) *Management Information Systems* by J. Dearden and F. W. McFarlan (Irwin) (especially Chapter 5).
(5) Feasibility and financial studies of a port installation, by A. C. C. Page and D. T. Steer, *Operational Research Quarterly* (1961), vol. 12, pp. 145–60.
(6) *The Limits to Growth* by D. H. Meadows (Earth Island, 1972).

# 7 Inventory and stock control

## 7.1 Introduction

Holding stock, in whatever form, costs money. The capital tied up the stock itself has to be serviced by the payment of interest, and the land or warehouse needed for the stock has to be bought or rented. The handling and securing of the stock, and any quality deterioration that occurs, also cost money. Global figures of actual stocks held in Great Britain by manufacturing industry are given in the *Monthly Digest of Statistics*. At the end of 1982 the amounts were: materials and fuel, £11·0 billion; work in progress, £14·2 billion; finished goods, £10·9 billion; an overall total of £36·1 billion. The total value today is probably even higher but, taken at this figure, the annual cost of holding this stock must be around £4 billion and there is clearly a great incentive to keep stocks to an absolute minimum. Planning the correct amount of stock needed in a factory complex can be complicated, although the principles concerned are straightforward.

Many rules of thumb are operated by companies to control their stocks. For instance, one company has a rule which states that the quantity of any product to be carried in inventory (stock) should be kept (approximately) equal to the amount that customers normally buy in sixty days (or some other fixed period). Such crude rules as this one often exhibit serious shortcomings and could result in excess stocks of some items and insufficient stocks of others. Most businessmen will recognize these rules of thumb for what they are—rough but serviceable management tools—but it is nevertheless worth considering whether such a rule cannot be refined.

## 7.2 The square-root formula

Suppose a manufacturer confidently expects to sell $Q$ units of one of his commodities at a predetermined price over the next year, with the demand spread evenly over the year. How much stock should he keep on hand? Clearly he could stock up with a batch of $Q$ units made at the beginning of the year and sell it evenly over the year. The average stock in hand over the year as a whole would then be $\frac{1}{2}Q$, corresponding to the actual stock held midway through the year. Alternatively he could arrange for monthly mailings of $\frac{1}{12}Q$ and his average stock then becomes $\frac{1}{24}Q$, but he has twelve orderings to arrange and check in per year with all the attendant set-up costs. Figure 7.1 illustrates the situation. Indeed,

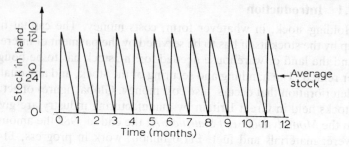

**Figure 7.1    Monthly stock pattern**

by having more and more frequent orders the average stock level in hand can be made as low as desired. A lower average stock, of course, saves money on carrying costs (storage, deterioration, interest on capital, etc.) but, on the other hand, there are re-order costs involved in placing, setting up, and delivering an order. Since a smaller stock involves more frequent orders and deliveries, the re-order costs may become prohibitive if management decides upon too small an average stock level.

In practice it is never deliberately planned to allow the stocks to run out altogether, as is tacitly assumed in the foregoing analysis, since unexpected demands or delays in deliveries could be embarrassing. In the formal analysis that follows some minimum extra safety or buffer stock level $B$ could be added throughout the year to allow for this possibility. The choice of value for $B$ is discussed later in the chapter. Such an allowance does not, however, affect the immediate analytical results derived below.

To find the optimal stock level (the level which results in minimum overall cost) mathematical expressions are required for the two types of cost, carrying and re-ordering.

## *Carrying cost*

The average stock level is one-half the amount received in a shipment. Thus if the quantity delivered to the retailer is $D$ units per shipment and demand is evenly spread over time, the average stock level must be

$$\tfrac{1}{2}D$$

Let $k$ be the variable cost of stocking one item for a year calculated as the interest on capital tied up plus other carrying costs involved in holding one item of stock for a year. Then the total carrying cost per annum will be

$$\tfrac{1}{2}Dk \tag{7.1}$$

## *Re-order cost*

Generally, if $Q$ items are to be sold per annum and there are $D$ items in each delivery made on re-ordering, the required number of deliveries per annum is $Q/D$. Suppose the cost per delivery is represented by

$$r + sD$$

where the number $s$ may be interpreted as the variable cost per item, whilst $r$ represents the fixed costs per order. For a producer mailing in batches the fixed costs would mainly be the set-up cost per run. For a retailer the fixed costs would be associated with book-keeping, telephoning, checking, etc. The total annual re-ordering cost is now

(cost per delivery) × (number of deliveries)

$$= (r + sD)\frac{Q}{D} \quad \text{or} \quad \frac{rQ}{D} + sQ \tag{7.2}$$

The total cost that the manufacturer lays out on his stock is the sum of the two costs (7.1) and (7.2) giving

$$C = \tfrac{1}{2}Dk + \frac{rQ}{D} + sQ \tag{7.3}$$

Now the only unknown in equation (7.3) will be the value of $D$ as $Q$, $r$ and $k$ need to be fixed by the conditions of the problem. Once $D$ is determined the inventory situation is completely fixed.

With equation (7.3) available the solution is, therefore, reduced to a simple one of computation. For example, suppose

$$Q = 200 \qquad k = 8 \qquad r = 20 \qquad s = 3$$

leading to the cost equation

$$C = 4D + \frac{4000}{D} + 600 \tag{7.4}$$

Trial and error could now be used to solve equation (7.4) and specimen values found as follows:

| D | 10 | 20 | 30 | 40 | 50 | 60 |
|---|----|----|----|----|----|----|
| C | 1040 | 880 | 853·3 | 860 | 880 | 906·7 |

Examination of this table and the associated Figure 7.2 suggests

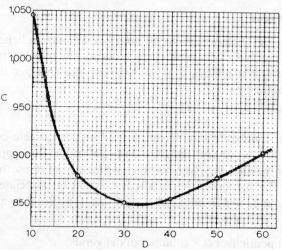

**Figure 7.2    Optimum value of *D***

(correctly) that the minimum value of *C* occurs when *D* is about 32. Thus the equation provides an objective function enabling the problem to be solved.

An extra piece of mathematical analysis, not given here, enables a generalization to be made which avoids the use of trial and error methods to solve equation (7.4). The mathematics leads to a further equation, deduced from (7.3), which states as a perfectly general result that the optimal value of *D*, i.e. the value of *D* which minimizes the cost in equation (7.3) is given by

$$\sqrt{\left(\frac{2rQ}{k}\right)} \tag{7.5}$$

This result is no longer tied to any particular set of numbers, but can be used perfectly generally for any set of values for $r$, $Q$ and $k$. Note that $s$, the variable cost, does not enter into the expression. Substitution of the appropriate figures for this particular example gives 31·6, or 32 to the nearest integer, as deduced graphically.

## 7.3 Sensitivity of the result

What is surprising, but important, about the result is that the general formula (7.5) indicates that the stock level should only increase in proportion to the square root of the sales. Thus the rule of thumb quoted earlier would, even if the total level of stocks held for a variety of products were right, lead to excessive stocks of the popular large sales volume items, and insufficient stocks of the goods whose sales are relatively modest.

A few further practical comments can be made. The optimal formula contains three quantities, namely $r$, $Q$ and $k$. Although these should, in theory, be susceptible to accurate estimation this may not really be so in practice. Concentrate attention on $r$ as an illustration. The quantity $r$ is the fixed cost of placing an order for items. As such it represents the costs that are broadly invariant with the size of the order, the machine set-up costs, the checking procedures, and so forth. Such costs may not be so easy to estimate as might be anticipated at a first glance. It is, therefore, of interest to see what effect any errors made in the estimation of $r$ would have on the cost structure of the optimal stock policy. Suppose, therefore, it is assumed that $r = 20$, whereas the value of $r$ is really $r' = 40$. The values of $Q = 200$ and $k = 8$ are assumed to be known without error. Now under the assumption that $r = 20$, the re-order quantity will be 32 and the true annual cost, from equation (7.3), will be

$$C = \tfrac{1}{2} \times 32 \times 8 + \frac{40 \times 200}{32} + 600$$

$$= 978 \tag{7.6}$$

But the *true* optimum value of $D$, using $r' = 40$, is

$$\sqrt{\frac{2 \times 40 \times 200}{8}} = 45 \text{ (approx.)}$$

from equation (7.5) and the annual cost of stockholding would then be

$$C = \frac{1}{2} \times 45 \times 8 + \frac{40 \times 200}{45} + 600$$

$$= 957 \cdot 8 \tag{7.7}$$

The difference between (7.6) and (7.7) is 20·2 or about 2 per cent. Hence an 'error' of −50 per cent in the estimation of $r$ has only affected the total costs by 2 per cent. This may still be a lot of money in absolute terms but, nevertheless, this stability should be borne in mind when judging how far to strive in the quest for accuracy in the quantities to be inserted in the formulae concerned. It must not be surmised from this calculation that the mathematical model has little or no use, rather that the method irons out inconsistencies in the treatment of the various items which need to be included and throws up the relative importance of the different items to be included.

## 7.4   Re-order levels

The next stage is to consider the re-order level, i.e. the level to which the stock is allowed to fall before a fresh order is placed, as well as the amount of stock that is then ordered. In the preceding section it was tacitly assumed that at the end of each period the stock could be allowed to run out, be replenished instantaneously, and then allowed to run out again, and so on. In practice, sales vary, replenishments are delayed, stocks deteriorate, perish, or go out of vogue. Uncertainty enters the system so that it is no longer strictly deterministic, but essentially *stochastic*. 'Stochastic' comes from a Greek word meaning marksman and, just as the archer's arrows group themselves round the bull's eye, so the weekly sales figures will vary, but group themselves round some average level.

The following simple example illustrates a problem relating to the stocking of raw material by a manufacturer, some basic quantities being defined first. Variations occur in demand and in the lead-time, whilst the buffer stock is the amount of extra stock that is kept in the system over and above what would otherwise be required to cater for these variations. The lead-time is the time taken for replenishments to arrive once they have been ordered.

A special delivery charge is made if a stock run-out occurs and an emergency supply has to be obtained. What is the stocking system that minimizes the total costs? The relevant data are as follows:

| | |
|---|---|
| Purchase price per article | £2 |
| Average consumption per week | 10 (distributed so that individual weeks vary in their consumption from 4 to 16, with a peak frequency at 10 and frequencies tailing off on either side). |
| Lead time (days) | 14 (distributed so that the time varies from 12 to 16 days, with a peak frequency at 14 days and frequencies tailing off on either side). |
| Cost of placing an order | £1 |
| Stock-holding costs | 20 per cent of value of stock per annum. |
| Special delivery charge when stock run-out occurs | £10 |

Using the square-root formula, with a year as the basic time interval, the appropriate re-order quantity will be

$$D = \sqrt{\frac{2 \times 1 \times 520}{0 \cdot 2 \times 2}} = 51$$

Hence the amount to re-order each time is 51. The remainder of the problem revolves around finding the re-order level $R$, i.e. the level to which the stock falls for a fresh order of 51 items to be made. This level has to cater for both a variable demand and a variable lead-time and will equal the average demand in the average lead-time, plus some buffer stock to allow for the variations in demand and lead-time. If $Q$ is the average demand per unit time, $L$ the average lead-time, and $B$ the buffer stock, then

$$R = Q \times L + B$$

The larger $B$ is made, the smaller will be the chance of running out of stock, but the larger will be the capital tied up. Hence the problem is now reduced to one of minimizing the combined cost of holding the buffer stock $B$, together with the run-out cost.

The number of orders placed per year is $520/51 = 10 \cdot 2$. If the probability, at each repetition of the order/demand cycle, of a stock run-out occurring is $p$, then the expected or average number of stock run-outs per year is $10 \cdot 2p$.[*] The expected cost of stock run-outs per year will then be £10 $\times$ 10·2p = £102p. The cost of

---

[*] Appendix B summarizes the statistical concepts concerning variability and expected values that are utilized in this, and later, chapters.

holding the buffer stock will be approximately $0.2B$, since the stock-holding cost $k$ is equal to 20 per cent of £1. The cost (£) that has now to be minimized is the sum of the two costs, namely

$$\text{Stock run-out cost + Buffer stock-holding cost}$$
$$= 102p + 0.4B \tag{7.8}$$

## 7.5   Choice of buffer stock

The size of $B$ which makes the last expression a minimum is required. Figure 7.3 illustrates a typical kind of situation which

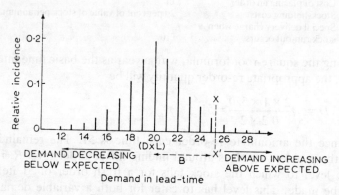

**Figure 7.3   Buffer stock distribution**

arises, giving the relative frequency or incidence of demand during the nominal lead-time $L$. The average is, by definition, $Q \times L$, but there are considerable variations about this level and on some occasions the actual demand observed is higher and, on some occasions, lower. If a buffer stock of size $B$ were held, it would imply that only on those occasions where the demand in the cycle exceeded $(Q \times L + B)$ would there be a stock run-out. Against this, however, an extra $B$ units would have to be held more or less permanently in stock. If $B$ were reduced, then the proportion of occasions on which a stock run-out would occur would be increased, but the holding of extra buffer stock would be reduced. Hence as $B$ increases, the value of $p$ reduces, and vice versa. For a particular situation, as in that defined in the last section, the combined cost expression (7.8) above, can be calculated mathematically for various values of $B$ and a graph plotted of cost against $B$. This is done in Figure 7.4 and from it the optimum

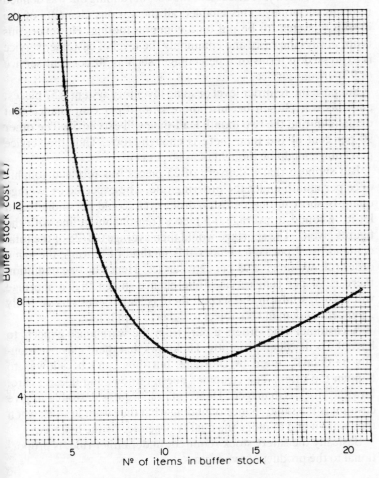

**Figure 7.4 Choice of buffer stock**

buffer stock for this particular situation is read off as 12 items. Since the average demand in the average lead-time is $Q \times L$ which is 20 items, the re-order level is $12 + 20$ or 32 items. The lowest possible overall cost is then obtained by re-ordering 51 items every time the stock falls to 32 items. If this system is followed the value of $p$ that has been imputed, from equation (7.8) above, is 0·008, i.e. the expected number of run-outs per annum is $12 \times 0·008$ or 0·09.

## 7.6 Safety stocks and service

In the illustration just discussed, the cost of running out was defined in terms of money. This enabled all the various elements of the inventory system to be put on a common footing. However, this is not always the case, and commonly the level of customer service is expressed in terms of a percentage, such as 90 per cent service or 95 per cent service.

Suppose the re-order level of some inventory system is 57 pieces, and this was chosen because there is a 10 per cent chance that demand during the two month lead-time will exceed 57. The other 90 per cent of the time there is enough stock. Thus the service percentage might be thought of as 90 per cent.

But suppose that a delivery of 25 pieces was received roughly once per month under the ordering rule. The expected or average quantity short in one delivery/order cycle could be studied, and let it be found to average 0·5 pieces (reasonably in line with the figures given). The shortage would then average 0·5/25 of the total demand, or 2 per cent. Under this method of scoring, the same order rule would give 98 per cent service. Hence by one definition there is 90 per cent service (one chance in ten that a shortage will occur), whilst in the second there is 98 per cent service (only 2 per cent of demand is subject to delay in supply).

A customer who orders a part from the warehouse expects to have the order filled promptly. He knows that there may occasionally be delays caused by shortage, but they can't be allowed to happen too often. The customer doesn't know, and doesn't care, how the stock is managed. Hence in practice it is desirable to give customers the same chance of finding what they want in stock when they want it and to judge the quality of service by the first rule.

Basically the safety stock required, under either rule, is proportional to the product of two factors

$$l \times v$$

where $l$ represents the level of service it is desired to give and $v$ represents the degree of variability in the forecast demand for the item during the lead-time. For a given level of service, the safety stock is proportional to the variability in demand, and vice versa. If variability is expressed in terms of standard deviation (see Appendix B) then there are tables available (see reference

4 from R. G. Brown at end of chapter) which will provide the value of *l* in terms of

D  Number of pieces per order placed.
M  Service (probability of filling order).
v  Standard deviation of forecast demand for item during lead-time.

For example, if $D = 15$, $v = 8·5$, $M = 98$ per cent, then *l* is found mathematically to be 1·4 and the safety stock is $1·4 \times 8·5 = 11·9$. This safety stock of 12 would be added to the normal stock required to meet demand during the lead-time in order to determine the order point.

## 7.7  Centralized stores

Many organizations have one or more central stores and a large number of branch stores. The hospital service, for example, has some central storehouses and depots in the country, and subsidiary storehouses in the individual hospitals fed from the central stores. A large company may have one big central stores organization with separate stores at factory or plant level, as illustrated in Figure 7.5(a).

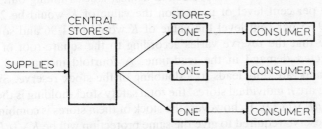

Figure 7.5a  Centralized store system

In such types of organization there is the problem of deciding which items should be centrally, as opposed to universally, stocked and how often items centrally held should be distributed to the subsidiary stores. Very often centralized store holdings can lead to economies in the level of overall stock-holding, and in the operation of the stores, as well as achieving better care of the material. In such instances, factors militating against central stores would be the poorer availability of goods on demand at the peripheral locations, and added transport costs to fulfil some requests. In any given situation it should be possible to enumerate the factors for and against, and to deduce conditions which determine the optimum location of the items to be held. The problem in its essence is the typical optimization problem of balancing two sets of costs: the costs arising from the overall stock levels of decentralized stores as opposed to the extra handling costs involved with central storage.

For an individual commodity, the following terms are defined:

$P$ = Purchase price per unit.
$Q$ = *Average* demand per week in units of an individual store.
$L$ = Lead-time (in weeks), i.e. the average time elapsing between the issue of an order and receipt of the goods.
$n$ = Number of subsidiary stores in the region.
$C_1$ = Stock-holding cost per week (assumed to be the same whether at the unit or the central store).
$C_2$ = Transport and handling cost per item between central and unit store.

If the variations in demand follow a similar pattern to that assumed earlier, then each store can be mathematically shown to need a stock reserve of $K\sqrt{(LQ)}$ where $K$ is a constant depending on the desired level of protection against stock running out. For a 99 per cent level of protection the value of $K$ would be 2·33; for 97·5 per cent level the value of $K$ would be 1·96 and so on. Note that the reserve varies according to the square-root of the expected demand in the lead-time. A fourfold increase in the demand rate only leads to a doubling of the stock reserve. Since there are $n$ individual stores, the total safety stock-holding is therefore $nK\sqrt{(LQ)}$. If, however, the stock of the $n$ stores is combined, the reserve required to give the same protection will be $K\sqrt{(nLQ)}$ since the expected demand in the lead-time is now $nLQ$ when all $n$ stores are centralized into one store. The saving in stock due to the centralizing of the stocks into a single depot will therefore be

$$nK\sqrt{(LQ)} - K\sqrt{(nLQ)}$$

or

$$K\sqrt{(nLQ)}(\sqrt{n} - 1)$$

Since the stock-holding cost is $C_1$ per item, the total money saving per week through central storage will be

$$C_1 \times K\sqrt{(nLQ)}(\sqrt{n} - 1)$$

But extra transport and handling costs are involved in getting the stocks from the central store to the individual store locations, and these costs must be set against the savings from the reduced level of safety stocks held. The total demand from the $n$ stores is $nQ$ per week and, since the transport and handling costs are $C_2$, it follows that the total cost of handling goods from a central depot is $nQC_2$. Clearly, it will pay to store goods centrally if, and only if, the extra handling costs are less than the savings, that is to say, if

$$nQC_2 < C_1K\sqrt{(nLQ)}(\sqrt{n} - 1)$$

or

$$Q < \frac{1}{n}\frac{C_1^2K^2L}{C_2^2}(\sqrt{n} - 1)^2$$

(The symbol $<$ means 'is less than'.)

Given the cost of holding stock ($C_1$), the handling and transport costs ($C_2$), the number of stores ($n$), and the lead-time ($L$), the formula gives the level of weekly demand at which it is economic to consider central storage. This condition can be demonstrated graphically, as shown in Figure 7.5($b$). The position of an item

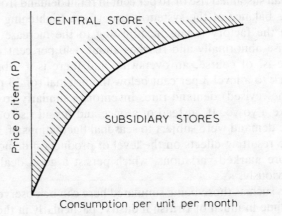

**Figure 7.5($b$)  Centralized store system**

on the figure is set by its price (proportional to $C_1$) and consumption. If the item falls in the shaded portion, then it is worthwhile storing the item centrally. If the item is below the line, then decentralized storage should be retained.

## 7.8   Industrial dynamics

Simulation can be a very valuable tool in the study of inventory and the corresponding production systems. One notable contributor in this field has been the American professor, J. W. Forrester who has considered the dynamics of a production/distribution system in some detail and, in particular, the effect that changes have on such systems. Figure 7.6 illustrates one of his studies relating to a production/distribution system for durable consumer goods with inventories at factory, wholesalers, and retailers. For this study, the time-lag between retail sales and the arrival of replacement orders at the factory via the wholesaler's office is 8 weeks. A further 6 weeks' delay occurs before factory output can be adjusted to respond to changes in demand. It is assumed that the various stages in the system aim to keep a fixed number of weeks' supply in stock and that the inventory held is therefore adjusted from time to time in line with changes in demand made by the next lower unit in the system. A computer simulation is then used to show the effect of changes on this otherwise stable system.

The figure shows the effects following an immediate and once-and-for-all sustained rise of 10 per cent in retail demand from January. The balance of the system is upset to a frightening degree. Because the factory is late in adjusting to the increase, output has to rise abnormally and reaches about +40 per cent in May. This rise is, of course, an overswing and there is a subsequent drop back to a level 3 per cent below the original (or 13 per cent below the revised) demand rate. Inventories similarly go up and down like a yo-yo. If, instead of a once-and-for-all rise of 10 per cent, the demand were subject to seasonal fluctuations of ±10 per cent, the resulting effects on the level of production demonstrate even more marked variations, which persist a good deal longer than previously.

Effects such as those being simulated here can be observed from time to time in much of British industry, particularly in the heavy sector of industry. Steel works are heard of operating at only 60 per cent of the normal rate at a time when the consumption of steel in the economy is only 5 per cent or 10 per cent down. It is those production units at the end of a long chain of processes

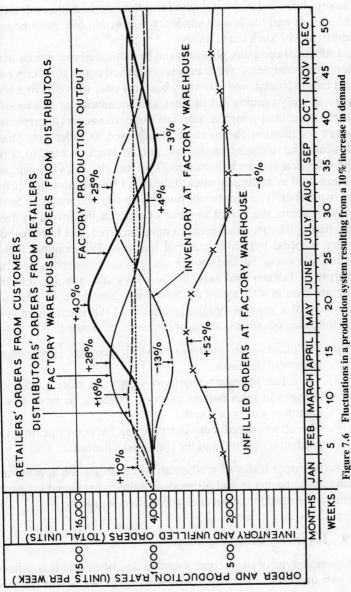

**Figure 7.6** Fluctuations in a production system resulting from a 10% increase in demand
(From 'Industrial dynamics'—a major breakthrough for decision-makers', by Jay W. Forrester, *Harvard Business Review*, July/August 1958.)

RETAILERS' ORDERS FROM CUSTOMERS
DISTRIBUTORS' ORDERS FROM RETAILERS
FACTORY WAREHOUSE ORDERS FROM DISTRIBUTORS
FACTORY PRODUCTION OUTPUT
INVENTORY AT FACTORY WAREHOUSE
UNFILLED ORDERS AT FACTORY WAREHOUSE

+10%  +16%  +28%  +40%  +25%  +4%  −3%
−13%  +52%  −6%

MONTHS  JAN  FEB  MARCH  APRIL  MAY  JUNE  JULY  AUG  SEP  OCT  NOV  DEC
WEEKS  5  10  15  20  25  30  35  40  45  50

INVENTORY AND UNFILLED ORDERS (TOTAL UNITS)
16,000  1500
4,000  1000
2000  500

ORDER AND PRODUCTION RATES (UNITS PER WEEK)

that are most exposed to this kind of apparently erratic variation. Analyses such as Forrester's can do a lot to assist in diagnosing the problems and thus helping to formulate methods that will soften the impact and the loss of efficiency that would otherwise be concomitant with such fluctuations.

Individual company positions can be simulated in a similar manner. For example, a tyre firm was concerned about the sharp rises and falls in its cash and inventory balances over the year. Problems of repeatedly running out of stock and then building up excessive stocks were hampering the company's operations, and management began to question the methods being used to order new stock. Basically the rule used was to have enough stock on hand to satisfy the sales demand for two months. Two months' sales demand was determined by adding up sales of the past 13 weeks and multiplying by two-thirds. The number of tyres to be ordered was then found by subtracting the actual number of tyres in the inventory from this figure. The trouble seems to have occurred, not from bad delivery records, but from seasonal business. For example, peaks commonly occurred in October and April, whilst sales declined sharply in January and July. These peaks and troughs were frequently around 40 per cent of the normal demand level. The construction of a general simulation model of the situation enabled the following questions, amongst others, to be studied:

(a) The effects of an ordering rule which recognized the seasonal pattern of demand.

(b) The effect of responding more slowly (or more quickly) to changes in sales pattern as far as ordering more or less in inventory was concerned.

(c) The effect of reducing the time lag between the time the product is ordered and the time it is delivered.

By setting up a series of mathematical equations the appropriate study could be made and alternative policies examined on paper without the need to try out each alternative in practice.

## 7.9 Inventory control systems

The simple type of stock control system described earlier is defined by two quantities. The first is the stock level below which a new order is to be placed, whilst the other gives the quantity then to be ordered. Such a system can be operated through what is referred o as the two-bin system. Under this system the units of stock, ay steel rods, are held in two bins 1 and 2. Stock is taken from ɔin 1 as required until this bin is empty. More rods are then ordered, he amount being determined from the standard formula given ɔn page 108. Meanwhile, until delivery occurs, stock is used from ɔin 2. The standard amount in bin 2 is calculated to be the expected demand in the lead-time plus the safety stock. When the replenishments arrive, bin 2 is filled up to its quota and the rest is placed in bin 1. The procedure is then repeated. If demand were changing, the amount ordered would vary and forecast changes in demand could be similarly allowed for.

An alternative system is the constant cycle system under which orders are placed at a constant interval of time, rather than at a fixed level of stock held. This time interval will often be chosen for administrative convenience, although it should properly be found by a minimum-cost procedure as outlined in earlier sections. The quantity ordered each time will be enough to meet the sales forecast for the next interval (adjusted for stock held, lead-time, demand, and safety stock). This system is especially advantageous when it is desired to co-ordinate the orders for several items from the same source.

For a stable situation (demand steady, lead-time constant, costs fixed) the two systems will generally be equally effective. If some of these factors are varying, differences may arise. The two-bin system responds to such changes by altering both the re-order quantity and the interval between orders. The constant cycle system can only change its re-order quantity and consequently needs to do so to a rather greater degree. This is reflected in the rather greater fluctuation in stock levels commonly observed under such conditions in the constant cycle system, in turn leading to a higher average stock. The constant cycle system loses some of its sluggishness if it is designed not only to meet expected demand, but also to apply a stock correction which depends on the difference between the measured stock and a target stock. Such systems can, however, become very unstable and give freak results in certain conditions, leading to a lack of confidence.

## 7.10 Feedback control systems

Any inventory control system needs to be of a feedback dynamic nature, able to take advantage of changing circumstances as quickly

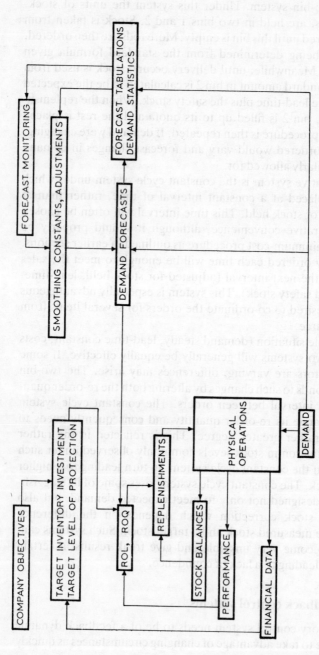

**Figure 7.7  Design for an inventory management control system**
ROL = Re-order level
ROQ = Re-order quantity

as is feasible. Such a feedback system aims to take account of past information from the system to make new rules for obtaining more effective control in the future. This may involve amending from time to time the order-quantity or lead-time or safety stock. Figure 7.7 shows schematically what is meant by such a control system. The physical operations of the system, concerned possibly with the steel held by a stock-holder, lead to replenishments of stock and demands being made on it. The decisions as to when and how much stock to replenish is gauged by the re-order level and the re-order quantity which will have been fixed by reference to the target level of investment and/or protection set by the management. The performance and financial data thrown up will be compared with the targets which were also set by the management. The re-order level (ROL) and re-order quantity (ROQ) will also be critically dependent upon the forecasting system used for the scheme, and the right-hand side of the figure is designed to show how the forecasting system itself both feeds into the re-ordering system and needs to be monitored. The dynamic system can then operate on a continuous basis updating the various key quantities as a regular routine and providing an automatic action procedure which can be operated at a clerical level.

## References

(1) *Introduction to Operations Research* by C. W. Churchman *et al.* (Wiley, 1957) (Chapters 8 to 10).
(2) *Production Planning and Inventory Control* by J. F. Magee (McGraw-Hill).
(3) *A Guide to Stock Control* by A. Battersby (Pitman, 1962).
(4) *Decision Rules for Inventory Management* by R. G. Brown (Holt, Rinehart and Winston).
(5) *Scientific Inventory Control* by C. D. Lewis (Butterworth, 1970).
(6) *Industrial Dynamics* by J. W. Forrester (MIT).
(7) *Problems of Stocks and Storage*, ICI Monograph No. 4 (Oliver and Boyd, 1967).

# 8 Forecasting techniques

## 8.1 Introduction

The resolution of many of the problems discussed in earlier chapters requires the provision of forecasts of future events, e.g. the level of sales next year, the likely market share, the rate of inflation, etc. Managers commonly assume that, when they ask a forecaster to prepare a specific projection, the request itself provides sufficient information for the forecaster to go to work and do the job. This is almost never true and successful forecasting must start with a discussion between the manager and the forecaster at which they will work out answers to questions such as the following:

— The purpose of forecast
— How it is to be used
— The components of the system for which the forecast is being made
— The importance of the past in estimating the future
— The benefit of the forecast to the company
— The time available.

When questions such as these have been answered, it is possible to decide upon the amount of effort that can be usefully employed on the forecast, and the possible methods open to the forecaster.

There are three basic types of forecasting methods available:

(a) Time series analysis and projections
(b) Causal models
(c) Qualitative techniques.

Type (a) focuses entirely on historical data. Type (b) uses highly refined and specific information about relationships between elements in the relevant economic system and is powerful enough to take special events formally into account. As with time series analysis and projection techniques, the past is important, but not exclusively, to causal methods. Type (c) uses qualitative data (expert opinions, for example) and possibly may take information about special events in the past into consideration.

These differences imply, quite correctly, that the same type of forecasting techniques is not appropriate to forecast the sales, say, at all stages of the life cycle of the product—for example, a technique that relies on historical data would not be useful in forecasting the future of a totally new product that has no history. A major problem is therefore to suit the technique to the situation and Table 8.1 gives some illustrative forecasting methods used under each

Table 8.1 **Illustrative forecasting methods**

| Time series analysis and projection | Causal methods | Qualitative methods |
| --- | --- | --- |
| Moving averages (exponential smoothing) | Regression models | Market research |
| Box-Jenkins forecasts | Econometric models | Historical analogy |
| Trend projection | Leading indicators | Delphi method |

of the three headings. The following sections sketch out the general functions of the three basic types of technique in more detail.

## 8.2 Time series analysis

The first group of methods uses past data to 'extrapolate' in some manner into the future. The data is allowed to speak for itself and no judgmental adjustments are made. It involves taking the past series of information and decomposing it into a number of components assignable to different effects.

A typical decomposition would be the following:

(1) Trend
(2) Seasonality
(3) Cycles
(4) Random variation.

Many forecasting methods use this type of decomposition, estimates of each component being computed and then combined to form a forecast. An important advantage of this approach is that the components are intuitively reasonable and can easily be explained to non-specialists.

The trend of a time series is defined as the systematic increase (or decrease) of the variable concerned over time. The trend line is essentially a smooth line indicating the path of the series after seasonal and random fluctuations have been removed (long-term cycles may or may not be left). The purpose of computing a trend line (it is usually a polynomial of low order) is to give an indication of the assumed 'true' progress of the variable.

A common approach to trend line estimation uses a *moving average* to smooth the series. Moving averages are the weighted average of a number of consecutive points, the number of data points being chosen so that the effects of seasonal or irregular fluctuations, or both, are eliminated, or at any rate considerably dampened. The choice of the number of data points to use is based on a judgment based on the stability of the phenomena under observation. If the phenomena is considered to be stable and most of the variation in the time series is random, then a simple moving average with a large number of points will give a good fit to the trend. If the opposite is true, fewer points must be used and, whilst the trend estimation will pick up big changes in the underlying trend, it may not be so sensitive to smaller changes.

Table 8.2 gives some data relating to the sales of sports shirts over two years. A moving annual average (that is the total for the last 12 months divided by a factor of 12 to give a monthly equivalent) is calculated to give a trend line. This is given in the table, being placed against the mid-point of the period. It will be noted that this moving average varies from a low of 1072 to a high of 1234, whereas the original monthly figures varied from 329 to 2430. However, there is a lag in the sense that the moving average refers basically to a period whose mid-point is some 6 months behind the latest piece of information (i.e. the current month) included.

Further, there is the question of the degree of seasonality in such a series. For example the weather affects the consumption of electricity, the time of the year the sales of Christmas goods, etc. There are two basic ways of estimating seasonal effects: the first is an additive model, where the seasonal variation is deemed to be independent of the overall level of the series, whilst the second is where the seasonal variation is proportional to the level of the series. Figure 8.1 gives the monthly time series for new

Table 8.2 **Twelve month moving average for sports shirt sales**

| Month | Sales in year 1 | Moving average | Sales in year 2 | Moving average |
|---|---|---|---|---|
| J | 437 | | 825 | |
| | | | | 1203 |
| F | 445 | | 329 | |
| | | | | 1179 |
| M | 1434 | | 512 | |
| | | | | 1179 |
| A | 768 | | 576 | |
| | | | | 1205 |
| M | 2052 | | 1332 | |
| | | | | 1221 |
| J | 1268 | | 1784 | |
| | | 1202 | | 1201 |
| J | 1231 | | 2417 | |
| | | 1234 | | |
| A | 2430 | | 2016 | |
| | | 1224 | | |
| S | 1311 | | 1309 | |
| | | 1148 | | |
| O | 1300 | | 1616 | |
| | | 1131 | | |
| N | 900 | | 1094 | |
| | | 1072 | | |
| D | 845 | | 596 | |
| | | 1115 | | |

car registration (GB) for a 7-year period with a 12-month moving average superimposed and, separately, the seasonal (month by month) profile calculated on a multiplicative basis. In some circumstances a combination of the two models is appropriate.

## 8.3 Exponential weights

In the foregoing, moving averages were used to indicate the underlying path of a time series, smoothing out the random fluctuations. The common property of these moving averages is that their weighting of observations are symmetrical about the mid-point of the

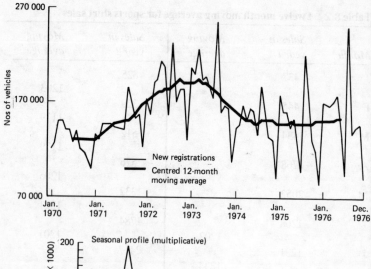

Figure 8.1    New registrations of road vehicles in GB

average. For forecasting ahead, the use of asymmetrical weights giving more weight to the more recent observations may be more effective. For a mathematically true average, the sum of weights must be unity and hence what is ideally required is an infinite series of weights with decreasing values which converge at infinity to produce a total sum of 1. Such a series is the exponential series with successive weights

$$\alpha, \alpha(1 - \alpha), \alpha(1 - \alpha)^2, \alpha(1 - \alpha)^3, \ldots$$

which sum to one at infinity, if $\alpha$ lies between zero and one. Choosing a value of 0·2, the first seven values of such a series would be

$$0·200, 0·160, 0·128, 0·102, 0·082, 0·066, 0·052$$

which sum to 0·79; it is apparent that if sufficient values are taken, the sum will be near enough 1.

Incorporating the exponential series as the weighting series yields an exponentially weighted average ($s_t$) defined by

$$s_t = \alpha d_t + \alpha(1 - \alpha)d_{t-1} + \alpha(1 - \alpha)^2 d_{t-2}$$

$$+ \ \alpha(1 - \alpha)^3 d_{t-3} + \ldots$$

or

$$s_t = \alpha d_t + (1 - \alpha)[\alpha d_{t-1} + \alpha(1 - \alpha)d_{t-2} + (1 - \alpha)^2 d_{t-2} + \ldots]$$

where $d_t$ is the demand in period $t$.

Since the term in square brackets is precisely $s_{t-1}$, the exponentially weighted average can be rewritten very simply as

$$s_t = \alpha d_t + (1 - \alpha)s_{t-1} \tag{8.1}$$

and $s_t$ is then used as a forecast for period $t + 1$. A numerical illustration is given in Table 8.3.

It is apparent that the exponentially weighted average overcomes the problem of strong data (since all previous data are neatly compacted into a single figure represented by $s_{t-1}$) and the problem of starting up with no previous data (since, once an initial guess for $s_{t-1}$ is made, when fresh data, $d_t$, arrive the next forecast can be directly evaluated). The sensitivity of the forecast can be changed at any time, simply by changing the value of $\alpha$, which is known as the *exponential smoothing constant*. This is typically chosen from a range of values between 0·05 and 0·3; the values of 0·1 and 0·2 being the most used. If the smoothing constant used is high, then the system is sensitive to sudden change, but random fluctuations are not well ironed out. If the smoothing constant is low, the converse applies in that any random fluctuations are smoothed out but the system, whilst responsive to slow gradual change, will not be responsive to sudden shifts.

In the stationary demand situations, because no growth or seasonality is assumed, the forecast for any month in the future is the same as for one month ahead. It is accepted, of course, that the further ahead that the forecast is made the wider will be the possible range of demand values that could be expected to fall either side of that average value.

An alternative method of calculating the exponentially weighted average is to re-organize the original equation into the form

$$s_t = s_{t-1} + \alpha(d_t - s_{t-1}) \tag{8.2}$$

In this form the forecast can be evaluated graphically by saying

**Table 8.3  Forecasting schedule for smoothing constant ($\alpha$) of 0·2**

| | | Jan. | Feb. | Mar. | Apr. | May | Jun. | Jul. | Aug. | Sep. | Oct. | Nov. | Dec. | Jan. |
|---|---|---|---|---|---|---|---|---|---|---|---|---|---|---|
| This month's demand | $d_t$ | 60·0 | 68·0 | 55·0 | 80·0 | 90·0 | 65·0 | 70·0 | 75·0 | 60·0 | 80·0 | 90·0 | 100·0 | 95·0 |
| Last month's forecast for this month | $s_{t-1}$ | 70·0* | 68·4 | 68·4 | 65·7 | 68·6 | 72·9 | 71·3 | 71·0 | 71·8 | 69·4 | 71·6 | 75·2 | 80·2 |
| $\alpha \times$ this month's demand | $\alpha d_t$ | 12·0 | 14·0 | 11·0 | 16·0 | 18·0 | 13·0 | 14·0 | 15·0 | 12·0 | 16·0 | 18·0 | 20·0 | 19·0 |
| $(1 - \alpha) \times$ last month's forecast for this month | $(1 - \alpha)s_{t-1}$ | 56·0 | 54·4 | 54·7 | 52·6 | 54·9 | 58·3 | 57·0 | 56·8 | 57·4 | 56·6 | 57·2 | 60·2 | 64·2 |
| This month's forecast for next month | $s_t = \alpha d_t + (1 - \alpha)s_{t-1}$ | 68·0 | 68·4 | 65·7 | 68·6 | 72·9 | 71·3 | 71·0 | 71·8 | 69·4 | 71·6 | 75·2 | 80·2 | 83·2 |

\* Obtained from estimated value in December of previous year.

that the new forecast $s_t$ will be equal to the old forecast $s_{t-1}$ plus one-fifth (with $\alpha = 0.2$) of the gap between the old forecast and the current demand value. The gap $(d_t - s_{t-1})$ is effectively the current value of the forecasting error denoted commonly by $e_t$ so that equation (8.2) can be re-written as

$$s_t = s_{t-1} + \alpha e_t \tag{8.3}$$

## 8.4 Causal methods

There are a number of forecasting models used where the quantity to be forecast is related to one or more other quantities which, it is believed, can themselves be estimated better than the quantity in question can itself be estimated directly. For example a regression model may relate sales (or the quality to be estimated) to other economic, competitive or internal variables and derive an appropriate equation for estimation using least-squares techniques. Relationships are primarily analysed statistically, although any relationship should be selected for testing on a rational ground. An econometric model is a system of interdependent regression equations that describe some sector of economic, sales or profit activity. The parameters of the regression equation are usually estimated simultaneously. As a rule, such models are expensive to develop, depending upon the details utilized. However, due to the system of equations inherent in such models, they will better express the causes involved than an ordinary regression equation, and hence will predict turning points more accurately. An inexpensive, but less effective, model is to use as a leading indicator some time series of an economic activity whose movement in a given direction precedes the movement of some other time series, of interest to the forecaster, in the same or opposite direction. An example of the latter is now discussed briefly.

Table 8.4 gives the consolidated sales (billings) of a market research organization over a 25-year period (the figures are disguised but are taken from a well known international firm). If these figures are plotted on ordinary graph paper the resultant plot suggests an upward curve. Fitting a straight line to such data would be of very limited value since it is clear that the absolute change year on year is rising. Yet, it is also likely that the *rate* of increase year on year is rather more constant. To test this it is useful to examine the logarithms of the billings and see whether these rise by constant amounts. If $x_1$ represents the billings in year

Table 8.4 **Annual billings of market research organization**

| Year | Billings (x) | Log x | Year | Billings (x) | Log x |
|---|---|---|---|---|---|
| 1 | 1915 | 3·282 | 14 | 10 975 | 4·040 |
| 2 | 2203 | 3·343 | 15 | 12 322 | 4·090 |
| 3 | 2342 | 3·370 | 16 | 14 377 | 4·158 |
| 4 | 3057 | 3·485 | 17 | 17 952 | 2·254 |
| 5 | 3708 | 3·569 | 18 | 20 823 | 4·319 |
| 6 | 4509 | 3·654 | 19 | 24 132 | 4·383 |
| 7 | 5125 | 3·718 | 20 | 26 858 | 4·429 |
| 8 | 5814 | 3·764 | 21 | 31 019 | 4·492 |
| 9 | 6540 | 3·816 | 22 | 36 162 | 4·558 |
| 10 | 6767 | 3·830 | 23 | 40 119 | 4·603 |
| 11 | 7354 | 3·867 | 24 | 45 349 | 4·657 |
| 12 | 8488 | 3·929 | 25 | 50 588 | 4·704 |
| 13 | 9895 | 3·995 | | | |

1 and $x_2$, representing the billings for year 2, is equal to $bx_1$ where $b$ is a constant, then

$$\log x_2 = \log bx_1 = \log b + \log x_1$$

or in words, the logarithms of the billings would go up by the amount $\log b$ each year where $b$, note again, is a constant. Figure 8.2 shows the logarithms of the billings plotted against the years. Clearly this is very close to a straight line and suggests a simple way of forecasting billings for the next few years ahead. The average increase in the logarithmic difference from one year to the next

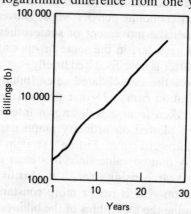

Figure 8.2 **Billings against time (log scale)**

is 0·0595. Hence a possible forecast for years 26 to 28 inclusive would be as follows:

Year 26     Logarithm 4·704 + 0·0595 = 4·7635
               (Forecast = 58 010)

Year 27     Logarithm 4·7635 + 0·0595 = 4·8230
               (Forecast = 66 520)

Year 28     Logarithm 4·8230 + 0·0595 = 4·8825
               (Forecast = 76 300)

Incidentally, the anti-logarithm of 0·0595 is 1·146, so that the annual rate of growth in billings may be expressed as 14·6 per cent per annum compound. This would in turn imply that billings would double in a period that is equal to log 2/0·0595, or 0·30103/0·0595, or about 5·1 years.

## 8.5 Qualitative techniques

Qualitative techniques are used when data are scarce, for example when a new product is first introduced into a market. They use human judgment and rating schemes to turn qualitative information into qualitative estimates. Their use is common in forecasts of long-range and new product sales. The objective here is to bring together in a logical, unbiased, and systematic way all information and judgments which relate to the factors being considered. Table 8.1 listed in the final column some of the ways used to do this. Market research is well known and readers are referred to Chapter 12 of reference (6) at the end of this chapter. Historical analogy, on the other hand, uses a comparative analysis of the introduction and growth of similar new products in the past and bases the forecast on similarity patterns.

The Delphi Method attempts to capitalize on this approach in a systematic way. The method was first formalized by Olaf Helmer in studies for the Rand organization reported in 1963. Since then, the Delphi technique has gained increasing popularity as a means for determining the pattern of expert opinion on future events. The aim is to reach the consensus opinions of a group of experts in a way which draws on the benefits of the committee approach (such as the dissemination of ideas and reasoning) but which removes the pressures inevitable in face-to-face discussions. The Delphi technique provides for a confrontation of ideas, rather than a confrontation of the people holding them.

A Delphi study consists of a series of questionnaires, with each questionnaire representing a 'round'. The responses and information yielded by the first round questionnaire become the basis for the second round questionnaire and feedback. This process is repeated, usually for a predetermined number of rounds. The nature of the questionnaires obviously depends on the purpose of the individual Delphi study. There is a common thread, however, in that studies concerned with forecasting all tend to require estimates of dates by which certain events will occur, or descriptions of the events expected to occur by a specified date.

Questions which elicit quantitative responses are usually summarized using medians and interquartile ranges. Hence, after the first round questionnaire responses have been analysed, respondents may be asked in the second round to reconsider their previous responses, in the light of the first round questionnaire, and revise them if they so desire. Furthermore, respondents that give a replication for an issue in the second round that falls outside the interquartile range of responses from the first round may be asked to give the reasoning behind their belief that the answers differ so much from the majority view of the first round. These reasons may then be provided as additional feedback in the third round. A similar, but less precise, method is employed in the case of questions yielding non-quantitative responses.

## 8.6   Delphi technique illustration

An illustration of the Delphi technique in the determination of the print run for a new, but unusual type of book, was described by J. R. C. Wensley (see reference (7) at end of chapter). The new book concerned was *The Shepherd* by Frederick Forsyth, which could be described broadly as a short ghost story from a writer who had made an enormous reputation for himself as a writer of fiction thrillers. Two facts summarized the sales forecasting problem: Forsyth was a dramatically successful author; and short stories, however, do not generally sell in substantial quantities. The general view of the publishing house was that a very restricted print-run should be produced for the 1975 Christmas trade of about 35 000 copies.

Since a print run of this order was, even if completely sold, likely to make only a modest profit for the publisher, it was decided to examine the forecasting problem more deeply and to employ the Delphi technique. For this purpose a panel was set up of some thirteen individuals

3 book sellers
2 critics
3 readers
2 publishing executives
2 sales representatives
1 overseas representative

} all from the publishing house

This panel was given a copy of the manuscript with the basic information that the book was to be 64 pages, hardback, and published in the third week of October at a price of £1·50. They were also given figures of sales of books from other popular authors of both full length and short stories. The panel made an initial assessment and then, in two repeat runs, they were allowed to modify their estimates on the basis of the panel ratings given by other individuals in earlier rounds. Table 8.5 gives a summary of

Table 8.5 **Most likely estimates by group and round**

|  | Round 1 | Round 2 | Round 3 |
|---|---|---|---|
| Booksellers (3) | 57 | 57 | 65 |
| Critics (2) | 34 | 36 | 46 |
| Readers (3) | 42 | 41 | 38 |
| Publishing Exec (2) | 26 | 31 | 31 |
| Sales Reps (2) | 29 | 30 | 41 |
| Overseas (1) | 35 | 35 | 50 |
| Publishers (5) | 29 | 31 | 39 |
| Outsiders (8) | 45 | 46 | 50 |

the most likely estimates for the three rounds made on an index scale (each index point approximately corresponded to sales of 1600 copies). The assessments are subdivided by the various categories of 'experts' and between publishers and outsiders.

For the first round of the Delphi the panel average for the most likely figures was 39, whilst for the third round it was 46, an increase of nearly 20 per cent. However, it is interesting to note the difference between the various categories, particularly between the publishers and the non-publishers, and the gap that still existed by the third round, even though it had by then narrowed. Table 8.6

shows the individual results for round 3, but also the results of asking for minimum and maximum estimates as well as the most likely estimate. The final two rows of the table give the weighted averages when each individual applied his own weights or, alternatively, when the panel weightings are applied. The changes in weightings have little affect on the estimated figures.

Table 8.6 **Delphi panel summary—round 3**

| | Min. | Most Likely | Max. | |
|---|---|---|---|---|
| | 25 | 75 | 80 | Booksellers |
| | 35 | 50 | 75 | |
| | 50 | 70 | 75 | |
| | 9 | 41 | 47 | Critics |
| | 25 | 50 | 75 | |
| | 25 | 35 | 60 | |
| | 20 | 35 | 60 | Readers |
| | 22 | 45 | 60 | |
| | 22 | 28 | 34 | Publishing |
| | 22 | 34 | 44 | |
| | 28 | 37 | 62 | Sales Reps |
| | 25 | 45 | 50 | |
| | 30 | 50 | 60 | Overseas |
| Panel average | 26 | 46 | 60 | |
| Self-weighted average | 25 | 45 | 59 | |
| Panel average weighting | 26 | 46 | 60 | |

Originally the publisher's favoured print run was 35 000 (an index of 22). After the Delphi forecasting procedure was ended they accepted a print run of 65 000 (index 41). This was an increase of some 85 per cent and, if achieved, raised the publisher's profits by some 300 per cent! In this sense the forecasting process had a very significant upward influence in the expectations of the publisher.

In the event the print run was, due to paper problems, reduced to 55 000. All the copies were sold by February 1976 and it appeared that a print run of 65 000 would have been the 'correct' figure. It would seem therefore that, even after three rounds, the booksellers were too optimistic and the publishers were too pessimistic. Next time . . . who knows?

# References

(1) *Demand Analysis and Inventory Control* by C. D. Lewis (Saxon House, 1975).

(2) *Time Series Analysis, Forecasting and Control* by G. E. P. Box and G. M. Jenkins (Holden Day, 1976).

(3) *Smoothing, Forecasting and Prediction of Discrete Time Series* by R. C. Brown (Prentice-Hall, 1962).

(4) Forecasting sales by exponentially weighted moving averages, by P. R. Winter, *Management Science*, 1960, vol 6, pp. 324–42.

(5) Monitoring a forecast system, by D. W. Trigg, *Operational Research Quarterly*, 1964, vol. 15, pp. 271–4.

(6) *Reason by Numbers* by P. G. Moore (Penguin, 1980).

(7) Short term forecasting using the Delphi approach by J. R. C. Wensley, *European Research*, March 1977, pp. 57–61.

(8) How to choose the right forecasting technique, by J. C. Chambers, S. K. Mullick and D. D. Smith, *Harvard Business Review*, July 1981, pp. 45–74.

# 9 Financial modelling

## 9.1 Introduction

The courses of actions recommended for most of the problems faced in operational research have, sooner or later, to be turned into financial terms in order that alternative courses of action can be compared. The profitability of a firm (and its survival) is primarily a function of its ability to generate projects or investments that provide returns greater than the cost of the funds used. Management must, therefore, have some consistent and accurate measures for appraising and comparing capital investments. This chapter examines three project appraisal methods, discussing their relative advantages and disadvantages, namely the Payback method, the Accounting Rate of Return method and the Discounted Cash Flow method. It will be seen that, for operational research purposes the third method examined has the greatest generality and applicability. Before discussing these different methods in detail, an illustration of a simple financial model is described.

## 9.2 A replacement situation

A firm's building contains 300 light bulbs. It is decided to examine two alternative policies relating to the replacement of the bulbs which will, after a variable length of time, fail. Failure data is given in Table 9.1 and the simplifying assumption is made that the bulbs fail at the end of the monthly intervals. The two policies to be examined are, first, whether individual bulbs should be replaced as they fail at a cost of £4 per bulb replaced, or, alternatively, whether to replace all bulbs at a set interval and, in the meantime, replace individual failures as they arise. The cost of a group replacement, i.e. all bulbs replaced whether or not they have failed, would be £360.

Table 9.1  **Failure data**

| Months from installation (i) | Average numbers failing (n_i) |
|---|---|
| 0 | 0 |
| 1 | 30 |
| 2 | 90 |
| 3 | 120 |
| 4 | 60 |
| Total | 300 |

To examine the cost of the first option the long-run situation should be considered, whereby the average number of months a bulb lasts is, from Table 9.1

$$\frac{1}{300}(30 \times 1 + 90 \times 2 + 120 \times 3 + 60 \times 4) = 2 \cdot 7$$

and the average number of bulbs failing per month will be

$$\frac{300}{2 \cdot 7} \text{ or } 111 \cdot 11.$$

The monthly cost of replacement will therefore be $4 \times 111 \cdot 11$ or £444·44. Note that initially the cost in early months fluctuates around this figure, but long term it would settle down to a steady £444·44 a month.

For the group replacement situation, the data and calculations are summarized in Table 9.2. Thus if the replacement interval is a month, then no individual failures are involved. If the interval is 2 months, then at the end of the first month 30 bulbs (shown in brackets) have to be individually replaced. Again if the interval is 3 months, then 30 have to be replaced at the end of the first month whilst 90, plus 10 per cent of the 30 replaced at the end of the first month, giving a total of 93 failures for the second month failures to be individually replaced. The final column of Table 9.2, gives the average monthly cost and the lowest is clearly 240, corresponding to a replacement interval of 2 months. Two caveats should be entered. First, because the approach has been one of enumeration, and not mathematical proof, replacement intervals greater than 5 months have been ignored. It seems reasonable to deduce that costs will continue to rise as the interval increases until the time will come when it approaches the £444·44 of the individual

Table 9.2  Group replacement costs

| Replacement interval (months | Group cost | Individual costs (and failures) in month | | | | Total cost | Monthly average |
|---|---|---|---|---|---|---|---|
| | | 1 | 2 | 3 | 4 | | |
| 1 | 360 | — | — | — | — | 360·0 | 360·0 |
| 2 | 360 | 120 (30) | — | — | — | 480·0 | 240·0 |
| 3 | 360 | 120 (30) | 372 (93) | — | — | 852·0 | 284·0 |
| 4 | 360 | 120 (30) | 372 (93) | 553·2 (138·3) | — | 1405·2 | 351·3 |
| 5 | 360 | 120 (30) | 372 (93) | 553·2 (138·3) | 454·9 (113·7) | 1860·1 | 372·0 |

All costs in £

eplacement method which would be reached if the replacement
interval became infinitely long. Hence group replacement with a
-month interval is the better policy.

The second caveat is that the timings of the emerging costs have
been ignored. Under the individual replacement model the costs
would be £444·44 per month every month. For the alternative preferred model the costs would alternate from month to month of
£120 followed by £360, followed by £120, and so on.

## 9.3 The payback method

The *payback* method is extremely popular in some quarters, largely
one suspects because of its simplicity. The payback period for a
project is defined simply as the number of years required to return
the project's initial outlay (including any working capital) and is
computed after tax and any investment allowances received. If
a project is forecast to produce constant net revenue the payback
period can be determined by the simple formula:

$$\text{Payback period} = \frac{\text{capital cost} - \text{cash grant} - (\text{initial allowances} \times \text{tax rate})}{\text{annual revenue} (1 - \text{tax rate})} \quad (9.1)$$

where the tax rate is expressed on the scale 0 to 1.

To illustrate the position consider the three projects outlined
in Table 9.3 for the first 6 years. Each project has the same initial

Table 9.3   **Calculation of payback period (cash £million, tax, etc. ignored)**

|  | Project 1 | | Project 2 | | Project 3 | |
|---|---|---|---|---|---|---|
| Year | Cash inflow | Cumulative cash inflow | Cash inflow | Cumulative cash inflow | Cash inflow | Cumulative cash inflow |
| 0 | −0·40 | −0·40 | −0·40 | −0·40 | −0·40 | −0·40 |
| 1 | +0·10 | −0·30 | +0·16 | −0·24 | +0·04 | −0·36 |
| 2 | +0·10 | −0·20 | +0·16 | −0·08 | +0·04 | −0·32 |
| 3 | +0·10 | −0·10 | +0·04 | −0·04 | +0·16 | −0·16 |
| 4 | +0·10 | 0·0 | +0·04 | 0·0 | +0·16 | 0·0 |
| 5 | +0·10 | +0·10 | +0·04 | +0·04 | +0·16 | +0·16 |

outlay of £0·4 million. If taxation and investment incentives are
ignored, all these projects have a payback period of 4 years as
shown by the zero cumulative cash inflow against the row marked
year 4. Note, however, that at the end of the first 2 years the

three projects have recovered entirely different percentages of their original capital costs, namely 50, 80, and 20 per cent respectively.

Suppose instead that corporation tax of 50 per cent was incurred and there was additionally a cash grant of £0·1 million, and a 100 per cent first year capital allowance of the £0·4 million. Then, from formula (9.1) the payback period for Project 1 would be:

$$\frac{0·4 - 0·1 - (0·4 \times 0·5)}{0·1 \times (1 - 0·5)} = 2 \text{ years}$$

Similar types of calculation could be made for the other two projects in Table 9.3, adapting formula (9.1), in each case reducing the payback period.

This method has a number of significant disadvantages as a measure of the effective use of resources, since it neglects the exact timing of the cash flows and excludes all cash flows after the payback period. The payback period for a mineral mine might be 8 years and not seem very desirable, but it could still be a very attractive investment if the cash flows extended significantly beyond the pay-back period. In this sense payback is not a good measure of a project's viability, as it understates profitability and the project's total cash flow. Conversely, on a short-term project where cash is generated rapidly, the payback would be short but cash flows may also terminate early. Clearly, therefore, payback is a quick and dirty approach that should not be used as the primary method of appraisal. It is, however, useful as a crude measure of liquidity, and for this reason many companies find it useful.

## 9.4    The accounting rate of return

The accounting rate of return (ARR) is defined as the average annual profits after tax and deprecation as a percentage of the capital outlay; or

$$\text{ARR} = \frac{(\text{net revenue} - \text{accounting depreciation}) \times (1 - \text{tax rate}) \times 100\%}{\text{net capital cost}}$$

(9.2)

In computing ARR the average net revenues over the life of the project are used, book depreciation rates are used and the capital costs include all capital involved, whether or not it was spent at the outset of the project. This procedure again normally under-states project profitability since it ignores the availability of high initial allowances for taxation purposes.

**Table 9.4 Cash inflows for three projects (£ million)**

| Year | Project 1 | Project 2 | Project 3 |
|------|-----------|-----------|-----------|
| | −1·0 | −1·0 | −1·0 |
| | +0·5 | +0·8 | +0·3 |
| | +0·5 | +0·8 | +0·4 |
| | +0·5 | +0·3 | +0·6 |
| | +0·5 | +0·3 | +0·6 |
| | +0·5 | +0·3 | +0·6 |

Table 9.4 gives the cash inflows for three projects, for each of which the initial capital costs are £1 million. The annual straight line (i.e. constant) depreciation is 20 per cent and corporation tax is 50 per cent. For each project the average annual revenue is 0·5, with depreciation equal to 0·2, and hence from (9.2).

$$\text{ARR} = \frac{(0·5 - 0·2)(1 - 0·5)}{1·0} \times 100 = 15 \text{ per cent}$$

All three projects are ranked equally on ARR, even though the timing of the cash flow differs substantially in each case. Clearly, managers would prefer project 2, since there is a much greater front-end loading of cash in the early years. Thus the method tends to confuse reported profits with net cash flow and, for this reason, is not in general use.

## 9.5 Discounted cash flow

The main criticism of the two methods just reviewed is that they fail to take account of the timing of the emerging cash flows in a consistent manner. They have not embodied a generally accepted concept which forms the basis of the DCF approach, namely that £1 available now is worth more than £1 available in a year's time. Discounting cash flows is conceptually the straightforward reverse of compounding sums of money which will be familiar to readers. For instance £1000 invested at 10 per cent compounded annually becomes £1331 in 3 years' time. Therefore £1331 received in 3 years' time *discounted* at 10 per cent has a value (its *present value*) of £1000 today. The arithmetic of this is that working forwards

$$£1000(1 + 0·1)(1 + 0·1)(1 + 0·1) = £1331$$

whilst the annual discount rate is $1/(1 + 0.1)$ so that working backwards

$$1331\left(\frac{1}{1 + 0.1}\right)\left(\frac{1}{1 + 0.1}\right)\left(\frac{1}{1 + 0.1}\right) = 1000$$

Appendix C gives a table of present values for various rate of interest up to 20 per cent and for annual periods up to 25 years Table 9.5 gives an illustrative calculation, using the table in Appendix C with an interest rate of 12 per cent, to determine the *ne*

Table 9.5   **Computation of net present value**

| End of year (1) | Net cash flows (£000) (2) | Discount factor at 12 per cent (3) | Present values (£000) (4) |
|---|---|---|---|
| 0 | −50 | 1·0000 | −50·000 |
| 1 | +20 | 0·8929 | 17·858 |
| 2 | +20 | 0·7972 | 15·944 |
| 3 | +20 | 0·7118 | 14·236 |
| 4 | +20 | 0·6355 | 12·710 |
| 5 | +20 | 0·5674 | 11·348 |
| | | Net present value | 22·096 |

present value (NPV) of a project which involved an initial expenditure of £50 000 and then annual inward cash flows of £20 000 for each of the following 5 years as shown in column (2). Column (3) contains the discount factors at 12 per cent for years 1 to 5 taken from the table in Appendix C. Column (4) is then the produc of columns (2) and (3), with the total of column (4) giving the net present value, or NPV, of £22 096. The next section gives a further illustration of the discounted cash flow approach.

## 9.6   Lease or buy

A firm has the opportunity to acquire an electronic telephone exchange that it needs with two alternative methods for its financing:

Method A   Outright purchase for £160 000

Method B   Rental payments   £60 000 annually for three years

£2 000 annually for next two years

Both methods involve exactly the same level of service and the
cost of this is included in the amounts given. Under method B
the firm owns the computer outright at the end of the fifth year,
whilst the annual payments are to be made in two equal 6-monthly
payments in arrear. The firm normally evaluates projects using
an interest rate of 12 per cent per annum. To evaluate the two
methods on a comparative basis, it is easiest to consider the differences between the two cash flows (£000) from Method A and B:

| Year | 0 | 1 | 2 | 3 | 4 | 5 |
|---|---|---|---|---|---|---|
| Difference A–B in cash flow (£000) | −160 | +60 | +60 | +60 | +2 | +2 |

In analysing these cash flows it is necessary to bear in mind
that the cash flows in years 1–5 are being paid 6-monthly in arrear,
whilst the Table in Appendix C deals with yearly and not 6 monthly
intervals. The problem can be overcome by using the discount
tables with an interest rate of 6 per cent (instead of 12 per cent)
and counting each 6 months as a unit of time (instead of each
12 months). The calculations are now developed as follows:

| Period (1) | Cash (£000) (2) | Discount factor (3) | (2) × (3) (4) | Period (1) | Cash (£000) (2) | Discount factor (3) | (2) × (3) (4) |
|---|---|---|---|---|---|---|---|
| 0 | −160 | 0·0 | −160·00 | 6 | +30 | 0·7050 | 21·15 |
| 1 | +30 | 0·9434 | 28·30 | 7 | +1 | 0·6651 | 0·67 |
| 2 | +30 | 0·8900 | 26·70 | 8 | +1 | 0·6274 | 0·63 |
| 3 | +30 | 0·8396 | 25·19 | 9 | +1 | 0·5919 | 0·59 |
| 4 | +30 | 0·7921 | 23·76 | 10 | +1 | 0·5584 | 0·56 |
| 5 | +30 | 0·7473 | 22·42 | | | | |
| | | | | | | Net present value | − 10·03 |

Since the NPV is negative, this demonstrates that method B
is the better approach to adopt, even though the total outlay (184)
for method B is greater than that for method A (160). Clearly
the interest rate used is critical—for example if the interest rate
used were zero, then method A would be preferable. The reader
is left to investigate, by trial and error the rate of interest at which
one would be indifferent between the two alternative methods of
financing. (Note that the assumption made of using 6 per cent
and 6-monthly intervals does introduce a small discrepancy in the
calculation, but this is negligible.)

## 9.7   Incremental analysis

In the previous section an incremental cash flow approach wa
used to determine whether to sign a contract to buy or to leas
a telephone exchange. The same principle can be used to discrimi
nate between different types of plant or alternative projects, indeed
in any situation where a choice has to be made between competing
schemes. The point is illustrated in Table 9.6 where a choice i

Table 9.6   **Choices between alternative plants**

| Plant | Initial capital (£000) | Annual cash flow years 1 – 10 (£000) | Net present value (£000) |
|---|---|---|---|
| L | −120 | +29 | 43·86 |
| M | −316 | +65 | 51·26 |

to be made between two mutually exclusive alternatives L and
M as regards plant size. Plant L has an initial capital cost of £120 000
with annual cash inflows for 10 years of £29 000; plant M has an
initial capital cost of £320 000 with annual cash inflows for 10 years
of £65 000. It is assumed that the company is looking for a 12
per cent return on this category of investment. If crude rates of
return are computed, that for plant L is $29/120 \times 100$ or 24 per
cent, and that for plant M is $65/316 \times 100$ or 21 per cent making
it appear that plant L is to be preferred. On a payback approach
the same ordering is achieved, namely 4·1 years for plant L and
4·9 years for plant M, again denoting a preference for plant L.

However, using net present values on a 12 per cent interest basis,
the net present values as shown in Table 9.6 are 43·9 for option
L and 51·3 for option M, thus making M the preferable option.
This could arise for two reasons. The first is connected with the
relative lengths of life of the plant, and is not applicable here as
both have a 10-year life. In general though, a steady cash flow
over a longer period elevates a project when put against another
project with the same cash flow over a shorter period under the
discounted cash flow approach, as opposed to payback or crude
rates of return. Secondly, the amount of capital involved is important and a simple rate of return calculation ignores this in its
approach. The NPV approach, whilst not perfect for all situations,
is very valuable in being able to discriminate between a large
number of mutually exclusive projects and, as will be seen in later

chapters, it provides a useful basis for appraisal into which risk can be incorporated.

## 9.8  A further replacement problem

Replacement decisions differ from other investments primarily in that they involve the displacement or scrapping of existing capital assets. With most assets it is usually clear that a replacement at some time is better than nothing, so that the comparison will commonly be between replacing the existing assets at once, or at some time over the next few years. The example discussed below based on Table 9.7 looks at the alternative of replacing now or waiting for 2 years when the economic life of the existing asset comes to an end.

The existing asset contributes £200 a year of net cash flows to the company for 2 more years, after which it will break down completely. A new replacement item costing £2000 would contribute a net cash flow of £900 per annum for 4 years before breaking down. Assuming no technical progress on future models and a zero resale value on the existing machine whenever it is scrapped, but 25 per cent per annum straight line depreciation of the new item, when should replacement take place; at once or in 2 years' time? It is assumed that the rate of interest for the company's normal cost of capital is 10 per cent per annum, and that a 20-year span is to be examined. Table 9.7 summarizes the cash flows for each alternative in rows (1) and (2), whilst row (3) gives the differences (1) − (2) in cash flow each year, i.e. the incremental effect. The process is given in detail for years 0–6 inclusive and then for the final year, namely year 20. The years in between repeat the pattern 0, −2000, 0, 2000, in a 4-year cycle. The final item reflects the worth of 1000 of the part-worn asset in year 20 under option (2) and the absence of any necessity under option (1) to buy a further new machine since the old one will have only just reached the end of its useful life.

The cash flows in row (3) can be evaluated at an interest rate of 10 per cent as follows:

$$-2000 + 700 \times 0{\cdot}9091 + 2700 \times 0{\cdot}8264 + 0 - 2000 \times 0{\cdot}6830$$
$$+ 0 + 2000 \times 0{\cdot}5645 + \ldots - 1000 \times 0{\cdot}1486$$

with the factors 0·9091, 0·8264 etc. taken from Appendix C and the column headed 10 per cent. The overall result is a total net

**Table 9.7  Annual cash flows of replacement investments (£)**

| Years | 0 | 1 | 2 | 3 | 4 | 5 | 6 | ... | 20 |
|---|---|---|---|---|---|---|---|---|---|
| (1) Replacement now | -2000 | 900 | 900 | 900 | -2000 900 | 900 | 900 | ... | 900 |
| (2) Replacement end of year 2 | — | 200 | -2000 200 | 900 | 900 | 900 | -2000 900 | ... | +1000 900 |
| (3) Incremental flows | -2000 | 700 | 2700 | 0 | -2000 | 0 | 2000 | ... | -1000 |

present value of +70·2 for row (3). This implies that (1) is more valuable than row (2) and hence replacement now is the better option to take. The reader is left to examine whether the cut-off point of 20 years is critical to the making of this particular decision, i.e. what difference would it make to take 25 or 30 years as the period.

More complex problems can be analysed along similar lines. For example, equipment items may become steadily less efficient and incur increasing repair bills as they age. This feature could be incorporated in the calculation. Again the method can cope with varying lengths of life of alternatives in ways in which payback and similar methods cannot, e.g. in comparing a bridge with a life of 100 years against a ferry service whose vessels need replacing every 25 years.

## References

(1) *Modern Managerial Finance* by J. R. Franks and J. E. Broyles (Wiley, 1979).
(2) *Corporate Financial Management* by J. R. Franks and H. Scholefield (Gower, 1977).
(3) *Capital Budgeting and Company Finance* by A. J. Merrett and A. Sykes (Longman, 1966).
(4) Replacement of equipment, by H. H. Scholefield, *Accounting and Business Research*, 1972, no. 8, pp. 316–24.

# 10 Decision analysis

## 10.1 Introduction

Decision-making contains both rational and psychological factors. For a 'satisfactory' decision, the two factors must be consistent. Decision theory studies the rational factor in order to clarify the situation and so increase the chance of attaining consistency. It does not make the final decision for the manager—the manager himself is paid to do that, and his ultimate success depends upon his ability to judge correctly the right blend of the two factors.

The primary elements involved in decision-making under conditions of uncertainty are:

(a) a number of possible *actions*, one of which is to be selected, whilst for each action there are

(b) a number of possible *outcomes*, dependent partly upon external factors, and for each outcome there is

(c) a *value* or consequence to the decision-maker, so that it is necessary to decide upon

(d) the *criterion* by which the decision-maker judges between alternative actions.

The range of actions to be considered depends upon the creativity and imagination of the decision-maker. No analytical technique as such will generate the alternatives to be considered; this can only be accomplished by careful evaluation of the situation by someone familiar with the basic problem. Many excellent actions are ignored because they were not considered until after the decision had been made. It should be remembered, too, that taking no action should itself be evaluated as an alternative. Doing nothing has consequences for the future, and is a choice under the control of the decision-maker.

Outcomes can be affected by the actions of a competitor, or the actions of consumers, or the state of the economy; the common characteristic is that they are beyond the complete control of the decision-maker. The decision-maker will need to make forecasts about future outcomes of events which is not so with actions, since even if they are to be taken in the future, they are completely within the decision-maker's control.

## 10.2  Illustrative example

To illustrate the issues, consider a problem concerning the weather and a swimming pool. Suppose that a ticket allowing the bearer to use a swimming pool all week-end costs 7 m.u.* if purchased during the preceding week, but a single day's admission costs 5 m.u. if paid on the day itself. Your alternative actions are, therefore, to buy a weekend ticket or to buy daily tickets, denoted by $a_1$ and $a_2$ respectively. You intend to go swimming whenever the weather is fine, but not otherwise. During the weekend there can be 0, 1 or 2 fine days and these outcomes are denoted by $b_1$, $b_2$ and $b_3$. These are the three possible outcomes that can arise. The pay-off matrix displaying the values of each action/outcome combinations would take the following form:

|  |  | Event (outcome) | | |
|---|---|---|---|---|
|  |  | $b_1$ | $b_2$ | $b_3$ |
|  |  | 0 | 1 | 2 | *fine days* |
| Action | $a_1$ Week-end ticket | −7 | −7 | −7 |
|  | $a_2$ Daily ticket | 0 | −5 | −10 |

The figures in the table represent the amount paid out for each action against the various outcomes. Under $a_1$ the cost is always 7; under $a_2$, it can be 0, 5 or 10. A negative sign is inserted since the quantities tabulated are paid out. Some criterion procedure is now needed to guide choice amongst the possible actions.

* All monetary units in this chapter are expressed as m.u. so as to make the arguments used independent of the particular currency concerned. The symbol m.u. is dropped unless required for clarity.

## 10.3    Minimax cost decision rule

Suppose you hold a pessimistic view of life and assume that whatever action is taken, nature will arrange the weather to your maximum pecuniary disadvantage. The safest action might be to take such a course as will make the best of a bad job, i.e. to take that action for which the maximum possible cost is least. This leads to the so-called *minimax* decision rule.

Applied to the swimming ticket problem the steps would be to take the minimum (or worst) pay-off for each action and then to select the action whose minimum is the maximum (i.e. the best amongst the minima):

| Action | Minimum pay-off for this action | Maximum of these minima |
|--------|--------------------------------|-------------------------|
| $a_1$ | −7 | −7 |
| $a_2$ | −10 | |

Hence action $a_1$ should be selected and a week-end ticket bought. By this action the maximum possible expenditure is limited to 7; with the other allowable action the possible expenditure could have been as high as 10. This rule is simple and straightforward, leading to an unequivocal solution, but it has certain snags.

To illustrate a major snag, consider a different problem when the rule is used to decide whether or not to undertake some research work. The two possible actions are either that the research is undertaken, or else that it is not. The two possible states (or outcomes) are that a cash return of $X$ is achieved for an expenditure of $C$, or alternatively that $C$ is expended with no return. The appropriate pay-off matrix will be as follows:

| | | Event (outcome) | | | |
|---|---|---|---|---|---|
| | | $b_1$ Research succeeds | $b_2$ Research fails | Minimum of row | Maximum of row minima |
| Action | $a_1$ Do research | $X − C$ | $×C$ | $×C$ | |
| | $a_2$ Don't do research | 0 | 0 | 0 | 0 |

Hence the decision under the minimax rule would be $a_2$ or 'don't do research'. Indeed, whatever the value of $X$, the answer would be the same and no research would be done. This is frankly unreasonable, and so the minimax rule cannot be adopted as a universal method of decision appraisal.

## 10.4 Minimax regret rule

It is obvious that in most practical problems, it is too pessimistic to assume that the worst will always happen. If such an attitude were adopted, the decison-maker would look with *regret* at lost opportunities. What is meant by regret in this connection? The regret for any action/outcome combination is defined as the difference between (i) the maximum possible pay-off under that outcome and (ii) the pay-off resulting from the action/outcome combination concerned, i.e. the amount of pay-off lost by not taking the optimal action for the (subsequently known) outcome concerned. In the swimming pool problem, under the combination $a_1/b_1$, the pay-off is $-7$. On the other hand, if outcome $b_1$ did in fact occur but action $a_2$ had been taken, the pay-off would be 0. Hence the subsequent regret at choosing $a_1$ rather than $a_2$ is $0 - (-7)$ or 7. A table (or matrix) can be written in which all the entries are not pay-offs as before, but regrets as calculated above. The table will run as follows:

|  |  | Outcome | | | Maximum | Minimum |
|---|---|---|---|---|---|---|
|  |  | $b_1$ | $b_2$ | $b_3$ | *of row* | *of maxima* |
| Action | $a_1$ | 7 | 2 | 0 | 7 |  |
|  | $a_2$ | 0 | 0 | 3 | 3 | 3 |

To select the best action the maximum (greatest) regret is tabulated for each action and that action chosen for which the maximum regret in a minimum (least). Action $a_2$ to buy daily tickets would now be selected, on the grounds that this minimizes the maximum possible regret.

How does this principle look when applied to the R & D matrix of the previous section? The appropriate regret matrix will be as shown on page 154.

Action $a_1$, do research, would be selected if $X - C$ is greater than $C$, which is equivalent to $X$ being greater than $2C$. Otherwise action $a_2$, don't do research, would be selected. This result is not

|  |  | Outcome | | Maximum | Minimum |
|---|---|---|---|---|---|
|  |  | $b_1$ | $b_2$ | of row | of maxima |
| Action | $a_1$ | 0 | $C$ | $C$ | ? |
|  | $a_2$ | $X - C$ | 0 | $X - C$ | ? |

(It is assumed, reasonably, that $X$ is greater than $2C$, i.e. that the successfu
outcome would more than cover the research cost.)

uncommonly quoted as a rule of thumb in research management
namely carry out an R & D project if the gross return from a
successful outcome is at least twice the cost, otherwise drop it.

Having derived rationally such a rule of thumb, suppose that
an inventor approached your firm and offered to develop a perpetual motion machine for £1 million, Success would certainly be
worth more than £2 million so that under this rule, you should
accept the offer. But you would be very unlikely to do so, since
although the rule is satisfied, there is a crucial missing element,
namely your belief in the feasibility of the proposal. This degree
of belief must, in practice, colour the decision you make and therefore needs to be brought into the assessment. To illustrate this,
a further example is analysed.

## 10.5    Installation of a boiler

You have to decide upon the best type of boiler to install in a
large factory. Basically, three alternatives are open:

(a) a coal-fired boiler,
(b) an oil-fired boiler,
(c) a dual-fired boiler capable of conversion from one fuel to
the other at negligible extra cost.

Table 10.1 gives the capital and annual running costs, as at the
appropriate date, for the three types of boiler.

Although the fuels would lead to identical running costs at present costs, the long-term fuel price position might be rather different. After taking advice, you decide that it is reasonable to
assume that the price differential, on a heat equivalent basis, which
could possibly arise will range from coal being $12\frac{1}{2}$ per cent higher
than oil to oil being $12\frac{1}{2}$ per cent higher than coal. Hence the three
extreme outcomes to be considered are set at

$b_1$    Coal $12\frac{1}{2}$ per cent up

Table 10.1  **Alternative boilers costs**

| | Boiler type | | |
|---|---|---|---|
| | I | II | III |
| | | | Dual-fired |
| | Coal only | Oil only | both fuels |
| | ($a_1$) | ($a_2$) | ($a_3$) |
| Capital cost | 1·95 | 1·50 | 2·40 |
| Annual running cost | 0·90 | 0·90 | 0·90 |

(All figures in 1000 m.u.)

  $b_2$  Prices equal
  $b_3$  Oil 12½ per cent up

You also decide that the period to be considered is 25 years
and that the appropriate interest factor to apply to the capital
invested is 15 per cent. The pay-off matrix has first to be calculated.
The capital involved for each action is amortised (written off) at
15 per cent over 25 years to convert the single capital payment
into a corresponding, but alternative, annual payment, by the discounting technique discussed in Chapter 9. These annual values
for the three types of boiler are

  $a_1$: 0·3016   $a_2$: 0·2320   $a_3$: 0·3712

The pay-off matrix can now be calculated on an annual basis.
It is assumed that the cheaper fuel remains at 0·9 annual cost,
the alternative rising by 12½ per cent or $12.5 \times 0.9/100 = 0.1125$.
The basic cost of 0·9 can be imputed as an extra addition to all
the possible combinations of action/outcome. Table 10.2 gives the

Table 10.2  **Matrix of pay-offs**

| | | Outcome | | Minimum | Maximum of |
|---|---|---|---|---|---|
| | $b_1$ | $b_2$ | $b_3$ | of row | row minima |
| | $a_1$ | −1·3141 | −1·2016 | −1·2016 | −1·3141 | |
| Action | $a_2$ | −1·1320 | −1·1320 | −1·2445 | −1·2445 | −1·2445 |
| | $a_3$ | −1·2712 | −1·2712 | −1·2712 | −1·2712 | |

combined costs for each action/outcome combination. For example, the action/outcome combination $a_1/b_1$ costs 0·3016 for capital
and $0.9 + 0.1125$ for running costs, 1·3141 in all. Under the maximin
procedure the optimum decision would be to install an oil-fired

boiler, since this will maximize the minimum possible pay-offs for each alternative action.

Suppose now that the minimax regret rule were considered in place of the maximin rule. Table 10.3 then gives the regrets for

Table 10.3 **Matrix of regrets**

|  |  | | *Outcome* | | *Maximum of row* | *Minimum of row minima* |
|---|---|---|---|---|---|---|
|  |  | $b_1$ | $b_2$ | $b_3$ |  |  |
|  | $a_1$ | 0·1821 | 0·0696 | 0 | 0·1821 | |
| *Action* | $a_2$ | 0 | 0 | 0·0429 | 0·0429 | 0·0429 |
|  | $a_3$ | 0·1392 | 0·1392 | 0·0696 | 0·1392 | |

the various actions, derived from the appropriate pay-offs in Table 10.2. Thus under outcome $b_1$, the best action is $a_2$; hence the regret for combination $a_2/b_1$ is zero. For combination $a_1/b_1$ it will accordingly be $-1·1320 - (-1·3141) = 0·1821$, etc.

The maximum regret is now found for each action and the action located for which the maximum is a minimum. Once again the same conclusion would be reached, namely to install an oil boiler. It can be seen, however, that the action deduced begs the question as to the likelihood of the various outcomes arising. The degree of belief in the various outcomes should be brought in, since they may be considered to have very different likelihood of occurrence, and this in turn could affect the desirability of the various actions. For instance, if it were thought that $b_3$ was the virtually certain outcome in practice, then action $a_1$, installing the coal boiler, should be followed.

## 10.6 Expected values

Return now to the R & D illustration of Sections 10.3 and 10.4 and assume that you have the choice between either being allowed to have the option of making the decision on the R & D project or alternatively taking part in a lottery. This lottery consists of 100 similar tickets in a big drum. The only difference between the tickets is that some are marked 'win' and the rest are marked 'lose'. You are given the straight choice:

either  to gamble on the success of the research

or  to draw one ticket at random from the drum, the writing on that ticket deciding the outcome of the research.

In each case the possible monetary outcome if the gamble succeeds is the same. How many winning tickets would you require there to be in the drum amongst the tickets for you to be indifferent as to which choice to accept? Note that if none of the tickets were marked 'win' you would prefer to gamble on the research, as there is presumably some finite chance of research success. Similarly, if all 100 tickets are marked 'win' you would prefer the lottery, as there must be some chance of the research failing whilst taking part in the lottery would give you a defined monetary profit. Hence there must be some changeover point between these two extremes.

For example, you might feel you were indifferent between a gamble on whether to go ahead with the research and a gamble in which you drew a single ticket from the 100 in the drum, of which 70 are marked 'win'. The probability of drawing a winning ticket is obviously 0·7, and this figure is therefore applied to your degree of belief that the research will succeed. It follows that your belief that the research will not succeed is measured by $1 - 0·7$, or 0·3. These 'subjective probabilities' are referred to as *a priori* probabilities and were first suggested by Thomas Bayes (an eighteenth century Englishman and Fellow of the Royal Society who had in the circumstances the rather unexpected occupation of clergyman). The suggested decision procedure is then to calculate a *weighted average* of the outcome of each action, the weights being the *a priori* probabilities attached to each outcome. The action showing the maximum weighted average is then selected as the best action to take. The method is commonly referred to as the *Expected Monetary Value* (EMV) approach.

Applying this principle to the R & D pay-off matrix with the *a priori* probability of success of 0·7 gives:

|  |  | *Outcome* |  |  |
|---|---|---|---|---|
|  |  | $b_1$ | $b_2$ |  |
| *Weights* |  | 0·7 | 0·3 | *Weighted average* |
| *Action* | $a_1$ | $X - C$ | $-C$ | $0·7(X - C) - 0·3C = 0·7X - C$ |
|  | $a_2$ | 0 | 0 | $0·7(0) + 0·3(0) = 0$ |

Hence action $a_1$ would be best, provided $0·7X - C$ were greater than 0, i.e. provided $X$ were greater than $\frac{10}{7}C$; otherwise action $a_2$ should be carried out.

In the case of the perpetual motion project you would probably visualize the drum with a million or more tickets, only one of which would read 'win'. Hence $X$ would need to be very large indeed for the project to be tempting; indeed, if there were just one winning ticket amongst a million tickets, $X$ would have to exceed $1\,000\,000C$ for the project to appear acceptable.

## 10.7  Concept of repeatablity

This translation to expected (or weighted) values introduces a new concept—the concept of repeatability or a sequence of decisions. For any single decision the outcome will be one from the set of possible outcomes; for the research problem the set consists of $X - C$ or 0. Hence expected value is meaningless when compared to that individual decision in isolation by itself; the action leads to the pay-off corresponding to one or other of the outcomes, not to some mixture of them. If the right choice is made there will be a high pay-off; if the wrong choice is made there will be a low pay-off. The expected value itself cannot and will not in general be precisely achieved, the actual results being sometimes better and sometimes worse than the expected value. But what is true is that if a large number of individual projects are each judged in this way and the appropriate decisions made, then the total gain from all projects combined will approximate to the total of the individual project expected values.

This effect can be seen by considering Figure 10.1. The figure relates to the accuracy of forecasting the return on capital investments for a sample of 100 large projects carried out in a big United Kingdom company over a 10-year period. The average cost per project exceeded £2 million. The comparison is between the forecast return when the projects were sanctioned and the return achieved in the first full year of operation. The degree of accuracy in forecasting has been estimated by taking the difference between the achieved return and the forecast return and expressing this as a percentage of the forecast return. Put formally

Inaccuracy of forecast (%)

$$= \frac{\text{Achieved return} - \text{Forecast return}}{\text{Forecast return}} \times 100$$

A positive result means that the achieved return was greater than the forecast return, whilst a negative answer shows that the

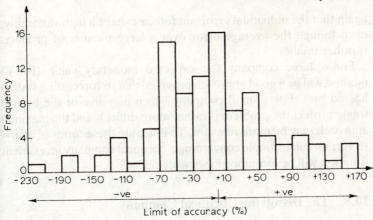

**Figure 10.1  Inaccuracy of forecasting**

achieved return failed to come up to the forecast figure. The results obtained on the 100 projects ranged from −220 per cent to +169 per cent (Figure 10.1). The overall average accuracy showed that the actual return was less than forecast, by some 9·6 per cent of the forecast. But it is interesting and revealing that, whilst the 100 projects individually showed such wide variations in achieved return, the average was so close to the expected overall average of zero. Bearing in mind, however, that the forecast return for any individual project must essentially be a weighted average of expectations, this is perhaps not so surprising.

The data just described were from a single large British company. D. S. Tull (see reference (8) at end of chapter) describes a similar kind of exercise carried out on sixty-three projects drawn from sixteen different companies with very similar results. In his case the criterion calculated is based on sales or profits over a five-year period, but the spread is of very much the same magnitude, namely:

Sales   −99%
             to +720% (+167% if one project is excluded)

Profits  −800% (−134% if two projects are excluded)
             to +140%

The mean forecast error, ignoring the sign of the error, was 65 per cent, and in 66 per cent of the projects the actual sales fell short of the forecast sales. It seems reasonable to conclude once again that the individual errors on forecasts have a high variability, even though the average error over a large number of products is rather smaller.

For a large company the expected monetary value (EMV) method will be a good approach provided that its forecasting system has no bias. For a small company which may live or die by one single project the problem is rather more difficult and the maximin approach may be more relevant. To illustrate these forms of analysis further, an example concerning a chemical company investment situation will be examined in some detail.

## 10.8   The Dissolving Chemical Company

The manager of this company has to decide whether to build a small plant or a large plant to manufacture a new product with an expected market life of 10 years. The decision hinges partly on the size of the market the company can obtain for the product.

Demand may possibly be high during the first 2 years but, if many of the initial users find the products unsatisfactory, the demand could then fall to a low level thereafter. High initial demand might alternatively indicate the possibility of a sustained high-volume market. If the demand is initially high and remains so and the company finds itself with insufficient capacity within the first 2 years, competitive products will certainly be introduced by other manufacturers.

If the company initially builds a big plant, it must live with it for the whole 10 years, whatever the size of the market demand. If it builds a small plant, there is the option of expanding the plant in 2 years' time, an option that it would only take up if demand were high during the introductory period. If a small plant is built initially and demand is low during the introductory period, the company will maintain operations in the small plant and make a good profit on the low-volume throughput.

The manager is uncertain as to the action he should take. The company grew rapidly during the early 1970s, keeping pace with the chemical industry generally. The new product, if the market turns out to be large, offers the company a chance to move into a new period of extremely profitable growth. The development department, particularly the development project engineer, is anxious to build the large-scale plant in order to exploit the first major product development the department has had in some years.

The chairman, a principal stockholder, is wary of the possibility of having a large amount of plant capacity lying idle. He favours a smaller initial plant commitment, but recognizes that possible later expansion to meet high-volume demand would, overall, require more investment and be less efficient to operate. The chairman also recognizes that, unless the company moves promptly to fill the demand which develops, once the product is on the market, competitors will be tempted to move in with equivalent products.

Various items of information have been obtained, or estimated, by the appropriate managers within the company, and are summarized as follows:

## (a) Marketing information

The marketing manager suggests a 60 per cent chance of a large market in the long run and a 40 per cent chance of a low demand, developing initially as follows:

| | | |
|---|---|---|
| Initially high, sustained high | 60% | |
| Initially high, long-term low | 10% | } Low 40% |
| Initially low, continuing low | 30% | |
| Initially low, subsequently high | 0% | |

## (b) Annual income

The management accounting section have put forward the following financial estimates:

(i)  A large plant with high market volume would yield £1 million annually in cash flow (for 10 years).

(ii)  A large plant with low market volume would yield only £0·1 million annually because of high fixed costs and inefficiencies.

(iii)  A small plant with low market demand would be economical and would yield annual cash income of £0·4 million per annum.

(iv)  A small plant, during an initial period of high demand, would yield £0·45 million per annum, but this would drop to £0·25 million per annum in the long run if high demand continued, because of competition from other manufacturers.

(v)  If an initial small plant were expanded after 2 years to meet sustained high demand, it would yield £0·7 million annually for the remaining 8 years and so would be less efficient than a large plant built initially.

(vi) If the small plant were expanded after 2 years, but high demand were not sustained, the estimated annual cash flow for the remaining 8 years would be £0·05 million.

## (c) Capital costs

Estimates obtained from construction companies indicate that a large plant would cost £3 million to build and put into operation, a small plant would cost £1·3 million initially and an additional £2·2 million if expanded after 2 years.

The manager must decide now upon his initial action. Should he recommend the company to build or not, and if it is to build, should it build big or small? It will be assumed that the firm uses expected monetary value (EMV) as its criterion for decision. Further, for purposes of simplicity, discounting of the cash flows will be ignored (equivalent to assuming an interest rate of zero). This does not affect the principles behind the analysis, but reduces the arithmetic enormously. The possible effects of discounting are discussed later.

## 10.9   The analysis of the problem

If no building is carried out at all, it is clear the EMV will be zero; no expenditure, no income. Hence the problem is reduced to a consideration of the other courses of action to see whether the best of them gives an EMV which exceeds zero. As a first step, it is useful to construct a *decision tree* to illustrate the structure of the decision which has to be made. Figure 10.2 gives this. Each path through the tree from the start to the finish (left to right) represents a separate logical possibility. Points where decision choices have to be made are indicated by squares. Points where alternative outcomes occur following some particular decision are indicated by circles. Thus the path AD represents the initial action 'build big' which is then followed by the outcome of low demand for all 10 years. The path AEH represents the initial action 'build small', then the outcome of high demand for the first 2 years, followed by action to expand the plant, resulting in the outcome of low demand for the remaining 8 years. Similarly for the other

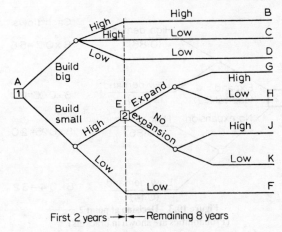

**Figure 10.2   Basic decision tree**

paths. A cursory examination of the original data will show that there would be no point in expanding a small initial plant if the demand in the first 2 years were low. This possibility has accordingly been omitted from path AF.

The power of the decision tree diagram rests in the opportunity it affords for the logical analysis of the various alternatives to be studied before making a decision. Decisions, as here, are often sequential in nature which the decision tree well illustrates. To analyse the diagram, various quantities are required, but notice first that there are basically two decision points, labelled 1 and 2. If the decision at point 1 is to be examined, it is necessary to know the values to be placed upon the two alternatives that are then open; the value of building a small plant can be assessed only if it is known what value can be expected if decision point 2 is reached. Hence it is necessary to evaluate decision point 2 first, i.e. the diagram is examined from right to left. This is sometimes referred to as the *roll-back principle*.

Decision point 2 is shown in more detail in Figure 10.3. The initial data given in section 10.8 enable the following deductions to be made for the last eight years:

$$\text{Probability of high demand} = \frac{0 \cdot 6}{0 \cdot 6 + 0 \cdot 1} = 0 \cdot 86$$

$$\text{Probability of low demand} = \frac{0 \cdot 1}{0 \cdot 6 + 0 \cdot 1} = 0 \cdot 14$$

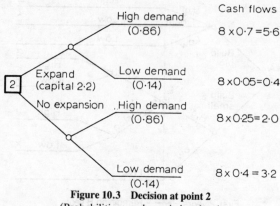

**Figure 10.3   Decision at point 2**
(Probabilities are shown in brackets)

The cash flows for the last 8 years of production are entered on Figure 10.3 at the right-hand side. These are calculated from the data in Section 10.8, remembering that the first 2 years must have given rise to high demand. Thus if the plant is expanded and there is high demand, the annual cash flow will be £0·7 million, from paragraph (*b*) (v) on page 161 in section 10.8, giving a total cash flow of $8 \times 0·7$, or £5·6 million. Similarly for the other possibilities.

Hence the EMV of expansion at point 2 will be:

$$\text{EMV (expansion)} = \underset{\substack{\text{(high} \\ \text{demand)}}}{0·86 \times 5·6} + \underset{\substack{\text{(low} \\ \text{demand)}}}{0·14 \times 0·4} - \underset{\substack{\text{(capital} \\ \text{cost)}}}{2·2}$$

$$= 4·82 + 0·06 - 2·2 = 2·68$$

(Note that since 2·2 represents an outlay as opposed to a gain, it is shown as a negative gain.)

Similarly, for no expansion the financial situation is:

$$\text{EMV (no expansion)} = \underset{\substack{\text{(high} \\ \text{demand)}}}{0·86 \times 2·0} + \underset{\substack{\text{(low} \\ \text{demand)}}}{0·14 \times 3·2}$$

$$= 1·72 + 0·45 = 2·17$$

(Note that there is no extra capital expenditure incurred by this action.)

As the former EMV exceeds the latter (2·68 versus 2·17) the decision, if point 2 were reached, would be to expand the plant, on the grounds that expansion gives rise to a higher EMV. The expected value of the decision at that moment of time would be 2·68.

Using this analysis for decision point 2 the original decision tree can now be modified to give the tree shown in Figure 10.4. In

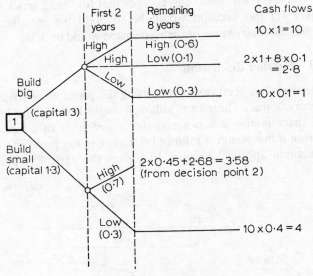

**Figure 10.4  Decision at point 1**
(Probabilities are shown in brackets)

this revised figure, decision point 2 has effectively been replaced by an EMV equivalent. The complete tree can now be evaluated on similar lines to those used above. For the decision to build big, this gives:

$$
\text{EMV (build big)}
$$

$$
= \underset{\substack{\text{(high} \\ \text{demand)}}}{0{\cdot}6 \times 10} + \underset{\substack{\text{(high/low} \\ \text{demand)}}}{0{\cdot}1 \times 2{\cdot}8} + \underset{\substack{\text{(low} \\ \text{demand)}}}{0{\cdot}3 \times 1} - \underset{\substack{\text{(capital} \\ \text{cost)}}}{3}
$$

$$
= 6 + 0{\cdot}28 + 0{\cdot}3 - 3
$$

$$
= 3{\cdot}58
$$

Similarly, for the decision to build small:

EMV (build small)

$$= 0.7 \times 3.58 + \underset{\substack{\text{(low} \\ \text{demand)}}}{0.3 \times 4} - \underset{\substack{\text{(capital} \\ \text{cost)}}}{1.3}$$
$$\underset{\substack{\text{(decision} \\ \text{point 2)}}}{}$$

$$= 2.51 + 1.2 - 1.3$$
$$= 2.41$$

Since the EMV for 'build big' exceeds that for 'build small' (3·58 versus 2·41) the decision would be to build big initially. The expected monetary value of such a decision would be 3·58.

## 10.10   Further discussion

The analysis has been carried out using the principle of Expected Monetary Value. Therefore, although 'build big' has the higher EMV there is also a non-negligible chance (0·3) of a loss of 2 occurring if this action is followed. Examining the problem under the maximin approach, Figure 10.5 gives the pay-off results for

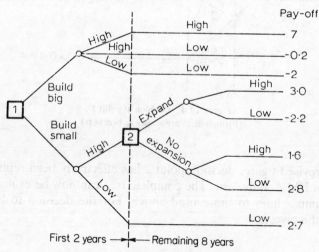

**Figure 10.5   Maximum approach to decision**

all possible decisions. Table 10.4 follows the usual approach of forming the row minima and then taking the maximum of these row minima. This table demonstrates that action $a_3$, namely 'build small' and never expand under any circumstances, would be the maximin solution and must give a profit of at least 1·6. Any other course could lead to a loss under certain circumstances. Hence

Table 10.4  **Pay-offs for various alternatives**

| Demand | *State (outcome)* | | | *Minimum of row* | *Maximum of row minima* |
| | $b_1$ High | $b_2$ High/Low | $b_3$ Low | | |
|---|---|---|---|---|---|
| Action $a_1$ (Build big) | 7·0 | −0·2 | −2·0 | −2·0 | |
| $a_2$ (Build small/ expand) | 3·0 | −2·2 | 2·7 | −2·2 | |
| $a_3$ (Build small/ not expand) | 1·6 | 2·8 | 2·7 | 1·6 | 1·6 |

a play-safe policy gives a rather different result from EMV, but such a decision process ignores possibilities such as a gain of 7 which could occur under a 'build big' action. For a small firm to whom a possible loss of 2·0 would be disastrous, the maximin approach is probably relevant; for larger firms for whom the current decision is one of a series of such decisions the EMV approach would be the more relevant.

This analysis has ignored any discounting of the cash flows. The principles of analysis would remain unaltered, but the effect of an interest rate above zero would be to take account of the precise timings of the cash inflows and outflows. The overall effect would be to increase the value of the second alternative (build small) in relation to the first alternative, since some part of the capital outlay is postponed, but the magnitude of the effect would depend upon the rate of interest used in the analysis.

## 10.11  General considerations

Use of the decision-tree approach as a basis for decision-making is a means of making more explicit the process which must be at least intuitively present in good decision-making. Such a method allows for, and indeed encourages, the revision of the nature of the decision from time to time and maximizes use of analysis, experience, and judgment. It helps to force out into the open those differences in assumptions or dimensions of value that underlie differences in judgment or choice. It keeps the manager from being trapped in the formalism of a rigid procedure in which there is little room for feedback, re-definition, or interplay between analysis and decision.

The abstraction followed in this chapter envisages that each action can be replaced by a hypothetical roulette wheel; further the average pay-off for that wheel, its expected value, can be calculated. If each action is represented by its appropriate fair roulette wheel, then the decision-maker should want to spin the wheel which has the highest expected value.

The recommendation, based on EMV, applies to this one decision and although he only makes this particular decision once, there are many other decisions of this type that he will make in the future. Hence, whilst he may not succeed in maximizing the possible pay-off on this one occasion, choosing the maximum EMV each time should maximize his total actual gain over a number of decisions.

In the next chapter the use of techniques to aid the assessment of probabilities is discussed. But the decision-maker should not allow his judgment to be entirely superseded by techniques. There are many aids, some simple and some complex, to assist the decision-maker in assessing probabilities. These techniques may be appropriate in many cases, but the decision-maker must realize that in the final analysis the probability assessment is his own judgment about future outcomes. This judgment can be guided, and hopefully improved, with techniques but it cannot be replaced.

The following chapter opens, however, with a discussion of how the approach used here can value the possibility of using further information, e.g. market research information, before making an initial choice between alternative courses of action.

# References

(1) *The Anatomy of Decisions* by P. G. Moore and H. Thomas (Penguin, 1976).
(2) *Elementary Decision Theory* by H. Chernoff and L. E. Moses (Chapman and Hall, 1959).
(3) *Decision Theory and the Manager* by Howard Thomas (Pitman, 1972).
(4) *Introduction to Statistics for Business Decisions* by R. Schlaifer (McGraw-Hill, 1961).
(5) *The Compleat Strategyst* by J. D. Williams (McGraw-Hill, 1954).
(6) Decision trees for decision-making, by J. F. Magee, *Harvard Business Review*, vol. 42, no. 4, 1964, pp. 126–38.

(7) How to use decision trees in capital investment, by J. F. Magee, *Harvard Business Review*, vol. 42, no. 5, 1964, pp. 79–96.
(8) The relationships of actual and predicted sales and profits in new-product introductions, by D. S. Tull, *Journal of Business*, vol. 40, no. 3, 1967, 233–50.
(9) *Making Decisions* by D. V. Lindley (Wiley, 1970).

# 11 The value of information

## 11.1 The modification of decisions

The natural reaction of anyone faced with making a decision when there is uncertainty present, perhaps displayed in the form of stated probabilities of the various alternative outcomes, is to try to remove the uncertainty by finding out just what is the true state of affairs. Knowledge in general is assumed to be beneficial to the making of a decision. Complete knowledge is certainly a way out of all difficulties provided one is clear as to the criteria to be used for decisions, but it is rarely practicable where decisions involve some consideration of the future, even if cost is of no concern. Thus a Stock Exchange investor trying to decide whether or not to invest in a particular share would not know for certain whether the stock was going to appreciate or not.

Again, cost may be a powerful deterrent to the removal of uncertainty; it may just be too expensive to find out the complete truth. An engineer designing a plant will not often be able to build a trial plant, but may alternatively think it useful to build a prototype to resolve some of the uncertainties in the design problem. A prototype may, however, in itself sometimes cost so much that it is better to build the plant in a fairly flexible manner and learn from experience as to the form of any modifications that are needed.

Thus, while it is usually a good thing to seek the removal of all uncertainty from a problem, it is commonly not a practicable aim. There is very often, however, a partial solution available in that, while it may not be possible to remove all the uncertainty, it is nevertheless feasible to reduce it by obtaining some relevant information. Thus, the investor may consult his stockbroker, who is presumed to be more knowledgeable than the investor, as to expectations concerning the particular share in question. The engineer, thwarted of his prototype, may obtain some information from calculations of the likely behaviour of the system or from visits of inspection to similar plants. In these situations it is still not possible to determine the true situation, but at least one will be more knowledgeable than without the information. If the extra information is combined with the original or *prior* probabilities to form revised probabilities, the latter are then referred to as *posterior* probabilities and provide a revised basis on which to make the decision.

## 11.2  Posterior probabilities

As an illustration of the formation of posterior probabilities consider the following example. A certain company is in the process of launching a new car. The marketing director assigns, on the basis of the information he currently has, a probability of 0·9 to the event 'the car is superior to its immediate competitor'. However, he is not sure if his assessment is correct because of his total commitment to, and enthusiasm for, the new car. He calls up a well-known market research company and asks for a quick and relatively inexpensive survey to confirm or reject his initial assessment. The market research executive reminds his client that the survey will only be 80 per cent reliable, because of the potential extent of measurement and sampling errors.

In operational terms, 80 per cent reliability means the following: the survey will indicate either 'winning' or 'losing' for the new car; if the car is really superior, the survey will indicate 'winning' with a probability of 0·8 and, similarly, if the car is really inferior the survey will indicate 'losing' with a probability of 0·8. Note that the words 'winning' and 'losing' have been used to avoid direct relationship and possible confusion with the terms superiority and inferiority.

The marketing director wants the market research firm to tell him what his revised probability assessment should be for the event 'the car is superior to its immediate competitor' after the completion of the survey. To assist in this evaluation refer to Figure 11.1. The horizontal scale is split in the ratio 90:10 and refers to the marketing director's assessments; the vertical scale refers to the market research outcomes. The vertical blocks are split 20:80 and 80:20 respectively to reflect the possible survey results for each of the two underlying possibilities.

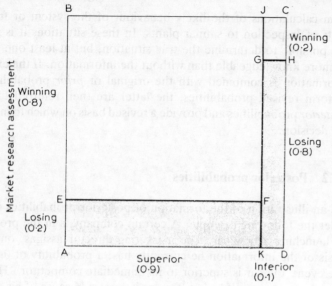

Marketing director's assessment

**Figure 11.1  Revision of probabilities**

Suppose now that the market research has been carried out and gave the indication 'winning'. Then the true situation must fall, not anywhere in the area ABCD, but in the smaller unshaded area EBCHGF. Moreover, the proportion of this latter area that corresponds to a superior situation is:

$$\frac{\text{Area EBJF}}{\text{Area EBCHGF}} = \frac{0.9 \times 0.8}{0.9 \times 0.8 + 0.2 \times 0.1} = 0.97$$

In other words, if the market research findings indicate that the new car is 'winning', the market director's *posterior* assessment for the probability of the new car being superior should be 0·97, i.e. very close to 'certainty', in place of the *prior* probability of 0·9.

If the other three possibilities are similarly computed the set of *posterior* probabilities turn out as follows:

|  |  | Market Research Findings | |
|---|---|---|---|
|  |  | *'Winning'* | *'Losing'* |
| Car status | Superior | 0·97 | 0·53 |
|  | Inferior | 0·03 | 0·47 |

Each column must add up to unity, but this is not necessarily true of the rows.

It is perhaps worth noting from the last column that, if the market research indicates 'losing', it then provides a very poor guide to the true situation as to superiority or inferiority.

What has been carried out here is an application of *Bayes's Theorem*, first formulated as a probability theorem by Thomas Bayes. It is extremely useful for obtaining revised probability estimates in those situations where the decision-maker has the option of collecting some additional evidence. (Readers who want to pursue the ramifications of the theorem further are referred to reference (1) at the end of the chapter.) Extra evidence normally has a cost attached to it and, as a general principle, one would feel it worth paying if the EMV of the revised optimum action (after deducting the cost of the extra evidence) is greater than the EMV of the optimum action without such extra evidence. The whole process is sometimes referred to as *Bayesian Decision Analysis* and is illustrated on a practical problem in the next section.

## 11.3   Oil wildcatter's problem

The background to the so-called oil wildcatter's decision problem is that, as part of a large ongoing programme of exploration, an oil wildcatter has to decide whether or not to drill for oil at a given site before his option on the site expires. He is uncertain about many things: the cost of drilling, the extent of the oil deposits at the site, the cost of raising the oil if there is any, and so forth. He has available the objective records of similar, and not quite so similar, drillings in the same area and he has already discussed the features peculiar to this particular option with his geologist, his geophysicist and his land agent. He could gain further relevant information (but still not necessarily perfect information) about the underlying geophysical structure at this particular site by arranging for seismic soundings to be taken. Such information, however, is quite costly and not of a stratigraphical nature (i.e. it does not indicate the kind of rock, sandstone, limestone, etc.). Only drilling can precisely determine this, and the wildcatter has to decide whether or not to purchase this information before he makes his basic decision whether to drill (D) or not to drill ($\overline{D}$).

To put the problem in a more formal framework, suppose that

a well sunk on the site can be either dry ($w_1$) or wet ($w_2$) or soaking ($w_3$). The former is bad and would lead to a net loss of £100 000. Outcome $w_2$ is so-so and would give a net profit of £100 000, while outcome $w_3$ is very good and would lead to a net profit of £500 000. Net profit or loss here is defined as the difference between sales revenue and all costs of production, including the sinking of the well. After appropriate discussions, but without taking any seismic soundings, the oil wildcatter estimates that the probabilities of the three possible outcomes are 0·5 for $w_1$, 0·25 for $w_2$ and 0·25 for $w_3$.

The seismic soundings, which could help him to determine more precisely the nature of the underlying geological structure, would cost £30 000. They will give a result in the form of a 'good' or 'not so good' indication. A 'good' indication ($\overline{G}$) is broadly linked to the presence of oil (i.e. to outcomes $w_2$ and $w_3$), while a 'not so good' indication ($\overline{G}$) is linked to the absence of oil (i.e. to outcome $w_1$). However, these are not precise deterministic relationships, but probabilistic ones. Past experience of seismic soundings, in this and other areas, shows that the probabilities given in Table 11.1 are a reasonable summary of the relationship between the

Table 11.1   **Seismic sounding results**

| | Seismic sounding | | |
| Drilled well | G (positive) | $\overline{G}$ (negative) | Total |
|---|---|---|---|
| $w_1$ dry | 0·2 | 0·8 | 1·0 |
| $w_2$ wet | 0·6 | 0·4 | 1·0 |
| $w_3$ soaking | 0·8 | 0·2 | 1·0 |

results of seismic soundings and subsequent drilled well results.

Thus if a drilled well at a site were wet ($w_2$), then a seismic survey carried out at the site prior to drilling would have a probability of 0·6 of giving a positive result and a probability of 0·4 of giving a negative result. Similarly, the corresponding probabilities are given for the other two possible drilling outcomes. Note that the seismic sounding results are very much linked to the drilling outcomes, and that such soundings do discriminate, albeit not very precisely, between good and bad situations. The whole situation and the alternatives open to the oil wildcatter are summarized in the decision tree shown in Figure 11.2.

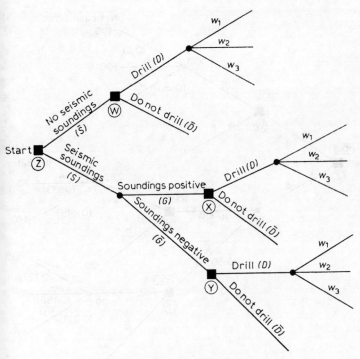

**Figure 11.2   Oil wildcatter's decision tree**

The analysis is outlined in the decision tree of Figure 11.3. The first step is to place against each possible route through the tree the total pay-off or net gain. This is done on the right-hand side of Figure 11.3, and includes, where appropriate, the cost of the seismic survey. All net gains are expressed in £000s and the £ symbol is dropped whenever there is no risk of confusion. The prior probabilities associated with the upper portion of the tree can also be entered. There are four decision points marked, as usual, with squares and labelled W, X, Y and Z.

The upper portion of the decision tree, namely the decision not to take seismic soundings, is analysed first. The EMV at decision point W for the decision 'drill' will be:

$$0 \cdot 5 \times (-100) + 0 \cdot 25 \times 100 + 0 \cdot 25 \times 500 = 100$$

The EMV for the decision not to drill is clearly zero. Hence, the decision at point W will be to drill (*D*), since this has the higher

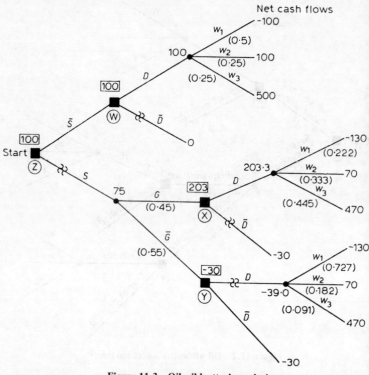

**Figure 11.3　Oil wildcatter's analysis**

EMV. The value of 100 is accordingly inserted on the decision tree at point W and branch $\overline{D}$ is barred.

The next point of analysis to be tackled is at decision point X. This point is only reached if seismic soundings are taken and they give a positive response ($G$). To evaluate the EMV for a decision to drill, the posterior probabilities of the three possible outcomes $w_1$, $w_2$ and $w_3$, given both the original prior probabilities and the seismic sounding evidence of a positive response, are required. The prior probabilities of the three outcomes are:

$$P(w_1) = 0.5; P(w_2) = 0.25; P(w_3) = 0.25$$

Using these prior probabilities and the probabilities given in Table 11.1, it is possible to construct the diagram shown in Figure 11.4. The shaded areas represent the situations where the seismic sounding results are positive, the unshaded areas where the results are negative. Consider the situation where the test result is positive.

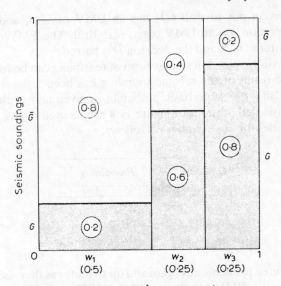

**Figure 11.4 Revision of oil wildcatter's probabilities**

Then the revised probability of situation $w_1$ is

$$\frac{0.5 \times 0.2}{0.5 \times 0.2 + 0.25 \times 0.6 + 0.25 \times 0.8} = \frac{2}{9}$$

being the ratio of the area of the left-hand shaded block to the total area of all three shaded blocks combined.

For $w_2$ the corresponding revised probability will be

$$\frac{0.25 \times 0.6}{0.5 \times 0.2 + 0.25 \times 0.6 + 0.25 \times 0.8} = \frac{3}{9}$$

and similarly the revised probability for $w_3$ will be

$$\frac{0.25 \times 0.8}{0.5 \times 0.2 + 0.25 \times 0.6 + 0.25 \times 0.8} = \frac{4}{9}$$

These three probabilities add up to unity, and are now entered on the appropriate branches of the decision tree. The EMV for the decision to drill (D) at decision point X is now given by:

$$\frac{2}{9} \times (-130) + \frac{3}{9} \times 70 + \frac{4}{9} \times 470 = 203 \cdot 3$$

The decision not to drill ($\overline{D}$) has an EMV of $-30$, and so the better decision, on an EMV basis, is to drill. The EMV of 203·3 is now entered at X and the decision $\overline{D}$ is barred.

At decision point Y a similar form of reasoning can be followed. Here the result of the seismic sounding has been a negative response. Using the same basic probabilities given above, the areas of the unshaded portions of Figure 11.4 can be used to give revised probabilities for $w_1$, $w_2$ and $w_3$ as follows:

| Outcome | Probability (given negative response) |
|---------|---------------------------------------|
| $w_1$ | 0·727 |
| $w_2$ | 0·182 |
| $w_3$ | 0·091 |

and the three probabilities again add up to unity, as they should.

Hence, the EMV for the decision to drill at decision point Y is:

$$0 \cdot 727 \times (-130) + 0 \cdot 182 \times 70 + 0 \cdot 091 \times 470 = -39 \cdot 0$$

Comparison of this EMV with that of the decision not to drill shows the latter to be the better, as the EMV of the latter is only $-30$ in comparison with $-39$. Hence, $-30$ is inserted at point Y and bar the decision to drill ($D$) barred. Note that the decisions made at points X and Y are different, as one would expect if the seismic results are to be of any real assistance.

The next step is to combine the two branches, $G$ and $\overline{G}$, weighting them according to the prior probabilities of obtaining $G$ or $\overline{G}$ results, assuming that it is decided to take seismic soundings. These probabilities can be computed from Figure 11.4 by noting that the shaded area relates to $G$ and the unshaded area to $\overline{G}$. The former is equal to

$$0 \cdot 5 \times 0 \cdot 2 + 0 \cdot 6 \times 0 \cdot 25 + 0 \cdot 8 \times 0 \cdot 25 = 0 \cdot 45$$

Similarly, the appropriate probability for $\overline{G}$ is 0·55. Note that the probabilities for $G$ and $\overline{G}$ add, as they must, to unity. The combined EMV for the decision to take seismic soundings can now be evaluated as:

$$0 \cdot 45 \times 203 \cdot 3 + 0 \cdot 55 \times (-30) = 74 \cdot 985 \text{ or } 75$$

Finally, the starting position denoted as decision point Z can be evaluated. The EMV for the decision to take a seismic sounding (S) is 75, while that for the decision not to have a seismic sounding (S̄) is 100. The latter is the higher EMV, and, hence, the oil wildcatter should go ahead without a survey and drill: his EMV will thereby be 100.

The cost of the seismic survey, on these data, would have to be reduced to 5 if it were to become a viable proposition on an EMV decision basis. Although in this instance EMV was the appropriate tool to use for choice it is, however, worth pointing out that the probabilities of a loss (any loss) under the two alternative initial decisions are rather different. Under the decision to take the seismic survey, the possible loss situations are as follows:

Loss of 130     Probability $0·45 \times \frac{2}{9}$ or $0·1$
Loss of  30     Probability $0·55$

Under the decision to drill straight away without a seismic survey at all, the only loss situation is:

Loss of 100     Probability $0·5$

Hence, if a loss of 100 or more is serious to the oil wildcatter but losses of less than that amount, whilst undesirable, are not so serious, then the decision to drill straightway carries with it certain important loss implications, and the wildcatter might prefer to take the survey. If *any* level of loss is of substantial consequence to the oil wildcatter, then the two decisions do not differ very materially in this respect. Indeed, under such circumstances the oil wildcatter might prefer to abandon the option.

## 11.4  The assessment of probabilities

The use of decision analysis necessarily involves the assessment of probabilities. There are basically two types of such assessments that have to be made. The first is for some defined future event, e.g. that there will be a Channel Tunnel in operation by 2000. The second is for some uncertain quantity, e.g. the volume of sales of new motor cars in the United Kingdom next year. Meaningful assessments cannot be carried out unless the assessor is absolutely clear as to the event or uncertain quantity in question. A few guidelines are therefore in order.

First, events or uncertain quantities must be defined unambiguously. A test of this characteristic is to ask whether a clairvoyant could reveal the value of the quantity concerned by specifying a single number without requesting further clarification. To cite an example, it is not meaningful to ask for 'the price of Imperial Chemical Industries ordinary shares in June next year', because the clairvoyant would need to know where the shares were to be purchased, the date, the number of shares, whether the price included commission and duties, etc. However, the average overall price per share of 1000 ICI ordinary shares bought at the close of business at the London Stock Exchange on the last business day of June next year would be a well defined quantity. Again, ask the man in the street if it rained yesterday and he will probably answer straight away with a 'yes' or 'no'. But the weatherman before answering will need to have a definition of what constitutes rain and where the rain must have fallen.

Secondly, uncertain quantities should be described in no more detail than is really necessary for the purposes in hand. Thus in many instances an uncertain quantity can be meaningfully translated into a few exclusive discrete events, and then probabilities assessed for these events. A discrete distribution of exclusive events is often easier to work with than a continuous uncertain quantity. For example, demand for a product in the next year might be broken down into these five exclusive events:

$E_1$    0–499 units
$E_2$    500–999 units
$E_3$    1000–1499 units
$E_4$    1500–1999 units
$E_5$    2000 units or more

The probabilities can now be assessed for each of these discrete events. One disadvantage of such a breakdown is that the process can easily lead to an excessively bushy tree, if the number of events concerned is at all large.

Thirdly, it is important to use a scale or units that are comfortable for the person giving the assessment: for example, don't use French francs if he usually thinks in terms of American dollars.

The most common technique used for estimating probabilities of events is that of preference. The assessor is asked to choose between two gambles and, depending upon his selection, the gambles are changed until he is indifferent between them. The point of indifference leads to his assessment. Suppose the probability of the successful development of a new product by the end of next year (M) is required. The assessor is initially offered the choice between the two gambles A and B. Gamble A relates to the development of the new product whilst for gamble B one ball is randomly drawn at the end of year M from an urn containing 900 black balls and 100 white balls. The prizes under the two gambles are as follows:

| Gamble A | Gamble B |
| --- | --- |
| £100 000 if development succeeds | £100 000 if ball drawn is black |
| £0 otherwise | £0 if ball drawn is white |

If the assessor chooses A the assessment is repeated, but with more black balls (and correspondingly fewer white balls) in gamble B; if he chooses B it is repeated with fewer black balls (and correspondingly more white balls). The process is repeated until the proportion of black balls in gamble B is such that he is indifferent between the two gambles. The required probability is then taken as the final proportion of black balls in B. At no time in this process is it necessary to ask the assessor a more difficult question than 'do you prefer this gamble, or that one, or can't you say'. Numerical measurement of an individual's degree of belief can thus be obtained by simply asking questions of preference.

When a decision tree involves the probabilities of several different levels of demand (say) then one may either break it up into a number of discrete events as described earlier, or else assess the complete distribution by the cumulative density function (CDF) method, reading off subsequently any required probabilities. This latter method has found great favours in experiments carried out with various groups of executives. For an explanation of CDF, see page 221. Typically the method is carried out in a number of steps:

(a) The assessor is asked to choose a value $x$ for the unknown quantity (e.g. sales of Whizzo in the next month) such that he thinks it equally likely that the true value will fall below or above $x$. (Call this value $x_{50}$).

(b) The assessor is now asked to consider only those values above $x_{50}$, and again asked to repeat the process of judgmentally subdividing this interval from $x_{50}$ to infinity into two equally likely parts. (Call this dividing point $x_{75}$.)

(c) The procedure in (b) is now repeated for values below $x_{50}$ and a value $x_{25}$ hence obtained.

(d) The procedure is further repeated for each of the four intervals now available, so that in all seven assessed values of $x$ are obtained.

(e) Finally, a graph of the cumulative percentage probability (12·5, 25, 37·5, 50, etc.) is plotted against the $x$ values and a smooth curve drawn by eye through the plotted points. Any required probabilities are now read off the graph.

An example of this approach has been given by R. L. Keeney in analysing the development of facilities at the Mexico City Airport. The procedure outlined above was carried out, the quantity to be estimated (in 1972) being the number of people who would be subjected annually to noise levels of 90 CNR (Composite Noise Rating) or above in 1985. The one major difference over the procedure described above was that the first step carried out was to estimate $x_{100}$ as 1·2 million and $x_0$ as 0·7 million (i.e. the absolute bounds for the variable $x$). Figure 11.5 illustrates part of the results obtained. As drawn, the probability of the true figure being between any two adjacent fractile points should be the same, namely 0·125 (or one-eighth). Thus, to check the consistency of the assessments, the assessor can be asked if in fact his judgmental probability of falling into any of the eight such ranges of impact is the same. If not, the assessor should adjust his various estimates until no more such discrepancies can be found.

Finally, it must be emphasized that training and experience in handling assessment methods is usually needed by executives, and this should form part of the general background of those executives likely to be concerned with decision analysis. To await the occasion when an assessment is urgently required is likely to cause difficulties and delays, and hence some experience of these methods should be accepted as a routine requirement for possible assessors. Readers are referred to references (5) and (6) for further discussion of assessment methods.

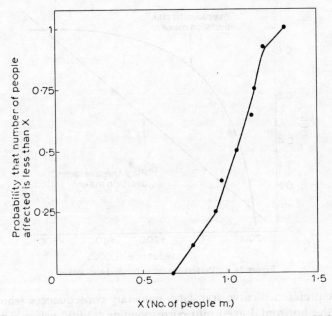

**Figure 11.5   Cumulative density function for aircraft noise nuisance above 90 CNR**

## 11.5   Risk aversion

As pointed out earlier, the risks of business decisions are commonly small enough in relation to the total asset base of the organization concerned to allow the decision-maker to base his analysis on expected consequences. This was so in the case of the chemical company in Chapter 10, and again for the oil wildcatter in this chapter. If, however, a substantial part of the business is at risk through the particular project concerned, an analysis which pushes aside the decision-maker's attitude to risk aversion may be seriously unsound. The collapse of Rolls Royce in 1971, over its difficulties with the RB 211 engine contract with Lockheed, illustrates a situation where full and proper consideration of the risks involved appeared to have been lacking. Fortunately, risk aversion can be incorporated quite straightforwardly into a decision tree as long as the decision-maker's general attitude towards risk can be quantified. This requires the construction of what is known as a preference or utility curve, of which an illustration is given in Figure 11.6.

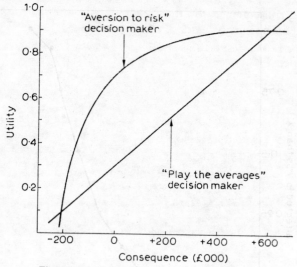

**Figure 11.6    Preference curve for decision-maker**

A preference curve translates monetary consequences (shown on the horizontal axis) into corresponding 'utility' values which typically range from 0 to 1. In this figure, using the top curve, a loss of £200 000 is shown to have a utility of 0·1, break-even has a utility of 0·7, and gaining £600 000 has a utility of 0·9. The effect of using a curve of this kind in order to read off utility values and using the latter in place of the original monetary values is to shift the decision tree analysis in the direction of risk avoidance, but in a precise and defined manner.

The technique of establishing a decision-maker's attitude to risk is discussed in detail elsewhere (see, for example, reference (2) by Raiffa at the end of this chapter). A common approach is to elicit the decision-maker's attitude to a few hypothetical gambling situations, e.g. how much would he take for sure in exchange for a 50:50 chance of receiving £0 or £600 000 in the prevailing economic condition? From such assessments, a few points on the curve can be deduced and the rest of the curve drawn in freehand. If the curve has been meaningfully assessed, the utility numbers can be used in place of the real monetary consequences to show the optimum strategy in accordance with the decision-maker's attitude towards risk. Note that if a straight line were used to translate monetary consequences into utilities, this would impart no more than a scaling effect to the original consequences, and replacement

of those consequences by the corresponding utilities would not
then alter the selection made as to the best action.

## References

(1) *Reason by Numbers* by P. G. Moore (Penguin, 1980).

(2) *Decision Analysis: Introductory Lectures on Choice under Uncertainty* by H. Raiffa (Addison-Wesley, 1968).

(3) *Decision Making* by D. V. Lindley (Wiley Interscience, 1971).

(4) *Case Studies in Decision Analysis* by P. G. Moore *et al*. (Penguin, 1976).

(5) Measuring uncertainty, by P. G. Moore and H. Thomas, *Omega* (1975), vol. 3, pp. 210–25.

(6) *The Business of Risk* by P. G. Moore (Cambridge, 1983).

(7) Decision analysis comes of age, by J. W. Ulvila and R. V. Brown, *Harvard Business Review*, 1981, pp. 210–18.

(8) The practice of decision analysis, by S. R. Watson (ed.), *Journal of the Operational Research Society*, 1982, vol. 33, no. 4.

(9) *Applied Decision Analysis* by D. W. Bunn (McGraw-Hill, 1984).

# 12 Some further operational research problems

## 12.1 Introduction

The earlier chapters of this book have developed much of the problem-solving activities of operational research through illustrative examples. These examples have been drawn from a wide variety of situations but, for reasons of exposition, the development has centred around applications that demonstrate each technique or approach as it is introduced. In this chapter some further illustrative problems, drawn from a wide variety of fields and using a combination of techniques, will be described to widen the range of applications. The first is taken from a problem involving the integration of transport and production facilities of a brewing organization. The second relates to the effect that the adherence to certain conventional financial ratios can have on the allocation of funds between competing capital projects. The third illustration relates to the selection of advertising media so as to maximize effectiveness for a given level of outlay. The fourth illustration is taken from a transportation situation to illustrate the use of decision theory in the analysis of a haulage problem for a perishable food. The fifth and final problem relates to an investigation concerning the true cost involved in the checking of invoices and goods received. Necessarily, the descriptions can only be given in outline but, where possible, followup references are given at the end of the chapter for those desiring to delve deeper.

## 12.2 Location problem

In the earlier chapters, problems concerning production and distribution have been discussed. The current problem under discussion is one linking together production and distribution in the sense that the siting of both the production units and the distribution depots was under consideration. The organization was a brewery company who had to incur some capital expenditure if the main brewery was to continue to operate efficiently. The site of the brewery was a valuable one and there seemed to be a good case for selling the site and building a new brewery elsewhere. The question was where and, more generally, should there be more than one brewery?

A schematic diagram of a brewery's distribution system is shown in Figure 12.1. Beer is manufactured in bulk in breweries and then

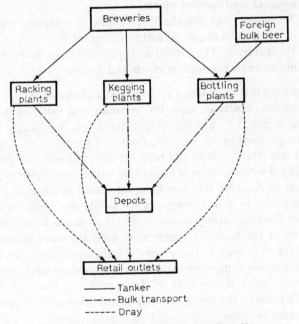

**Figure 12.1 Schematic diagram of the flow of beer**

packed in casks (racking), kegs, or bottles. Bottling plants are frequently at separate locations from the breweries and, although there is no technical reason why racking and kegging should not be done at separate locations, it is unusual. The possibility that this separation might be economic arises because of the considerably greater transport costs by bulk transport and by dray as opposed to tanker. So-called 'foreign' beers are brewed by other companies and sold in bulk to the present company for bottling in their own plant. Beer in cask, keg, or bottle is transported in bulk to depots, or by dray to individual public houses, either from the depots or direct from the packaging plants.

To tackle this problem a considerable amount of data, falling under four main headings, was required:

(*a*) *Demand forecasts* for the time during which the new system would be expected to be operational, broken down by area and separated into draught and bottled, in-company, and foreign beers.

(*b*) *Handling costs* separately for the depots and the racking, kegging, and bottling plants.

(*c*) *Transport costs* for the three types of company transport in terms of an overhead and a mileage cost.

(*d*) *Process costs*. The capital and operating costs for both existing and new production plants and depots.

Obtaining this data was a relatively straightforward, but extremely tedious, exercise. Since the accuracy and value of the final solution depends to a considerable extent on the quality of the information used in the analysis, time well spent at this stage was of vital importance. With the relevant data to hand, the problem was tackled with the help of a specially written computer program designed to describe the flow diagram shown in Figure 12.2. To use the program it was necessary to specify the numbers of the different kinds of facility available and their initial locations. The locations of the facilities which minimized the total distribution costs were then found. The program had considerable flexibility; for example, it was possible to fix the positions of any of the facilities and obtain optimal locations of the remainder. One use of this was to determine the effects on total distribution costs of retaining any existing facilities.

Nearly 100 runs were made with the computer program to gain information using the existing site pattern, to optimize the positions chosen, and to test the stability of the answers. These runs were not all made together but singly or in small batches. Each set of results was analysed to incorporate the net cost of building and operating new facilities and closing old ones. On the basis of these results, further computer runs were made and fresh analyses carried out. The process can be described as interrogating the model—a common procedure used with models of complex systems. The recommendations that were eventually made included moving existing bottling plants as well as two of the company's depots.

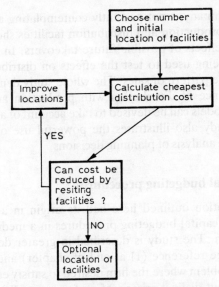

**Figure 12.2 Flow diagram of computer program**

These recommendations were based on the best assumptions that could be made about future demand and costs. Some of these assumptions appeared to be particularly liable to error—and the computer program was re-run to determine how they affected, not so much the distribution costs themselves, but the recommendations. Among the changes tested were:

(a) Increased utilization of the transport fleet.
(b) Increased depot handling costs.
(c) Changes in the assumed manning of company vehicles.

In the first two cases, there was no effect on the recommendations, but in the third case the recommendation on depot locations was changed.

The model was also used to test out the effects of possible future acquisitions of small breweries on the optimal locations of plants and depots. A brewery takeover is made, not only for the plant and buildings, but also for the outlets, particularly the tied licensed premises. Indeed, the latter may be the prime reason for the take-over. Such an acquisition affects the geographical pattern of demand and hence the optimal location of the plant and depots.

Even if a company is not presently contemplating a takeover, its planning of production and distribution facilities should take into account the effects of possible future takeovers. In this sense the model was being used to test the effects on distribution costs of changes in the pattern of sales. The whole study demonstrates the interdependence of distribution with production and sales, and shows that models can be devised to take account of all these activities. This study also illustrates the powerful use of a computer model for the analysis of planning decisions.

## 12.3   Capital budgeting procedures

The investigation outlined here had its origin in a study aimed at improving capital budgeting procedures in a medium-sized engineering firm. The study is described in greater detail by D. J. Chambers (see reference (1) at end of chapter) and relates to a budgeting problem where the firm desired to satisfy each of several overlapping but distinct criteria of performance. When managers planned major internal investments in plant and equipment, they were unwilling to restrict their attention solely to the cash flows which each investment would generate. They were concerned also with the effects on quantities shown in the balance sheet, on published profits, and on various earnings-to-assets ratios. They were very conscious that alternative investment plans could have markedly different effects on these results, and they ruled out of court those plans which, although they offered attractive rates of return, would have given rise to poor published results at some point in the planning interval.

The problem the managers posed was not, therefore, the well-known one of choosing the list of projects whose cash flows had the highest present worth or equivalent rate of return. It was a problem of maximization subject to constraints on the published financial results.

A further aspect of their problem resulted from a policy that a large proportion of the firm's finance should come from internal sources. At the same time it was possible to make reasonable estimates of the kinds of investment opportunities that would occur in the next few years. Financial managers considered that an important part of their skill lay in so dovetailing projects that funds would be released by some projects just as they were required for profitable investment in others. Current projects could not be considered in isolation, and managers wished to know to what extent a future opportunity cast its shadow forward to affect the optimal current allocation of investment funds.

At the risk of some over-simplification, procedures currently followed by many progressive firms in the management and allocation of disposable funds could be characterized as follows:

(*a*) Decisions on the firm's financing taken at a comparatively rarefied level: on debt management, on the raising of new funds, on relations with the capital markets.

(*b*) Decisions at a more mundane level: recurrent decisions on the allocation of available funds between competing projects.

The two types of decision are linked through a figure which purports to represent the cost of new funds. If many individual projects appear to offer returns greater than this, a case can be made for increasing the volume of outside financing; and if finance becomes tighter the total amount available for allocation can be reduced.

The allocation is often made in several stages. When planning budgets have been prepared to show how the 'optimal' allocation affects future financial statements, the results implied for some future period may turn out to be unacceptable. In this event the 'optimal' allocation will be adjusted until it yields tolerable results. The full effects on financial statements are probably worked out for just a few alternative plans.

The method used in this particular study takes account of the financial implications of all possible plans right at the start, and proceeds to investigate further only those plans whose financial implications are acceptable.

In this situation, four constraints on reported financial results were incorporated. These were constraints which managers selected as being the most important, although different versions could easily be substituted in the analysis. The four constraints were:

(*a*) Company policy dictated that, short of dire emergency, published profits should increase from year to year. In the particular case concerned, profits were required to increase by 5 per cent each year.

(b) To retain the confidence of the firm's creditors, it was thought desirable to keep the ratio of current assets to current liabilities, as reported on the balance sheet, at or above a specified value. In this case the value was taken as 3.

(c) A third restriction applied to dividends. It was again company policy that, subject to the usual provisos, dividends should not fall below a specified value. The case concerned illustrated a policy of maintaining dividend payment at one-third of earnings after tax, although other policies had also been investigated.

(d) The final restriction referred to a measure of performance: the return on gross assets. This ratio was defined as earnings before tax or depreciation, expressed as a fraction of total assets minus current liabilities. In the company under discussion, this ratio was not allowed to fall below 0·15.

Other obvious constraints were also included, e.g. a restriction on the scale at which particular projects could be undertaken.

The limitations of the information conveyed by any one of these published values or ratios need hardly be emphasized. When the National Economic Development Council (an official British Government advisory body) issued recently a league table ranking firms in the British clothing industry in the order of their return on gross assets, comments in the press from firms near the bottom of the list neatly summarized the objections to return on assets as a measure of performance. Alternatively, a high return may mean no more than that a revaluation of assets is long overdue. But while this particular return should certainly not be used in isolation, it is likely to appear on any short-list of measures of the performance either of the whole firm or of divisions within the firm.

In a world of perfect information, the published return on assets could no doubt be ignored, as a veil cloaking the reality of the underlying cash flows. But where public information about the performance and prospects of firms is imperfect and scrappy, such a measure provides the market with extra evidence. In such a world it is not irrational for managers to attempt to meet conventionally accepted requirements on published financial results.

How are managers to choose between different feasible investment plans? What is to be maximized? It was agreed that the point of view to be adopted should be that of the current owners of the firm. Managers should choose the plan most advantageous to current shareholders. It followed that the criterion adopted would have to depend in some way on the dividend policy to be followed. If a firm pays no dividend, and instead reinvests all earnings, the best plan will be the one giving the firm its highest value at the horizon. But in cases such as this one, where dividends are paid and where they are related to earnings, the shareholder will be interested both in how the investment plan affects the horizon value and in the stream of dividends he will receive in the meantime.

If management is to identify the plan most advantageous to current shareholders, it must therefore take a position on how shareholders weigh current as against future receipts. In this case a rate of 7 per cent was used to express shareholders' preferences, although it was found that the results were broadly unaffected by reasonable variations in this figure.

The analysis was carried out through a linear programming formulation which allowed managers to take account of the diverse and complicated measures, such as those mentioned above, which the market appears to use in assessing the condition and progress of the firm. Evaluation of a firm's performance is notoriously difficult, and managers are justly sceptical of any single measure of how their capital budgeting decisions contribute to overall performance. No current system can offer more than partial and provisional solutions to a firm's capital budgeting problem. But the linear programming model can at least take account of diverse financial criteria, and it can be used to evaluate the consequential financial effects that flow from trade-offs between the various criteria. In this way it handles systematically some of the complexities and interactions managers have to weigh up. The sorts of problem which it could answer are

(a) The optimal initial allocation between projects.
(b) The effects of borrowing extra funds at any particular time.
(c) The timing of future opportunities in the sense of how they cast their shadows forward to present actions.

Examples given in the paper quoted show that the effects can be quite marked and that the use of linear programming techniques can give results which differ widely from, and are commonly better than, those obtained by using standard methods of investment appraisal.

## 12.4   Optimum media schedules

This section provides a brief description of some work carried out by D. M. Ellis (see reference (2) at end of chapter) on determining an optimum media schedule in terms of its response to an advertising campaign in 1965. A sum of money is available to spend on an advertising campaign designed to evoke a response from a certain section of the population, and various different media can be included in the campaign. Certain information has been made available and some assumptions have been made:

(a) *Information*

    (i) The cost of a single insertion of the type of advertisement intended in each medium. Adjustments may have to be made to deal with varying costs, discounts, etc.

    (ii) The effect of exposure is known, i.e. the probability that a person reads the issue in which an insertion appears, notices the advertisement, and is sufficiently impressed to respond. This probability will differ from person to person, i.e. a distribution of personal probability values is assumed to exist.

(b) *Assumptions*

    (i) The cost of each insertion in each medium can be specified before construction of the schedule.

    (ii) The effect of an individual exposure is not altered with the passage of time, nor by the previous history of a person's response to the campaign.

    (iii) The basic response to an advertisement for all members of the target population, and for each medium, is independent as between one person and another.

    (iv) The effects of advertising in different media are independent.

A mathematical model can now be formulated to estimate the average response to various media combinations, bearing in mind that a model based on such assumptions is obviously a considerable simplification of the complicated business of advertising. The assumption about costs is not a serious restriction. Its main implication is that the format, size, and colour of insertions must be decided before beginning the optimization. This is primarily a creative decision, to be made before the media planner gets to work. For exposure values there are two elements: the probability of reading the issue concerned and the probability, having read it, of being affected by the advertisement. The former is accurately known, but only limited data are available on this second aspect, although considerable field-work is going on. Until more data become available, there is little value in discussing the effect of the assumption.

The most serious assumption, however, is that concerning the independence of exposure values. A lot of data are available on the 'readership' of different media and this is the basis of the work. To be able to assume independence is desirable for two reasons. First, it gives a model which is amenable to analysis, though not too divergent from reality. Second, although readership data are plentiful, even these are insufficient to give accurate estimates of joint readership in some cases.

The IPA/NRS survey uses 15 000 to 17 000 interviews per year. For a 12 month period, a sample of roughly 7200 male readers gave readership for the *Daily Mirror*, *Daily Express*, and *Daily Telegraph* of 41, 34, and 9 per cent respectively. On the independence assumption: the number of persons reading all three would be, on average, 91, and sampling variations on such a number would be quite high (see Appendix B). A few errors such as this will, however, probably have little effect in a schedule involving a reasonable number of media. But if the data are further split by status etc. direct estimates may well be inaccurate, unless based on prohibitively large amounts of data.

In the face of such difficulties, simulation is often used. (See, for example, the article by E. M. L. Beale, reference (3) at end of chapter.) This has the advantage that all the complexities of the situation can, in theory, be incorporated. Against this, no computer program has yet been prepared which leads automatically to optimum schedules. At best, such a program simulates response to given schedules and perhaps evaluates minor alterations which might improve them. The information available on certain of the points mentioned above hardly justifies a high level of sophistication. Hence the two approaches may be profitably combined. The model, and the method of optimization used with it, can indicate an optimum and the way in which the optimum response increases with cost. A simulation programme can then be used to estimate the average response more accurately and to cast around for slight changes in the schedule which improve the response. The following example illustrates the kind of results obtained from such an approach.

Suppose that the sum of £80 000 is available for a campaign directed at men only. Table 12.1 shows the relevant data, and a simplified method is used whereby the exposure value depends

Table 12.1  **Short-list of media**

| Medium | Cost of insertion (£) | Readership amongst sample (%) | Conditional exposure value |
|---|---|---|---|
| Daily Mirror | 3225 | 41 | 0·50 |
| Daily Express | 3000 | 34 | 0·40 |
| Daily Mail | 2480 | 17 | 0·40 |
| Daily Telegraph | 1930 | 9 | 0·45 |
| News of the World | 4224 | 44 | 0·30 |
| People | 3750 | 41 | 0·30 |
| Sunday Express | 3750 | 27 | 0·30 |
| Sunday Times (Colour) | 2277 | 9 | 0·45 |
| ITV Publications | 3003 | 35 | 0·40 |
| Radio Times | 3600 | 33 | 0·50 |

a simplified method is used whereby the exposure value depends on two factors:

(a) The percentage readership $b_i$ of the $i$th medium amongst the target population; these readerships are assumed to be basically static and distributed independently of each other.

(b) The conditional exposure value $v_i$, which is the (conditional) probability that a person who reads the issue in which an insertion appears, notices the advertisement and responds to it.

It was decided to have at least one insertion in each medium, but a maximum of two insertions in each weekly paper. The coverage was to be maximized. The final schedule, using the type of model outlined earlier, and maximizing the effective coverage, is built up in Table 12.2. This schedule shows two insertions in each paper except the *Daily Mirror* (4 insertions), *Daily Express* (5), and *Daily Mail* (3). Examination of the table reveals, however, that approximately £16 000 spent on obtaining the last 2 per cent of effective coverage might not be thought worth the return. The schedule would then be terminated at 20 insertions, costing £65 000. At this point, the marginal gain from an extra £1000 of advertising

Table 12.2 **Construction of optimum insertion schedule**

| Total insertions | Medium | Cumulated cost (£) | Effective coverage (%) |
|---|---|---|---|
| 10 | 1 insertion each | 31 239 | 70·4 |
| 11 | *Daily Mirror* | 34 464 | 74·2 |
| 12 | *ITV Publications* | 37 467 | 76·7 |
| 13 | *Daily Express* | 40 467 | 78·9 |
| 14 | *Radio Times* | 44 067 | 81·0 |
| 15 | *People* | 47 817 | 82·9 |
| 16 | *News of the World* | 52 041 | 84·7 |
| 17 | *Daily Mirror* | 55 266 | 85·8 |
| 18 | *Daily Express* | 58 266 | 86·7 |
| 19 | *Daily Mail* | 60 746 | 87·3 |
| 20 | *Sunday Express* | 64 496 | 88·1 |
| 21 | *Daily Express* | 67 496 | 88·6 |
| 22 | *Daily Mirror* | 70 721 | 89·0 |
| 23 | *Daily Telegraph* | 72 651 | 89·3 |
| 24 | *Daily Mail* | 75 131 | 89·6 |
| 25 | *Sunday Times* (Colour) | 77 408 | 89·8 |
| 26 | *Daily Express* | 80 408 | 90·1 |

(Note that each line is incremental to the previous line, i.e. assumes that all insertions up to and including that line are made.)

is approximately 0·16 per cent effective coverage; or, put alternatively, the cut-off point is being put where 1 per cent extra effective coverage is equated with £6000 extra advertising expenditure. The situation is summarized graphically in Figure 12.3.

## 12.5 A food transportion problem

Young's Seafoods, part of Imperial's Food Division, are well known for their products, and possibly for their vehicles in white livery with a large red prawn. Until 1979 they distributed to their depots around the country, using 23 trunkers based at the distribution centre in Yorkshire. This is a very large cold store that acts as a buffer between Young's factories and their depots. Any trunking operation is expensive, but refrigerated goods are even more so. Three points were giving concern to the distribution director: firstly the forthcoming EEC regulation on mileage would make it difficult to achieve several more of their journeys in a day; second, the industrial relations environment at the depot was very poor

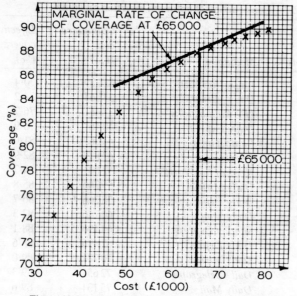

**Figure 12.3** Advertising costs and marginal coverage

with friction between inside workers and the trunker drivers and considerable problems with the interpretation of payments system; and third, the very high cost of the operation. The distribution director had considered several alternative solutions to the problem and invited two consultants (one from the Food Division and one from Imperial Group) to help him evaluate the costs and risks of the alternatives.

The analytical work involved about 10 man days in total, over a period of 6 weeks or so. During this period a dozen or so decision trees were produced, with the following sequence of events. The first task was the problem definition, and a half day was spent with the client discussing the options, at the end of which an initial tree structure was drawn. This was broadly agreed after a few changes, and a couple of days later an outline tree (with broad costs) was prepared for the client. This was used by the client for the first task, which was to have board approval for a more detailed study of the options. A simplified version of the tree is given in Figure 12.4. The most attractive option from a cost point of view was the move to an outside haulier. They were quoting, in broad terms, prices that gave a substantial saving on the Young's

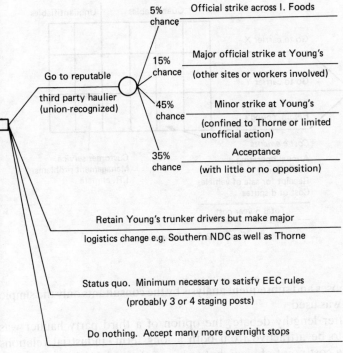

5% chance — Official strike across I. Foods

15% chance — Major official strike at Young's (other sites or workers involved)

45% chance — Minor strike at Young's (confined to Thorne or limited unofficial action)

35% chance — Acceptance (with little or no opposition)

Go to reputable third party haulier (union-recognized)

Retain Young's trunker drivers but make major logistics change e.g. Southern NDC as well as Thorne

Status quo. Minimum necessary to satisfy EEC rules (probably 3 or 4 staging posts)

Do nothing. Accept many more overnight stops

**Figure 12.4  Simplified decision tree**

own fleet. The discussion at board level was aided by the tree, and agreement given for a detailed study.

It was possible to eliminate several options (such as building a new distribution centre) fairly quickly on grounds of cost, and the work concentrated on the elements of the tree (Figure 12.5). It should be emphasized that, in both the early problem structuring stage and this more detailed phase, the trees eventually selected were chosen after several false starts and an interactive procedure with the client. Much work was spent on examining the possible contracts with the outside hauliers to see how they compared in cost terms, what inflation clauses were present, the service level they offered and what arrangement could be reached for the tractors and trailers owned by Young's. An interesting use of a tree is the simple example (Figure 12.6), which showed what happened if Young's moved to a carrier, sold its vehicles and then was dissatisfied with the carrier. This could have been built into the main tree (and was, briefly, by the consultants) but for client discussion

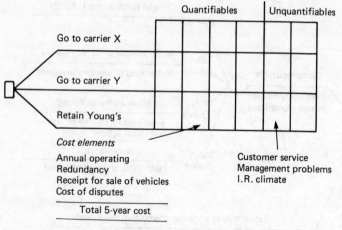

**Figure 12.5    Five-year costs**

purposes and subsequent analysis by the consultants only the simple tree was used.

After lengthy debate, the option of a third party haulier was felt to be attractive from both a long term, industrial relations and a cost point of view, but to have substantial risks in the short term (the Young's drivers would effectively be made redundant, but would possibly be taken on by the third party). The early soundings and negotiations with the union were not the subject of the tree (one could have had a branch of 'raise possibility of move with union'). However, it became clear that, provided the third party involved was union recognized, the union would not oppose the move and indeed would be, to some extent, happy to have the anomalous Young's payments system removed.

As a result of the decision the drivers left the company and the tractors were sold. The trailers remained the property of

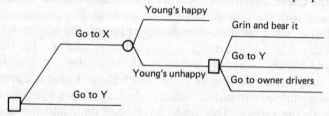

**Figure 12.6    The switch to carriers**

Young's and still carried the famous red prawn. The business is effectively split between several third party hauliers who operate specific journeys for specific rates, agreed every 6 months or so. The service to the depots is excellent, and the costs are advantageous. One of the problems for Young's when it owned the fleet was a journey that took 1·3 days, for example. This can be more easily accommodated by the third party haulier who can tender for a wide variety of business to make use of spare time.

## 12.6   The checking of invoices and bills

All organizations have some routine for checking and paying the bills which they incur. This may seem a trivial affair, but throughout the world there must be millions of people engaged upon the meticulous examination of documents and accounts. In many cases the scrutiny is costing more than the mistakes found thereby are worth. The typical sequence of events is:

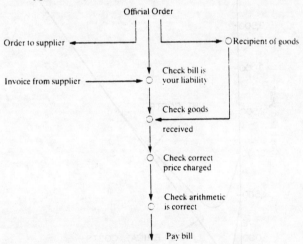

Four checks are therefore involved:

(*a*)  Ensuring bill is your liability.
(*b*)  Ensuring goods were received and correct.
(*c*)  Ensuring correct price was charged.
(*d*)  Ensuring arithmetic on invoice was correct.

A study made of these checks in the supplies department of a large local authority has been described by R. A. Ward (director of the Local Government O.R. Unit, see reference (5)).

After discussion it was decided that check (*a*) had to be retained at 100 per cent, and attention was accordingly transferred to the other three checks. Consider what would happen if, instead of asking the recipient of goods to confirm all deliveries, he were required simply to report when defective deliveries had occurred, so that payment could be stopped when the invoice was received. If this principle were adopted, the bill would be passed for payment without confirmation of delivery. If the delivery failed completely, however, the recipient would also remain silent, believing that the goods were still due to arrive. Lost goods might then be paid for by the purchasing section in the mistaken belief that they had been received in good condition and on time.

By examining the extent to which goods had been lost in the past, it was possible to derive Figure 12.7. In this figure it was

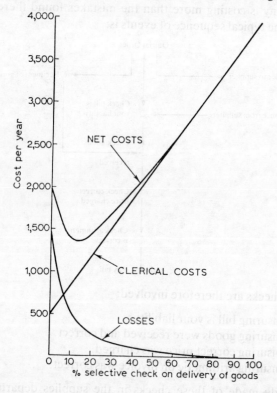

**Figure 12.7 The effect of selective checking for receipt of goods on losses and clerical costs**

assumed that selective checking would be on the most expensive invoices first. For example, against 12 per cent the result shown implies that all invoices above £100 in value were checked. When the balance was struck, by adding together the losses and clerical costs shown from the figure, the optimum point of balance did, in fact, come out at 12 per cent. The incidence of overcharging which occurred on invoices was next examined. The frequency of such mistakes was again small and, by a coincidence, the optimum cost balance once more corresponded to a checking rate of the 12 per cent most valuable invoices.

Finally, the incidence of arithmetical errors was examined. Here an interesting phenomenon, shown in Figure 12.8, emerged. At

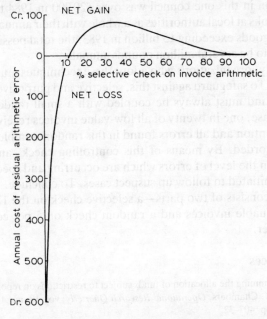

**Figure 12.8  Effect of various checking levels on residual arithmetic error**

first sight, it might be expected that such errors would occur completely by chance and tend to cancel one another out. In turn, this would suggest that arithmetical errors are not worth looking for, since in the long run the gains would cancel the losses. A thorough examination of the situation, however, showed that the elimination of checking led to quite serious losses. Even more surprising is the fact that a 25 per cent check produces a slight profit which is not obtained on a 100 per cent check. This must be due to the fact that the direction of the errors tends to be correlated with the size of the invoice, with the consequence that undercharging is more likely to occur on low-value invoices than on high-value invoices. In turn, this points out a feature of operational research worth stressing, namely that a thorough and quantitative examination of a familiar idea can sometimes produce a remarkable new insight. The decision taken here was to continue with the 12 per cent sample check.

The results of this study were implemented by the council concerned, and similar schemes are being introduced by other authorities. The estimated annual savings as a result of 2 years' successful operation in this one council was over £20 000 in 1984 terms and, if one looks at local authorities as a whole with their annual expenditure on goods exceeding £5 billion in 1983, the total possible saving is likely to be several million pounds annually.

Clearly, organizations who adopt these techniques must not lose control. To safeguard against this, selective and purposive checking of this kind must always be coupled with a small random check. In this case, one in twenty of all low-value invoices receive meticulous attention and all errors found in this random sample are carefully recorded. By means of this controlling check, an estimate is kept on the level of errors which are occurring and special action can be initiated to follow up suspect cases. To conclude: the whole process consists of two parts—a selective check on the 12 per cent most valuable invoices and a random check on 5 per cent of the remainder.

# References

(1) Programming the allocation of funds subject to restrictions on reported results, by D. J. Chambers, *Operational Research Quarterly*, vol. 18, no. 4, December 1967, pp. 407–32.

(2) Building up a sequence of optimum media schedules, by D. M. Ellis, *Operational Research Quarterly*, vol. 17, no. 4, December 1966, pp. 413–24.

(3) A computer assessment of media schedules, by E. M. L. Beale, P. A. B. Hughes and S. R. Broadbent, *Operational Research Quarterly*, vol. 17, no. 4, December 1966, pp. 381–412.

(4) The use of decision analysis in Imperial Group, by G. E. Wells, *Journal of the Operational Research Society*, 1982, vol. 33, no. 4, pp. 313–18.

(5) *Developing Operational Research in Local Government* by R. A. Ward, OECD Symposium on Contribution of Operational Research to Urban and Regional Planning, December 1966.

# Appendix A
# The Simplex method for linear programming

## A.1 Introduction

The standard algebraic technique used for solving linear programming problems is known as the Simplex method. Essentially the method consists of defining the problem in a standard form, and then finding by inspection a feasible solution (i.e. a solution that satisfies all the conditions and constraints, but does not necessarily produce maximum profit, assuming profit to be the quantity that is to be optimized). This first feasible solution is then amended by a series of steps, each step being chosen so as to improve the profit until a situation is reached where no further improvement can be achieved. The procedure is, therefore, an iterative one which satisfies the conditions:

(a) There is a mathematical rule which determines after each step exactly what the next step is to be, on the basis of the step just completed (a consequence of this feature is that it makes electronic computation possible); and

(b) The method is constructed in such a way that it guarantees that each trial yields values which are closer to the final answer than the preceding ones.

The details of the method are best illustrated through an example.

## A.2 The Simplex procedure

To keep the problem simple and also to be able to demonstrate the solution graphically, as well as algebraically, the problem used will again be a two-product one, but on this occasion the method is capable of generalization to three or more types. The following illustration, of a product mix problem, relates to the manufacture of two products, 1 and 2, which use the same two sequential processes, A and B. The processing times are given in Table A.1, together with the available time and profits.

Table A.1 **Basic data**

| Process | Processing time per unit (hours) 1 | Product 2 | Maximum available processing time (hours) |
|---|---|---|---|
| A | 4 | 2 | 24 |
| B | 3 | 6 | 36 |
| Profit per unit (£) | 3 | 2 | — |

Put formally, it is desired to maximize the profit function:

$$P = 3x_1 + 2x_2 \tag{A.1}$$

where $x_1$ and $x_2$ are the number of units made of products 1 and 2 respectively, subject to the constraints:

$$\text{Process A} \qquad 4x_1 + 2x_2 \leqslant 24 \tag{A.2}$$

$$\text{Process B} \qquad 3x_1 + 6x_2 \leqslant 36 \tag{A.3}$$

where the symbol $\leqslant$ is the mathematical shorthand for 'less than or equal to'.

The solution proceeds by a series of steps.

## Step 1

Write the capacity restrictions in the form of equations of equality by adding a 'slack variable' to each equation. Then:

$$(\text{A.2}) \text{ becomes} \qquad 4x_1 + 2x_2 + x_3 = 24 \tag{A.4}$$

$$(\text{A.3}) \text{ becomes} \qquad 3x_1 + 6x_2 + x_4 = 36 \tag{A.5}$$

$x_3$ represents the quantity of a fictitious product with unit processing time which utilizes the available unused capacity (if any) in process A; $x_4$ performs a similar role for process B.

## Step 2

Construct an array, referred to as a 'matrix', of the coefficients of these equations of restrictions, labelling the columns with the

ppropriate variables. The rows are labelled with the appropriate
lack variables and maximum capacity, as shown in Table A.2.

Table A.2  **Matrix for step 2**

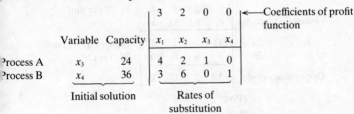

| | Variable | Capacity | $x_1$ | $x_2$ | $x_3$ | $x_4$ |
|---|---|---|---|---|---|---|
| | | | 3 | 2 | 0 | 0 | ←——Coefficients of profit function |
| Process A | $x_3$ | 24 | 4 | 2 | 1 | 0 |
| Process B | $x_4$ | 36 | 3 | 6 | 0 | 1 |

Initial solution      Rates of substitution

The two left-hand columns in Table A.2 give the values of the
non-zero variables in the current solution. Thus initially a solution
with $x_3 = 24$, $x_4 = 36$ units is chosen, which means that there is
no production and no profit. (Note that the number of non-zero
variables does not exceed the number of constraints and that these
constraints, defined by equations (A.4) and (A.5), are satisfied.
Such a solution is called a 'basic feasible solution'.)

The matrix array can then be interpreted in the following manner. If a unit of product 1 is made, this will displace 4 units of
product 3 and 3 units of products 4. Since the unit profits associated
with the products 1, 3 and 4 are 3, 0 and 0 respectively, then the
opportunity profit associated with making 1 unit of product 1 is

$$(3 \times 1) - (4 \times 0) - (3 \times 0) = 3$$

Similarly, the opportunity profits for the other column variables
can be calculated and are 2, 0 and 0 for the products 2, 3 and
4 respectively. The solution which must be tested for optimality
is shown in the left-hand side.

As stated above, with this initial solution, there is no production
and no profit.

## Step 3

Calculate the opportunity profits for each column variable and identify the column with the greatest positive opportunity profit. This
is known as the pivotal column. Divide the coefficients in the capacity column by the respective coefficients in the pivotal column.
Identify the row with the smallest positive value so calculated.

This is known as the pivotal row, and the coefficient at the intersection of this row and column is known as the pivot. Table A.3

### Table A.3  **Matrix for Step 3**

| Variable | Capacity | 3 | 2 | 0 | 0 | Profit per unit |
| | | $x_1$ | $x_2$ | $x_3$ | $x_4$ | |
|---|---|---|---|---|---|---|
| $x_1$ | 24 | (4) | 2 | 1 | 0 | 24/4 = 6 (Pivot row) |
| $x_4$ | 36 | 3 | 6 | 0 | 1 | 36/3 = 12 |
| Opportunity profit | | 3 | 2 | 0 | 0 | |

(Pivot
column)

illustrates the procedure.

This process is the mathematical equivalent of saying that product 1 offers the greatest opportunity to increase profits, but that no more than 6(=24/4) units can be made without exceeding the capacity available from process A.

### Step 4

Next construct a new matrix array of coefficients from the existing one by following these rules:

(*a*) The pivot row is reconstructed by dividing all the coefficients in it (including the capacity label in that row) by the pivot coefficient.

(*b*) Calculate the new coefficients of the other row(s) of the array by subtracting from each such row the reconstructed pivot row multiplied by the coefficient lying at the intersection of the row being transformed and the pivot column. This ensures that the pivot, which now has the value 1, is the only non-zero coefficient in the pivot column.

The result of these calculations is shown in Table A.4 below.

### Table A.4  **Matrix for step 4**

| Variable | Capacity | 3 | 2 | 0 | 0 | Profit per unit |
| | | $x_1$ | $x_2$ | $x_3$ | $x_4$ | |
|---|---|---|---|---|---|---|
| $x_1$ | 6 | 1 | $\frac{1}{2}$ | $\frac{1}{4}$ | 0 | 6 × 2 = 12 |
| $x_4$ | 18 | 0 | $\left(\frac{9}{2}\right)$ | $-\frac{3}{4}$ | 1 | 18 × 2/9 = 4 (Pivot row) |
| Opportunity profit | | 0 | $\frac{1}{2}$ | $-\frac{3}{4}$ | 0 | |

(Pivot
column)

The opportunity profits are now recalculated. Thus under $x_2$, a unit of $x_2$ would displace $\frac{1}{2}$ a unit of $x_1$ and $\frac{9}{2}$ of a unit of $x_4$. Hence the profit would be $2 - \frac{1}{2} \times 3 - \frac{9}{2} \times 0$, or $\frac{1}{2}$. For $x_1$ the opportunity profit would be $3 - 3$, or 0, as $x_1$ is merely replaced by $x_1$. Similarly for the other columns. The highest column opportunity profit is $x_2$, hence that column is the pivot. The corresponding row values will be $6/\frac{1}{2}$, or 12, and $18/\frac{9}{2}$, or 4. Hence the latter is the new pivotal row, and the value $\frac{9}{2}$ is the new pivot.

## Step 5

The procedure described under steps 3 and 4 are now repeated until a matrix array is obtained which has no positive opportunity profits. At this stage there is no point in making further substitution and the optimum has been reached. In the present example, the new matrix array becomes as shown in Table A.5 and when the

Table A.5 **Matrix for Step 5**

| Variable | Capacity | 3 | 2 | 0 | 0 | Profit per unit |
| | | $x_1$ | $x_2$ | $x_3$ | $x_4$ | |
|---|---|---|---|---|---|---|
| $x_1$ | 4 | 1 | 0 | $\frac{1}{3}$ | $-\frac{1}{9}$ | |
| $x_2$ | 4 | 0 | 1 | $-\frac{1}{6}$ | $\frac{2}{9}$ | |
| Opportunity profit | | 0 | 0 | $-\frac{2}{3}$ | $-\frac{1}{9}$ | |

revised opportunity profits are calculated it will be seen that they are all zero or negative. Hence there is no point in making further substitution and the optimum has been reached. Under this optimum, $x_1 = 4$, $x_2 = 4$, and the profit will be

$$4 \times 3 + 4 \times 2 = 20$$

Note that from the final array, if there were a profit per unit of $\frac{1}{9}$ associated with $x_4$, then $x_4$ would have a zero opportunity profit and could be brought into the solution without decreasing the total profit. Thus if $x_4$ represented the amount of some product being manufactured, its price would have to be increased by this amount to make its production worthwhile. In fact, it represents the number of hours for which process B is unused, so losing an hour of process B would represent a loss of £$\frac{1}{9}$. Thus the marginal value of process B is £$\frac{1}{9}$, and similarly that of process A is £$\frac{2}{3}$.

## A.3  A graphical analysis

Figure A.1 shows the same problem treated graphically as for the Transrad Company in Chapter 3. The constraints imposed on the capacity of the two processes as given in Table A.1, lead to capacity boundaries in Figure A.1 given by the line JK for process A and by the line LM for process B. Lines of iso-profit (i.e. the same profit for any point on the line) are shown for profits between £12 and £21 and it can be readily deduced that the point of maximum profit will be that marked Q. This corresponds to $x_1 = 4$, $x_2 = 4$ as above, giving a total profit of 20. Note that in the Simplex solution the first solution under step 2 above is the point (0, 0). The next solution under step 3 is the point J (0, 6). The third solution, step 4, is the point Q (4, 4), and step 5 shows that no further improvement can then be made.

## A.4  References to programming techniques

The Simplex technique for linear programming is fully dealt with in

*Elements of Operational Research* by F. M. Wilkes (McGraw-Hill, 1980),

*Linear Programming* by G. Hadley (Addison-Wesley 1962),

*Using Operational Research* by R. Taffler (Prentice Hall, 1979).

There are three other forms of programming to which reference may usefully be made. The first is *quadratic programming* where the constraints amongst the variables are still linear, but the function which it is desired to maximize or minimize is quadratic amongst the variables concerned. For example, a firm produces five varieties of cakes and makes use of three types of raw material, all in limited supply. The various kinds of cakes use the raw material types in different proportions. The contribution to income depends upon the amounts produced of the five varieties and the overall profit becomes a quadratic function of the proportion of cakes produced in the five varieties. Two additional references to methods of solution for such problems are

On quadratic programming, by E. M. L. Beale, *Naval Research Logistics Quarterly*, 1959, vol. 6, pp. 227–43,

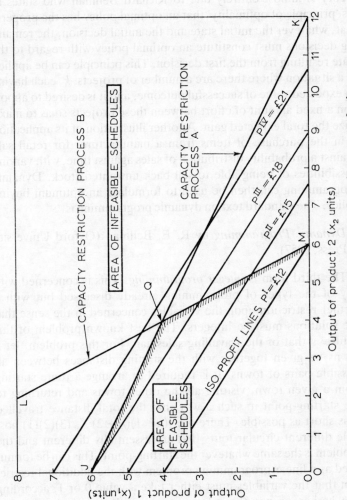

**Figure A.1 Capacity relationships between two products sharing same production resources**

The simplex method for quadratic programming, by P. Wolfe, *Econometrica*, 1959, vol. 27, pp. 382-98.

The second form is *dynamic programming* which arises where the approach requires a sequence of decisions to be made. The theory is almost entirely due to Richard Bellman who states as his 'principle of optimality' that an optimal policy has the property that, whatever the initial state and the initial decision, the remaining decisions must constitute an optimal policy with regard to the state resulting from the first decision. This principle can be applied to a situation where there are a number of projects, $k$, each having an expected value of successful outcome, and it is desired to apportion a fixed amount of effort between these projects so as to maximize the total expected gain. Another illustration of its application is in the purchase of items from a manufacturer for retail sale against a probability distribution of sales against time, with varying possibilities of being able to sell back unwanted stock. Dynamic programming can then be used to formulate an optimum buying policy. The standard text on dynamic programming is

*Dynamic Programming* by R. E. Bellman (Oxford University Press, 1957).

The third form is *integer programming*. This is concerned with any of the types of programming already discussed but with a further restriction upon the variables concerned in the sense that the solutions must be integers. The best known problem of this nature is that of the travelling salesman. For this problem, let $n$ towns be given together with the starting distances between all possible pairs of towns. It is required to arrange a route starting from a given town, visiting all the other towns and returning to the starting-point in such a way that the total distance travelled is as short as possible. There are $\frac{1}{2}(n-1)(n-2)\ldots(3)(2)(1)$ possible different circular tours that are essentially different and the problem is the same whatever the starting-point. This can be formulated as a linear programming problem with the additional restriction that the variables must either take a value 0 or 1, according to whether or not the salesman makes the particular journey between two possible points. If no restrictions of an integer nature are placed on the problem it is quite possible to obtain absurd results by use of the ordinary linear programming techniques, i.e. fractional numbers of salesmen being sent along given routes in a particular situation. Comprehensive surveys of integer programming are given in

*Linear Programming and Extensions* by G. B. Dantzig (Oxford University Press 1963),

Survey of integer programming, by E. M. L. Beale, *Operational Research Quarterly* (1965), vol. 16, pp. 219–28.

# Appendix B
# Some statistical concepts

## B.1 Inferential statistics

Inferential statistics is concerned with the drawing of an inference concerning a population (or 'universe' which is used as an interchangeable term with population). A universe consists of all possible objects, states, or events within defined bounds, and it may be very large or very small. If the universe is large, it may sometimes be assumed to be effectively infinite in order to ease computation without loss of accuracy. A universe may not always be large; it may be defined as only a dozen events or even as only one object. The relative usefulness of the universe as an entity will be paramount in its definition.

All males over 21 years old in the United Kingdom make up a universe. The schoolchildren in Oxford make up another. The car accidents occurring in Kent in 1984 make up yet another. All these populations are finite. They constitute populations that could, with sufficient care and patience, be counted and enumerated. In some cases they may be so large, for example the pebbles on the beach at Hastings, that they are effectively infinite and would have to be treated as such. Other populations are truly infinite. For example, the number of points on a line is infinite. The possible different lengths of life of light bulbs are infinite; the possible lengths of steel bars are infinite. In practice even in these cases the number of different values that can be recorded is finite, as there will always be a limit to the precision with which such quantities can be measured.

## B.2 The sample

A sample is a part or portion of a universe. It may range in size from one unit (or individual) to one less than the number of units in the universe. A sample is drawn from the universe and observations, e.g. lengths of life of light bulbs, are made on the units contained in the sample. The sample is assessed and inferences are made from it with regard to the universe as a whole. This procedure of sampling and inferring is followed for one or more of the following reasons:

(a) The universe is infinite (or virtually infinite) in size or scope (the manufacturer of electric light bulbs may produce millions in a year).

(b) The universe is inaccessible as a whole (to carry out a market research investigation on every individual in the United Kingdom would be a physical impossibility).

(c) To sample the complete universe would destroy it (light bulbs are destroyed by testing for length of life).

(d) The cost of a complete enumeration would not be economically justified with respect to the value of the information obtained (if it were desired to establish whether or not the average length of life of the light bulbs were 1500 hours, there would normally be a limit to the amount of money it would be worth expending to establish this fact, linked to the purpose for which the information was required).

The efficacy of a sampling procedure must depend upon the representative nature of the sample. Basically, and unless it is stated to the contrary, a representative sample is a random sample, by which is meant that every unit in the universe has the same chance of appearing in the sample. It is simple to state this definition, but often rather more difficult to implement it in the sampling operation itself. But, assuming this is so, then the characteristics of the sample can be related to the characteristics of the universe in a defined manner, albeit on a probability basis.

Consider, as a simplified illustration, tossing a coin 12 times and counting the number of heads that occur. Experience suggests that the 13 possible results, namely 0, 1, 2, ... 11, 12 heads, are not all equally likely to occur. If you don't believe this statement, ask any gambler if he would give the same odds on all the 13 results. If the experiment (of tossing the coin 12 times) were carried through just once it would be impossible to predict the outcome precisely. There are 13 possibilities, all of which could occur, but only one actually will occur. The outcome could, however, be predicted in the shape of odds, i.e. likelihood of each possible outcome. For this particular experiment, these have been calculated (the details need not be given here) to two decimal places and are as follows:

| Number of heads | 0 | 1 | 2 | 3 | 4 | 5 | 6 | 7 | 8 | 9 | 10 | 11 | 12 |
|---|---|---|---|---|---|---|---|---|---|---|---|---|---|
| Probability | 0·00 | 0·00 | 0·02 | 0·06 | 0·12 | 0·19 | 0·22 | 0·19 | 0·12 | 0·06 | 0·02 | 0·00 | 0·00 |

If the experiment were repeated many times, the relative frequencies with which the 13 possible results occurred would approximate to the figures in the second line of the table. Clearly, if the experiment is done once or twice only, this cannot be so, but as the number of trials get larger and larger, the proportions observed of the different results will come closer and closer to those shown.

Now suppose alternatively that, instead of a coin being tossed 12 times, a fair six-sided die were tossed 12 times and the number of sixes counted. Calculations show that the revised table of probabilities will be:

| Number of sixes | 0 | 1 | 2 | 3 | 4 | 5 | 6 | 7 or over |
|---|---|---|---|---|---|---|---|---|
| Probability | 0·11 | 0·26 | 0·30 | 0·20 | 0·09 | 0·03 | 0·01 | 0·00 |

Comparison of this table with the previous one shows quite a different pattern, and it is precisely this difference which enables inference to take place. Suppose, rather unusually, that it was not known whether a coin or a die were being tossed. The result was merely quoted as: 'In a single experiment of 12 tosses, 2 successes were obtained out of the 12 tosses.' Now if it were the coin, the result, although technically possible, would be a very unlikely one. Hence in the absence of any prior knowledge of the likelihood of its being the coin rather than the die, the result of the experiment would throw heavy support behind its being the latter. Of course, if there were some prior information that the item being tossed was more likely to be one rather than the other this would, for any given experimental result, change the odds one way or the other.

## B.3 The accuracy of a proportion

Experiments along the lines described in the previous section will show that if there is a large drum containing a very large number of beads of which a proportion $p$ are red and the rest are blue, then in samples of size $n$ drawn from this drum, the observed proportion of red beads in the sample will vary from sample to sample. This observed proportion will average out to $p$ in a long run of samples, but the individual sample red bead proportions will vary a lot. This variation is not completely haphazard, however, and it will be found that the sample results are almost invariably contained between

$$p - 2\sqrt{\left(\frac{p(1-p)}{n}\right)} \quad \text{and} \quad p + 2\sqrt{\left(\frac{p(1-p)}{n}\right)}$$

To illustrate this, suppose $p = 0.3$ and $n = 100$. Then the limits are

$$0.3 - 2\sqrt{\frac{0.03 \times 0.7}{100}} \quad \text{and} \quad 0.3 + 2\sqrt{\frac{0.03 \times 0.7}{100}}$$

or $\qquad 0.21 \qquad$ and $\qquad 0.39$

Hence, an individual sample drawn from such a drum, would be very unlikely to show a proportion of red beads outside the range 0.21 to 0.39.

The results may also be used the other way round. The households in a random sample of 100 from amongst all London households are approached and asked whether they intend to purchase a dishwasher in the next 12 months; 30 reply yes. Then the likely range of proportion of 'yes' answers in the whole population, had every household been asked, is 0.21 to 0.39. Such an interval is termed a confidence interval. This may or may not be precise enough for the purpose in hand. If it is not, then further samples would have to be taken, but it is better to know the likely range of accuracy than to pretend that the proportion is exactly 0.3. Note that if 1000 households had been approached and 300 reply yes (the same proportion as before) the confidence interval, following the same calculation, narrows to the band 0.27 to 0.33. The greater the size of the sample, the narrower in general will be the confidence interval.

## B.4 The interpretation of a sampling distribution

As a rather different illustration of how a sample result can give confidence in the result for a whole universe, consider the use of the following procedure to estimate the value of a large engineering spare parts store.

From lists it was known that 5128 different commodities were stocked, with holdings at any one moment of time ranging from zero items to several thousand items. A random sample of 571 commodities was taken from the store, the holdings counted, and the value of each commodity obtained as the product holding times the price per unit. These values were added up for the 571 commodities and the total thus obtained multiplied by 5128/571 to estimate the overall value of the store. This overall value came to be £46 000 (all overall values are rounded to the nearest thousand).

Now the sampling procedure used here amounted (in a slightly simplified way) to having 5128 numbered but otherwise identical tickets in a box thoroughly mixed and drawing out 571 of them. Now suppose that this sample of tickets were replaced, the tickets were remixed and a second sample of 571 tickets drawn out. The estimate of the overall value of the store obtained from following up the commodities denoted by this second sample of tickets would most likely be different from that obtained with the first sample. Suppose further that this procedure of replacing the sample tickets and re-sampling were to be repeated a number of times. The estimated total store value would vary from occasion to occasion and the results might well take the form shown in Figure B.1, where

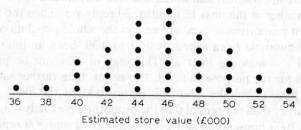

**Figure B.1   Distribution of sample estimates**

each dot represents the result obtained from a single sampling process (the values being rounded to the nearest £2000 for purposes of presentation). The results show, from 34 completely separate samplings, one value at £36 000, one value at £38 000, three values at £40 000, and so on up to one value at £54 000. Immediately certain features stand out. First the store values obtained by such a procedure do not roam over the whole spectrum of theoretically possible values; they are concentrated in a band of values. Second, even within the defined band, the values are more likely at the centre and fall away in likelihood at the two extremes, so that 18 out of 34 (or 53 per cent) of the values are either £44 000, £46 000, or £48 000, and only 3 out of 34 (9 per cent) are as much as £8000 above or below the central peak at £46 000.

Extending the above approach, if a very large number of samples were similarly taken, store values estimated from each but not rounded off, and plotted as in Figure B.1, the outline of the distribution thus formed would be along the line shown in Figure B.2, curve A. This sampling distribution, so-called, of an estimated total

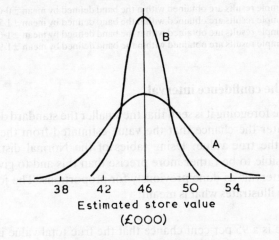

**Figure B.2 Idealized distribution**

value will, for all practical purposes, always have the characteristic symmetrical bell-shaped outline shown. The shape or form of the distribution is referred to as the 'Normal' or 'Gaussian' distribution. Such a distribution is characterized by two values: the mean or average value which will fall at the point of symmetry, and the standard deviation which is a statistical measure of the spread of the distribution. The range (i.e. the highest minus the lowest value) of the distribution is approximately four standard deviations for this case of some 30 observations, so that a spread from £36 000 to £54 000 suggests a standard deviation of $\frac{1}{4}(54\,000 - 36\,000)$, or £4500. Curve B shows another Normal distribution with a narrower spread than curve A; the standard deviation in this instance would probably be around £3000, or about two-thirds that of curve A. The practical implication is that an estimated total value having sampling distribution B will have a greater chance of being within a defined amount from the true (but unknown) total than one with sampling distribution A. Differences in standard deviation can arise from a number of sources, but in the present instance the most likely source would be the size of the sample—the larger the sample used the smaller would be the standard deviation of the sampling distribution.

Extensive tables of areas of the Normal distribution are available in terms of multiples of the standard deviation (s.d.). For example, extracts from the tables give the following:

50% of sample results are obtained within the band defined by mean ±0·67 s.d.
80% of sample results are obtained within the band defined by mean ±1·28 s.d.
90% of sample results are obtained within the band defined by mean ±1·64 s.d.
95% of sample results are obtained within the band defined by mean ±1·96 s.d.

## B.5   The confidence interval

From the foregoing it is seen that the smaller the standard deviation the greater the chance that the value estimated from the sample is near the true value. Using tables of the Normal distribution it is possible to be rather more precise than this and to give confidence intervals as done previously for proportions. The following example illustrates what is meant:

'There is a 95 per cent chance that the true total value is within the range:
     estimated total value ± 1·96 × standard deviation.'

The beauty of this approach is that, provided the sampling method used is basically a random method, it is possible to estimate the standard deviation of the sampling distribution from the sample itself. Hence even though only a single sample (consisting of a number of units) is taken, some idea of the possible range of the true unknown value is possible. Suppose, therefore, that a sample estimate of a store value gave an estimated value of £42 500 and an estimated standard deviation of £2300. This could then be interpreted as meaning that there is a 95 per cent chance that the true total value is within the range £42 500 ± £4554 (or £38 000 to £47 000). If this is not accurate enough for the purpose in hand, it will be necessary to devise a sampling method giving a smaller standard deviation, but to do so may well mean that some extra cost will be incurred.

# B.6 Cumulative density functions

A sample distribution is sometimes expressed in an alternative form to that used above, being put in terms of the probability that the variable of interest (say the store value) is less than some given value (say £48 000). If this cumulative probability (approximately 0·68) is graphed against the value of the variable (£48 000), an S-shaped form of curve is obtained from which individual probabilities of falling in any required ranges can be read off. This is referred to as a *cumulative density* function (or CDF). An example of a CDF is given on page 181 when the possible noise levels at Mexico City Airport were being estimated. For many purposes such a form of distribution is found easier to handle than the straight sampling distribution, although the two are mathematically and arithmetically equivalent.

# Appendix C
# Present value table

The table gives the present value of £1 due at the end of *n* years at rates of interest from 1% to 20% per annum.

| n | 1% | 2% | 3% | 4% | 5% |
|----|---------|---------|---------|---------|---------|
| 1 | 0·99010 | 0·98039 | 0·97007 | 0·96154 | 0·95238 |
| 2 | 0·98030 | 0·96117 | 0·94260 | 0·92456 | 0·90703 |
| 3 | 0·97059 | 0·94232 | 0·91514 | 0·88900 | 0·86384 |
| 4 | 0·96098 | 0·92385 | 0·88849 | 0·85480 | 0·82270 |
| 5 | 0·95147 | 0·90573 | 0·86261 | 0·82193 | 0·78353 |
| 6 | 0·94204 | 0·88797 | 0·83748 | 0·79031 | 0·74622 |
| 7 | 0·93272 | 0·87056 | 0·81309 | 0·75992 | 0·71068 |
| 8 | 0·92348 | 0·85349 | 0·78941 | 0·73069 | 0·67684 |
| 9 | 0·91434 | 0·83675 | 0·76642 | 0·70259 | 0·64461 |
| 10 | 0·90529 | 0·82035 | 0·74409 | 0·67556 | 0·61391 |
| 11 | 0·89632 | 0·80426 | 0·72242 | 0·64958 | 0·58468 |
| 12 | 0·88745 | 0·78849 | 0·70138 | 0·62460 | 0·55684 |
| 13 | 0·87866 | 0·77303 | 0·68095 | 0·60057 | 0·53032 |
| 14 | 0·86996 | 0·75787 | 0·66112 | 0·57747 | 0·50507 |
| 15 | 0·86135 | 0·74301 | 0·64186 | 0·55526 | 0·48102 |
| 16 | 0·85282 | 0·72845 | 0·62317 | 0·53391 | 0·45811 |
| 17 | 0·84438 | 0·71416 | 0·60502 | 0·51337 | 0·43630 |
| 18 | 0·83602 | 0·70016 | 0·58739 | 0·49363 | 0·41552 |
| 19 | 0·82774 | 0·68643 | 0·57029 | 0·47464 | 0·39573 |
| 20 | 0·81954 | 0·67297 | 0·55367 | 0·45639 | 0·37689 |
| 21 | 0·81143 | 0·65978 | 0·53755 | 0·43883 | 0·35894 |
| 22 | 0·80340 | 0·64684 | 0·52189 | 0·42195 | 0·34185 |
| 23 | 0·79544 | 0·63414 | 0·50669 | 0·40573 | 0·32557 |
| 24 | 0·78757 | 0·62172 | 0·49193 | 0·39012 | 0·31007 |
| 25 | 0·77977 | 0·60953 | 0·47760 | 0·37512 | 0·29530 |

| 6% | 7% | 8% | 9% | 10% | $n$ |
|---|---|---|---|---|---|
| 0·94340 | 0·93458 | 0·92593 | 0·91743 | 0·90909 | 1 |
| 0·89000 | 0·87344 | 0·85734 | 0·84168 | 0·82645 | 2 |
| 0·83962 | 0·81630 | 0·79383 | 0·77218 | 0·75131 | 3 |
| 0·79209 | 0·76290 | 0·73503 | 0·70843 | 0·68301 | 4 |
| 0·74726 | 0·71299 | 0·68058 | 0·64993 | 0·62092 | 5 |
| 0·70496 | 0·66634 | 0·63017 | 0·59627 | 0·56447 | 6 |
| 0·66506 | 0·62275 | 0·58349 | 0·54703 | 0·51316 | 7 |
| 0·62741 | 0·58201 | 0·54027 | 0·50187 | 0·46651 | 8 |
| 0·59190 | 0·54393 | 0·50025 | 0·46043 | 0·42410 | 9 |
| 0·55839 | 0·50835 | 0·46319 | 0·42241 | 0·38554 | 10 |
| 0·52679 | 0·47509 | 0·42888 | 0·38753 | 0·35049 | 11 |
| 0·49697 | 0·44401 | 0·39711 | 0·35553 | 0·31863 | 12 |
| 0·46884 | 0·41496 | 0·36770 | 0·32618 | 0·28966 | 13 |
| 0·44230 | 0·38782 | 0·34046 | 0·29925 | 0·26333 | 14 |
| 0·41726 | 0·36245 | 0·31524 | 0·27454 | 0·23939 | 15 |
| 0·39365 | 0·33873 | 0·29189 | 0·25187 | 0·21763 | 16 |
| 0·37136 | 0·31657 | 0·27027 | 0·23107 | 0·19784 | 17 |
| 0·35034 | 0·29586 | 0·25025 | 0·21199 | 0·17986 | 18 |
| 0·33051 | 0·27651 | 0·23171 | 0·19449 | 0·16351 | 19 |
| 0·31180 | 0·25842 | 0·21455 | 0·17843 | 0·14864 | 20 |
| 0·29415 | 0·24151 | 0·19866 | 0·16370 | 0·13513 | 21 |
| 0·27750 | 0·22571 | 0·18394 | 0·15018 | 0·12285 | 22 |
| 0·26180 | 0·21095 | 0·17031 | 0·13778 | 0·11168 | 23 |
| 0·24698 | 0·19715 | 0·15770 | 0·12640 | 0·10153 | 24 |
| 0·23300 | 0·18425 | 0·14602 | 0·11597 | 0·09230 | 25 |

| n | 11% | 12% | 13% | 14% | 15% |
|---|------|------|------|------|------|
| 1 | 0·90090 | 0·89286 | 0·88496 | 0·87719 | 0·86957 |
| 2 | 0·81162 | 0·79719 | 0·78315 | 0·76947 | 0·75614 |
| 3 | 0·73119 | 0·71178 | 0·69305 | 0·67497 | 0·65752 |
| 4 | 0·65873 | 0·63552 | 0·61332 | 0·59208 | 0·57175 |
| 5 | 0·59345 | 0·56743 | 0·54276 | 0·51937 | 0·49718 |
| 6 | 0·53464 | 0·50663 | 0·48032 | 0·45559 | 0·43233 |
| 7 | 0·48166 | 0·45235 | 0·42506 | 0·39964 | 0·37594 |
| 8 | 0·43393 | 0·40388 | 0·37616 | 0·35056 | 0·32690 |
| 9 | 0·39092 | 0·36061 | 0·33288 | 0·30751 | 0·28426 |
| 10 | 0·35218 | 0·32197 | 0·29459 | 0·26974 | 0·24718 |
| 11 | 0·31728 | 0·28748 | 0·26070 | 0·23662 | 0·21494 |
| 12 | 0·28584 | 0·25667 | 0·23071 | 0·20756 | 0·18691 |
| 13 | 0·25751 | 0·22917 | 0·20416 | 0·18207 | 0·16253 |
| 14 | 0·23199 | 0·20462 | 0·18068 | 0·15971 | 0·14133 |
| 15 | 0·20900 | 0·18270 | 0·15989 | 0·14010 | 0·12289 |
| 16 | 0·18829 | 0·16312 | 0·14150 | 0·12289 | 0·10686 |
| 17 | 0·16963 | 0·14564 | 0·12522 | 0·10780 | 0·09393 |
| 18 | 0·15282 | 0·13004 | 0·11081 | 0·09456 | 0·08080 |
| 19 | 0·13768 | 0·11611 | 0·09806 | 0·08295 | 0·07026 |
| 20 | 0·12403 | 0·10367 | 0·08678 | 0·07276 | 0·06110 |
| 21 | 0·11174 | 0·09256 | 0·07680 | 0·06383 | 0·05313 |
| 22 | 0·10067 | 0·08264 | 0·06796 | 0·05599 | 0·04620 |
| 23 | 0·09069 | 0·07379 | 0·06014 | 0·04911 | 0·04017 |
| 24 | 0·08170 | 0·06588 | 0·05322 | 0·04308 | 0·03493 |
| 25 | 0·07361 | 0·05882 | 0·04710 | 0·03779 | 0·03038 |

| 16% | 17% | 18% | 19% | 20% | n |
|---|---|---|---|---|---|
| 0·86207 | 0·85470 | 0·84746 | 0·84034 | 0·83333 | 1 |
| 0·74316 | 0·73051 | 0·71818 | 0·70616 | 0·69444 | 2 |
| 0·64066 | 0·62437 | 0·60863 | 0·59342 | 0·57870 | 3 |
| 0·55229 | 0·53365 | 0·51579 | 0·49867 | 0·48225 | 4 |
| 0·47611 | 0·45611 | 0·43711 | 0·41905 | 0·40188 | 5 |
| 0·41044 | 0·38984 | 0·37043 | 0·35214 | 0·33490 | 6 |
| 0·35383 | 0·33320 | 0·31392 | 0·29592 | 0·27908 | 7 |
| 0·30503 | 0·28487 | 0·26604 | 0·24867 | 0·23257 | 8 |
| 0·26295 | 0·24340 | 0·22546 | 0·20897 | 0·19381 | 9 |
| 0·22668 | 0·20804 | 0·19106 | 0·17560 | 0·16151 | 10 |
| 0·19542 | 0·17781 | 0·16192 | 0·14756 | 0·13459 | 11 |
| 0·16846 | 0·15197 | 0·13722 | 0·12400 | 0·11216 | 12 |
| 0·14523 | 0·12989 | 0·11629 | 0·10420 | 0·09346 | 13 |
| 0·12520 | 0·11102 | 0·09855 | 0·08757 | 0·07789 | 14 |
| 0·10793 | 0·09489 | 0·08352 | 0·07359 | 0·06491 | 15 |
| 0·09304 | 0·08110 | 0·07078 | 0·06184 | 0·05409 | 16 |
| 0·08021 | 0·06932 | 0·05998 | 0·05196 | 0·04507 | 17 |
| 0·06914 | 0·05925 | 0·05083 | 0·04367 | 0·03756 | 18 |
| 0·05961 | 0·05064 | 0·04308 | 0·03669 | 0·03130 | 19 |
| 0·05139 | 0·04328 | 0·03651 | 0·03084 | 0·02608 | 20 |
| 0·04430 | 0·03699 | 0·03094 | 0·02591 | 0·02174 | 21 |
| 0·03819 | 0·03162 | 0·02622 | 0·02178 | 0·01811 | 22 |
| 0·03292 | 0·02702 | 0·02222 | 0·01830 | 0·01509 | 23 |
| 0·02838 | 0·02310 | 0·01883 | 0·01538 | 0·01258 | 24 |
| 0·02447 | 0·01974 | 0·01596 | 0·01292 | 0·01048 | 25 |

# Exercises

1. The following data relate to the planning and coordination of a sales management training programme next year.

| Activity | Description | Immediate predecessors | Expected time to complete (weeks) |
|---|---|---|---|
| A | Plan topic | — | 2 |
| B | Obtain speakers | A | 2·5 |
| C | List meeting locations possible | — | 2 |
| D | Select meeting location | C | 2 |
| E | Speaker travel plans | B, D | 1 |
| F | Final check with speakers | E | 2 |
| G | Prepare and mail brochure | B, D | 3·5 |
| H | Take reservations | G | 4 |
| I | Last minute details | F, H | 2 |

(a) Draw a network for this project.

(b) Which are the critical path activities and the expected project completion time?

(c) If it were necessary to save time, which activities would you examine first in order to achieve such a saving?

2. Stereopes Ltd undertakes special contracts. The table gives estimates of the time and cost for activities involved in completing one contract that has just been offered to the firm.

'Previous activities' must be completed before the activity in question can be started. The minimum time represents shortest time in which the activity can be completed given the use of especially costly methods of operation. Assume that it is possible to reduce the normal time to the minimum time in small steps and that the extra cost incurred will be proportional to the time saved.

| Activity | Previous activities | Normal time (days) | Normal cost (£) | Minimum time (days) | Cost for minimum time (£) |
|---|---|---|---|---|---|
| A | | 12 | 10 000 | 8 | 14 000 |
| B | | 10 | 5 000 | 10 | 5 000 |
| C | A | 0 | 0 | 0 | 0 |
| D | A | 6 | 4 000 | 4 | 5 000 |
| E | B, C | 16 | 9 000 | 14 | 12 000 |
| F | D | 16 | 3 200 | 8 | 8 000 |
| | | 60 | 31 200 | 44 | 44 000 |

You are required to:

(a) Draw a network diagram for the contract and identify the critical path assuming that normal procedures are adopted.

(b) Recommend what programme should be followed if the job must be completed in 30 days, and calculate the total cost for that programme.

(c) Explain how you would modify your analysis if the estimates were subject to uncertainty. Illustrate your answer by assuming that estimates of the time required for E are uncertain. Normal time is expected to be in the range 12 to 20 days, but 2 days could still be saved by spending an extra £3000. You remain confident about the estimates for other activities. Target time for the contract is 30 days and there would be a penalty of £5000 for late completion.

3. A weaver makes two kinds of cloth, both containing red and white wool. Type X uses 0·2 kg of red wool and 0·3 kg of white wool per metre of cloth, whilst type Y uses 0·4 kg and 0·1 kg respectively per metre of cloth. The weaver has maximum amounts of 200 kg of red wool and 150 kg of white wool available, at prices of £4 per kg of red wool and £2 per kg of white wool. Find the amounts of type X and type Y cloth that should be manufactured so as to maximize contribution, if type X sells at £4 per metre and type Y at £6 per metre.

4. A printing company manufactures two qualities of notepaper: standard and deluxe. Each quality goes through four processes. The table below shows the time necessary in each process to make one unit of each quality, the capacity in hours of each process during the coming production period, and the profit obtained per unit of each quality.

| Quality | Process (hours) | | | | Profit per unit |
|---|---|---|---|---|---|
| | A | B | C | D | |
| Deluxe | $2\frac{1}{2}$ | 2 | 2 | 2 | 5 |
| Standard | 1 | $1\frac{1}{3}$ | 2 | $1\frac{2}{3}$ | 3 |
| Capacity (hours) | 900 | 800 | 950 | 900 | |

(a) Determine the production schedule that will maximize the overall profit.

(b) If the selling price of the standard product remains constant, by how much would the selling price of the de luxe product have to be increased in order that it would be more profitable for the company to manufacture only the de luxe quality?

(c) It is proposed to introduce a new process which would have the effect of replacing processes A and B by a single process, the remaining processes C and D being unaltered. This new process requires 4 hours per unit for the de luxe quality paper and 3 hours for the standard quality, and will have a total capacity of 1680 hours. Determine whether it is more profitable to install the new process if the profit obtainable from each quality of paper remains the same. Assume that there are no set-up costs associated with such a change-over.

5.  Curlew Diagnostics Ltd, a firm specializing in the diagnosis of car engine problems, is planning to open a new service centre and is attempting to decide if one or two diagnostic bays should be built. Based on the experience at other locations, it has been found that the service times for customers have the following frequency distribution: 1 time-period (20 per cent), 2 time-periods (60 per cent), and 3 time-periods (20 per cent). A time-period is a 15-minute time-slot.

Based on its historical experience but making subjective adjustments for differing locations, Curlew feels that the probability distribution for the number of cars arriving at the proposed location during any time-period is 0·6 probability of zero arrivals, 0·3 of one arrival, and 0·1 of two arrivals. Assume that if any customers arrive, they do so at the beginning of the time interval.

(a) Simulate 10 hours of operations (i.e. 40 time-periods) with a one-bay facility and also, using the same arrival pattern, with a two-bay facility, recording for each level of facility the following measures of performance:

(i) Average waiting time before service.
(ii) Maximum waiting time before service.
(iii) Average number of cars waiting for service.
(iv) Maximum number of cars waiting for service.
(v) Number of idle hours for the diagnostic bays.

(*b*) What is the significance of those performance measures with regard to the choice between a one-bay or a two-bay facility?

6.  A model devised for predicting a company's sales volume by periods assumes that sales are affected by four factors: trend, business cycle, seasonal and random fluctuations. Suppose that the trend of sales is increasing by 2000 units per quarter, that the long-term business cycle is expected to affect sales in the next twelve quarters according to schedule A below, that the deviation of sales from average in each of the four quarters of a year is given by schedule B, and that the probabilities of various random fluctuations are given by schedule C.

| Schedule A | | | Schedule B | | | Schedule C | |
|---|---|---|---|---|---|---|---|
| Qtr | | Cyclical deviations | Qtr | | Seasonal deviations | Random fluctuations | Probability |
| 1 | + | 3 000 | 1 | − | 8 000 | −10 000 | 0·02 |
| 2 | + | 5 000 | 2 | − | 2 000 | − 8 000 | 0·04 |
| 3 | + | 6 000 | 3 | + | 1 000 | − 6 000 | 0·08 |
| 4 | + | 7 000 | 4 | + | 9 000 | − 4 000 | 0·11 |
| 5 | + | 7 000 | | (repeating for | | − 2 000 | 0·15 |
| 6 | + | 6 000 | | successive quarters) | | 0 | 0·20 |
| 7 | + | 4 000 | | | | + 2 000 | 0·15 |
| 8 | + | 2 000 | | | | + 4 000 | 0·11 |
| 9 | − | 1 000 | | | | + 6 000 | 0·08 |
| 10 | − | 3 000 | | | | + 8 000 | 0·04 |
| 11 | − | 4 000 | | | | +10 000 | 0·02 |
| 12 | + | 4000 | | | | | |

Simulate 3 years' sales by quarters if the next quarter's basic sales level (i.e. Qtr 1) including trend but excluding cyclical, seasonal and random factors in 150 000 units. Plot a graph showing the simulated results and the original trend figures. Comment on the main features shown by your simulation.

7.  Telcol Ltd have just begun to hire out a total of 200 colour television sets. Market research has shown that out of a hundred hirings the pattern of the length of hire is as follows:

| Length of hire (years) | 1 | 2 | 3 | 4 |
|---|---|---|---|---|
| Number of hirings | 20 | 40 | 30 | 10 |

Required:

- (a) Determine the number of new rentals required each year for the next 4 years to maintain Telcol's total rentals at 200 (round to nearest whole number in your calculations).
- (b) What is the average length of hire period?
- (c) What is the average number of new rentals required each year?
- (d) Telcol Ltd, in an attempt to reduce their administrative overheads, are launching an advertising campaign aimed at their existing customers to encourage them to rent for longer periods. They would regard their campaign as successful if the following pattern of hiring was achieved in the long-run:

| Length of hire (years) | 1 | 2 | 3 | 4 | 5 |
|---|---|---|---|---|---|
| Number of hirings | 10 | 30 | 35 | 15 | 10 |

If the administrative cost of arranging a hire is £20, what is the maximum amount Telcol Ltd should spend on their advertising campaign each year?

8.  The following data relate to Mr Everyman's electricity consumption over a period of four years.

| Year | Quarter | Electricity consumed (kwh) |
|---|---|---|
| 1 | 1 | 3000 |
|   | 2 | 2900 |
|   | 3 | 2400 |
|   | 4 | 2710 |
| 2 | 1 | 3120 |
|   | 2 | 3100 |
|   | 3 | 2720 |
|   | 4 | 3040 |
| 3 | 1 | 3200 |
|   | 2 | 2120 |
|   | 3 | 2760 |
|   | 4 | 3170 |
| 4 | 1 | 3460 |
|   | 2 | 3350 |
|   | 3 | 3050 |
|   | 4 | 3180 |

- (a) Calculate annual moving average based on the quantity consumption figures.
- (b) Estimate the seasonal (quarterly) adjustments to be made to the trend line derived in (a).
- (c) Estimate the quarter by quarter consumption in year 5.

9. An asset belonging to the HKL company has worn out. However, it can be completely overhauled at a cost of £1000 and continue producing net cash flows of £200 per year. If sold as is, the asset would bring in cash of £1000. A brand new replacement can be purchased for £2000. The economic life is the same for overhaul as for purchase. The required rate of return is 15 per cent per annum. What should the management of HKL Ltd do? (All figures given are net of taxes and investment allowances etc.)

10. A company has the opportunity to purchase a machine at the price of £2200. It will have a productive lifetime of 3 years, and the net additions to cash flows (after tax and including scrap value at the end of the third year) at the end of each of 3 years are respectively £770, £968, and £1331. The company has sufficient funds to buy the machine without recourse to borrowing and the best alternative is investment elsewhere at an annually compounded interest rate of 10 per cent. Should the machine be bought?

11. Consider the mutually exclusive projects A to E having the following net incremental cash flows (£s):

| End of year | 0 | 1 | 2 | 3 | 4 | 5 |
|---|---|---|---|---|---|---|
| Project A | −900 | 300 | 300 | 300 | 300 | 300 |
| Project B | −225 | 85 | 85 | 85 | 85 | 85 |
| Project C | −350 | 120 | 120 | 120 | 120 | 120 |
| Project D | −550 | 165 | 165 | 165 | 165 | 165 |
| Project E | −400 | 155 | 155 | 155 | 155 | 155 |

With the aid of present value tables determine:

(a) The net present value for each project if the required rate of return is 12 per cent.
(b) Which projects you would accept if the capital budget available for these projects in year 0 is only £1000.

12. The following description is extracted from the current British Civil Service nationality rules for eligibility to appointment in the Diplomatic Service:

You will be eligible for appointment to a situation in the Diplomatic Service only if

(i) at all times since your birth you have been a British subject, and
(ii) each of your parents has always been, or (if dead) always was, a British subject, and

(iii) the Secretary of State is satisfied that you are so closely connected with the United Kingdom, taking into account such considerations as ancestry, upbringing and residence, that you may properly be appointed, and

(iv) you undertake to become a citizen of the United Kingdom and Colonies as soon as possible after your appointment if you are not already such a citizen.

(v) If condition (ii) is not satisfied, you may nevertheless be admitted to appointment, by special permission of State, if

    (*a*) one of your parents has always been, or (if dead) always was, a British subject (see below), and

    (*b*) your father, if not always a British subject, is or was at death a British subject.

    (*c*) For the purpose of (v)(*a*) above, any period before 1 January 1949 during which your mother lost British nationality as a result of marriage to an alien may be disregarded.

Construct a suitable form of algorithm from which it is possible to determine eligibility for the Diplomatic Service.

13.  Under the Social Security Act of 1973, certain requirements are placed on the right to the preservation of benefits under occupational pension schemes when members leave their employment. Two relevant extracts from the Act are given below:

*Basic principle as to short service benefit*

6.  A scheme must provide so that where a member's service in relevant employment is terminated before normal pension age and—

    (a)  he has attained the age of 26; and

    (b)  he has at least 5 years' qualifying service,

he is entitled to benefit (calculated in accordance with the following provisions of this Schedule and there referred to as 'short service benefit'), consisting of or comprising benefit of any description which would have been payable under the scheme as long service benefit, whether for himself or for others.

*Qualifying service*

7.  (1) '5 years' qualifying service' means 5 years (whether a single period of that duration or two or more periods, continuous or discontinuous, totalling 5 years) in which the member was at all times employed either—

    (a)  in pensionable service under the scheme; or

    (b)  in service in recognized pensionable employment by reference to the scheme; or

    (c)  in linked qualifying service under another scheme,

no regard being had to whether or not it was the same description of service in the whole of the 5 years.

(2) A period of service previously terminated is not to count towards the 5 years' qualifying service unless it counts towards qualification for long service benefit, and need then count only to the same extent and in the same way.

Draw up an algorithm to determine whether or not a pension scheme member leaving the employment of his or her organization before normal retirement is entitled under the Act to the preservation of benefits.

14.  Some time ago, Consolidated Chemicals agreed to supply Morgan Manufacturers with a batch of a rare chemical reagent, PQ-73. The contract drawn up between the two companies included two penalty clauses:

(a) A penalty of £20 000 in the event of late delivery.
(b) A penalty of £50 000 in the event of PQ-73 being substandard and ruining Morgan's production process.

This morning, just as he was about to ship the batch to Morgans, the production manager of Consolidated learned that his supplies of an important constituent chemical of PQ-73 might have become contaminated and that the batch of PQ-73 already produced might therefore be substandard. He assessed the probability of this to be 0·2.

Instead of shipping the batch as planned, the production manager could decide to scrap it and attempt to produce another batch (which he is certain would be up to the required standard) in time to meet Morgan's deadline. Working normal time on this second batch would cost £4000 and give a 50 per cent chance of the batch being ready for shipment within a week. Working overtime would cost £6000 and give a 90 per cent chance of this. In either case it is certain that this second batch would be ready for shipment within two weeks.

Experts estimate that there is a 90 per cent chance of a batch of PQ-73 reaching Morgans on time if it is shipped by sea now; 70 per cent if it is shipped by sea within the next week, 50 per cent if it is shipped by sea within the week after next. However, at any time right up to the last minute the decision to ship by air can be taken. This would cost £8000 more than shipping by sea, but would ensure delivery on time.

(a) Draw a decision tree of the situation facing Consolidated and recommend a course of action.
(b) How sensitive is this recommendation to the probability of the batch being substandard?

15.  A chemical firm is about to invest in a plant for producing a plastic. The firm has a choice of two methods of producing this plastic. The first

method involves the use of an established process and the cost of the plant using this manufacturing process is £2·4 million. The plant for producing the plastic by the second method would cost £2 million and involves using a process which has not been tested commercially. The firm's chief chemical engineer feels that there is a 70 per cent chance of the new process being successful commercially and a 30 per cent chance of the process being unsuccessful. If the process is unsuccessful commercially the plant would have to be modified at a cost of £2 million to produce the plastic by the established process.

In view of the uncertainty about the new process, the chief chemical engineer has suggested that the firm could build a pilot plant, at a cost of £100 000, to provide the further information on the commercial viability of the new process. The chemical engineer feels that there is an 80 per cent chance of the pilot plant being successful and a 20 per cent chance of it being unsuccessful. If the pilot plant does prove successful, the chemical engineer feels that there is a 90 per cent chance of the commercial plant being successful and a 10 per cent chance that it will be unsuccessful. If the pilot plant is unsuccessful, then the commercial plant using the new process would definitely be unsuccessful.

Use a decision tree approach to help management with their investment decision.

16. M. Borel, the owner of a French cargo shipping line, is offered two ships of a European line that is going out of business, in exchange for an ongoing interest in M. Borel's line. M. Borel proposes either to accept the European line's offer or to reject it outright. The condition of the two ships (i.e. whether or not they require a major overhaul) is a key determinant of the pay-off that M. Borel will receive if he accepts the offer. If he rejects the offer, his pay-off is zero in any case.

M. Borel decides to base his decisions on an EMV approach. He has no precise information on the condition of the two ships, but is able to assign the prior probabilities shown in the table below as to the condition of the ships as a set, on the basis of judgment and experience. (He does not attempt to apply probabilities to the individual ships.) Also shown are M. Borel's specific estimates of the total discounted pay-offs that he would receive if he accepts the offer under the different possible outcomes (in millions of French francs).

| No. of ships requiring major overhaul | Prior probability | Pay-off if accepted |
|---|---|---|
| 0 | 0·30 | 60 |
| 1 | 0·10 | 10 |
| 2 | 0·60 | −40 |

(a) Suppose M. Borel must make his decision between accepting and rejecting the offer without obtaining further information on the condition of the two ships. Which decision should he make?

(b) M. Borel has the option of having one or both ships taken to a reliable inspection station in a second foreign country before he makes his decision. The cost (to be paid by M. Borel) is 0·6 million francs per ship so inspected. What is M. Borel's best strategy? Give the number of ships he should inspect (i.e. 0, 1 or 2) together with the action he should take in each eventuality (e.g. inspect two, one fails and he accepts the offer, etc.) and the EMV of following your proposed strategy.

(c) Suggest conditions under which M. Borel might not be willing to take the action proposed under (b).

17. (a) Mill Hill Equipment (MHE) is currently developing a new model in its typewriter range with which it expects to make a significant impact on the UK market and also hopes to penetrate the European market. They are confident of total sales of 20 000 units, but success in Europe, which they rate at a 50:50 chance, would raise this total sales figure to 50 000.

A decision must shortly be made on production facilities. It is possible to manufacture the new model essentially using the existing plant with modification costs of £0·25 million; alternatively a new production line costing £2·5 million could be set up (capacity is not seen as a problem). It is expected that production costs per unit utilizing the existing plant would be £520, while this figure would be reduced to £460 on the new line. The typewriter is intended to sell at £600 in both markets. Show how decision analysis could guide MHE in its decision between the two options.

(b) As MHE have had only limited experience in the European market, they are also considering commissioning a market analysis by a firm of marketing consultants. The analysis would contain a prediction of either success or failure in the European market. A quotation of £50 000 for this work has been received. The consultants concerned have a high reputation, and the probabilities of their predictions being correct, based on MHE's previous experiences with them and their initial comments on the European typewriter market, have been summarized in the table below:

| | Prediction | |
| *Actual conditions in Europe* | *Success* | *Failure* |
| --- | --- | --- |
| Excellent: product would succeed | 0·6 | 0·4 |
| Poor: product would fail | 0·2 | 0·8 |

Should MHE commission the analysis and, if so, how should they react to the possible predictions?

# Notes on exercises

1. (b) A, B, G, H, I; 14 weeks
   (c) H, G, B, I, A
2. (a) 34 days at normal times
   (b) Save 2 days in D and 2 days in F at an additional cost of £2200
   (c) Data unclear, but saving 2 days in job A at a cost of £2000 seems best
3. 400 metres of $X$, 30 metres of $Y$; contribution 3400
4. (a) 300 de luxe, 150 standard; profit 1950
   (b) Raise price by 2·5
   (c) Yes; make 291·4 de luxe, 171·4 standard; profit 1971·3
5. (a) One specimen simulation for a two-bay situation gave the following results: (i) 15, (ii) 14, (iii) 13, (iv) 12, (v) 11
6. Look to see how far cyclical and seasonal fluctuations are masked by the random fluctuations
7. (a) 40, 88, 94, 85 sets respectively
   (b) 2·3 years
   (c) 87
   (d) £340
8. (a) Ranging from 2752 to 3260
   (b) +300, 0, −400, +100
9. Overhaul or buy new asset (and sell old) if life is greater than 10 years, otherwise sell old asset.
10. Yes, the NPV is +300
11. (a) 200, 10, 150, 180, 200
    (b) D and E
14. (a) Make a new batch through normal working
    (b) If p rises, a new batch through normal working is still the optimal action; if it falls below 0·18, ship now
15. Build pilot
16. (a) Reject offer
    (b) Inspect both, accept if either ship is acceptable
17. (b) Yes; new plant if success predicted, otherwise modify existing plant

# Index